# Studies in Space Policy

Volume 32

The use of outer space is of growing strategic and technological relevance. The development of robotic exploration to distant planets and bodies across the solar system, as well as pioneering human space exploration in earth orbit and of the moon, paved the way for ambitious long-term space exploration. Today, space exploration goes far beyond a merely technological endeavour, as its further development will have a tremendous social, cultural and economic impact. Space activities are entering an era in which contributions of the humanities — history, philosophy, anthropology —, the arts, and the social sciences — political science, economics, law — will become crucial for the future of space exploration. Space policy thus will gain in visibility and relevance. The series Studies in Space Policy shall become the European reference compilation edited by the leading institute in the field, the European Space Policy Institute. It will contain both monographs and collections dealing with their subjects in a transdisciplinary way.

The volumes of the series are single-blind peer-reviewed.

More information about this series at http://www.springer.com/series/8167

Annette Froehlich · Diego Alonso Amante Soria

# A Regional Space Agency for Latin America

## Legal and Political Perspectives

ESPI
European Space Policy Institute

Springer

Annette Froehlich
European Space Policy Institute
Vienna, Austria

Diego Alonso Amante Soria
European Space Policy Institute
Vienna, Austria

ISSN 1868-5307 ISSN 1868-5315 (electronic)
Studies in Space Policy
ISBN 978-3-030-79433-0 ISBN 978-3-030-79434-7 (eBook)
https://doi.org/10.1007/978-3-030-79434-7



This Springer imprint is published by the registered company Springer Nature Switzerland AG
The registered company address is: Gewerbestrasse 11, 6330 Cham, Switzerland

# Acknowledgements

Special acknowledgment is expressed to Salvador Landeros Ayala (Mexican Space Agency), César Duarte Muñoz (Mexican Space Agency), Martha Mejía-Kaiser (International Institute of Space Law), Cynthia Jiménez Monroy (Mexican space lawyer), Victoria Cocca y Esquivel (Latin American and Caribbean Space Network), Juan Manuel de Faramiñán Gilbert (University of Jaén), and Brenda Ulate (Central American Association for Aeronautics and Space) for their comments, ideas and inputs for the elaboration of this study.

# Introduction

States are free to choose the cooperation mechanisms that they consider the most convenient and effective to develop their space sectors and promote their national interests in the regional and international space arenas. In many regions, space cooperation has taken different forms since the beginning of the space era. Non-institutional space cooperation mechanisms, such as regional space conferences and multilateral space cooperation agreements, have largely been adopted by a great array of countries. The Asia-Pacific Regional Space Agency Forum (APRSAF), and the African Association of Remote Sensing of the Environment (AARSE) are current examples of these mechanisms. Moreover, some countries have joined their efforts to establish regional institutional space cooperation mechanisms, for example, the European Space Agency (ESA), the Asia-Pacific Space Cooperation Organization (APSCO), the Arab Satellite Communications Organization (ARABSAT), and the Intersputnik International Organization of Space Communications (INTERSPUTNIK).[1] These institutional and non-institutional mechanisms are embedded in specific regional contexts and are influenced by geographical, historic, political, economic, social, technical and scientific considerations.

In Latin America, there are several space related cooperation mechanisms. On one side there are non-institutional space cooperation mechanisms such as the Space Conference of the Americas (SCA) and the RELACA-Espacio Network (RELACA-Espacio), which promote national and regional space activities and function as hemispheric forums to discuss and exchange ideas on space matters. On the other side there are institutional space cooperation mechanisms such as the Regional Centre for Space Science and Technology Education for Latin America and the Caribbean (CRECTEALC),[2] the Inter-American Telecommunications Commission (CITEL),[3]

[1] Several states are members of more than one regional institutional space cooperation mechanism, such as Germany (ESA and INTERSPUTNIK) and Egypt (APSCO—as associated member state—and the African Space Agency (AfSA)). Many European states are members of ESA and the European Organisation for the Exploitation of Meteorological Satellites (EUMETSAT).

[2] Centro Regional de Enseñanza de Ciencia y Tecnología del Espacio para América Latina y el Caribe (CRECTEALC).

[3] Comisión Interamericana de Telecomunicaciones (CITEL).

and the Andean Telecommunications Authorities Committee (CAATEL)[4] that have largely contributed to the development of telecommunications and space related activities in the region.

However, there is not yet a regional institutional body or multilateral cooperation mechanism in Latin America that coordinates space initiatives in all the region, functions as a permanent and stable discussion forum on space issues or operates regional space programs. The lack of an institutional space cooperation mechanism in the region and the existence of successful institutional mechanisms in other parts of the world have prompted some Latin American countries and academics to propose the creation of a regional space agency in the Americas. Actually, this idea has been suggested since the 1980's on multiple occasions, but for multiple reasons the agency has never materialized. To overcome this impasse, Latin American countries should consider if a multilateral space agency is necessary, desirable, and possible in the region, and answer some essential questions, such as the following:

- Does Latin America need a regional space agency? More specifically, is the Latin American Space Agency (LASA) the most appropriate mechanism to promote regional space cooperation and develop the space sector for the benefit of Latin American countries?
- Who wants to create LASA and is willing to launch or collaborate in this endeavour?
- Who is willing to participate in LASA's overall budget and what formula should be adopted to calculate the contributions of its members?
- Which is the most appropriate forum to discuss and prepare the creation of LASA?
- What would LASA's mission and main objectives be? What should be its legal and administrative framework?
- Can ESA serve as the best model for LASA? If so, what kind of European space activities, policies and programmes should be replicated by LASA?
- Are other institutional cooperation mechanisms more suitable than ESA as models for LASA?
- Who should be a member of LASA and which criteria should be used to join LASA membership?
- Should one or more regional space cooperation mechanisms (non-institutional mechanisms, for example) be created or reinforced before creating LASA?
- Are Latin American countries capable of setting up LASA in the short or medium term?
- What does it take to establish LASA in terms of political, legal, financial, scientific and technical considerations?

Clearly, this is not a comprehensive list of possible questions to be answered, and different approaches to the subject may generate further and more complex questions. Moreover, the present study will not deal with all these questions. Instead, it will focus on the essential legal and political issues concerning the creation of LASA.

[4] Comité Andino de Autoridades de Telecomunicaciones (CAATEL).

Therefore, the study is divided into four chapters: Chap. 1 examines the implementation of the principle of international space cooperation by Latin American countries; Chap. 2 presents a historical analysis of the proposals on the creation of a regional space agency in Latin America; Chap. 3 deals with the main conditions to set up this entity, and Chap. 4 examines several of the potential issues to be included in a convention on LASA.

Finally, this study uses the words "Latin America" to refer to the region or group of countries of the American continent where Romance languages, such as Spanish, Portuguese, and French are predominantly spoken. Therefore, reference to countries or subregions of the American continent in which English or other non-Romance languages are predominantly spoken, for example, Canada, the United States of America, and the Caribbean, are not considered part of Latin America. To clear doubts, for the purposes of this report, Latin America comprises the following 20 countries: Argentina, Bolivia, Brazil, Chile, Colombia, Costa Rica, Cuba, Dominican Republic, Ecuador, El Salvador, Guatemala, Haiti, Honduras, Mexico, Nicaragua, Panama, Paraguay, Peru, Uruguay and Venezuela.

# Contents

# About the Authors

**Dr. Annette Froehlich** is a scientific expert seconded from the German Aerospace Center (DLR) to the European Space Policy Institute (Vienna), and an honorary adjunct senior lecturer at the University of Cape Town (SA) at SpaceLab. She graduated in European and International Law at the University of Strasbourg (France), followed by business oriented postgraduate studies and her Ph.D. at the University of Vienna (Austria). Responsible for DLR and German representation to the United Nations and International Organizations, she was also a member/alternate head of delegation of the German delegation to UNCOPUOS. Dr. Froehlich is an author of a multitude of specialist publications and serves as a lecturer at various universities worldwide in space policy, law and society aspects. Her main areas of scientific interest are European space policy, international and regional space law, emerging space countries, space security and space and culture. She has also launched, as editor, the new scientific series Southern Space Studies (Springer publishing house) dedicated to Latin America and Africa.

**Diego Alonso Amante Soria** holds a bachelor's degree in law from the National Autonomous University of Mexico (UNAM) and a master's degree in international law from the University of Grenoble Alpes (France). His main areas of interest are space law and policy, international security and international organisations. His master's dissertation was about the legal challenges of the exploitation of natural space resources. He has acquired professional experience at the Legal Research Institute of UNAM, the Mexican Ministries of the Interior, Economy and Foreign Affairs and the European Space Policy Institute (Vienna, Austria). Passionate about astronomy, he volunteered at a Mexican Astronomical society for several years. He has already co-authored previous space related publication in this series on Space Supporting Latin America: Latin America's Emerging Space Middle Powers.

# Abbreviations

| | |
|---|---|
| AARSE | African Association of Remote Sensing of the Environment |
| ABAE | Agencia Bolivariana de Actividades Espaciales (Bolivarian Agency for Space Activities)—Venezuela |
| ABE | Agencia Boliviana Espacial (Bolivian Space Agency) |
| ACE | Agencia Chilena del Espacio (Chilean Space Agency) |
| AEB | Agência Espacial Brasileira (Brazilian Space Agency) |
| AEC | Agencia Espacial Colombiana (Colombian Space Agency) |
| AECA | Agencia Espacial de Centroamérica y el Caribe (Space Agency for Central American and the Caribbean) |
| AECR | Agencia Espacial Costarricense (Costa Rican Space Agency) |
| AEM | Agencia Espacial Mexicana (Mexican Space Agency) |
| AEP | Agencia Espacial del Paraguay (Space Agency of Paraguay) |
| AfSA | African Space Agency |
| AfSP | African Space Policy |
| AfSS | African Space Strategy |
| ALADA | Asociación Latino Americana de Derecho Aeronáutico y Espacial (Latin-American Association of Aeronautical and Space Law) |
| ALAS | Alianza Latinoamericana de Agencias Espaciales (Alliance of Latin American Space Agencies) |
| ALCE | Agencia Latinoamericana y Caribeña del Espacio (Latin American and Caribbean Space Agency) |
| ALMA | Atacama Large Millimetre/submillimetre Array |
| AMEXCID | Agencia Mexicana de Cooperación Internacional para el Desarrollo (Mexican Agency for International Development Cooperation) |
| AMRO/WHO | World Health Organization's Regional Office for the Americas |
| AP-MCSTA | Asia-Pacific Workshop on Multilateral Cooperation in Space Technology and Applications |
| APOSOS | Ground-Based Space Object Observation Network |
| APRSAF | Asia-Pacific Regional Space Agency Forum |
| APSCO | Asia-Pacific Space Cooperation Organization |

| | |
|---|---|
| ARABSAT | Arab Satellite Communications Organization |
| ARRA | UN Rescue Agreement |
| ASEAN | Association of Southeast Asian Nations |
| ASI | Agenzia Spatiale Italiana (Italian Space Agency) |
| AU | African Union (formerly OAU) |
| BCIE | Banco Centroamericano de Integración Económica (Central American Bank of Economic Integration) |
| CAATEL | Comité Andino de Autoridades de Telecomunicaciones (Andean Telecommunications Authorities Committee) |
| CELAC | Comunidad de Estados Latinoamericanos y Caribeños (Community of Latin American and Caribbean States) |
| CERN | European Organization for Nuclear Research |
| CIM | Inter-American Commission of Women |
| CIREN | Centro de Información de Recursos Naturales (Information Centre of Natural Resources)—Chile |
| CITEL | Comisión Interamericana de Telecomunicaciones (Inter-American Telecommunications Commission) |
| CJI | Inter-American Juridical Committee |
| CMSD | Council of Ministers for Space Development—Chile |
| CNES | Centre National d'Études Spatiales (National Centre for Space Studies)—France |
| CONACYT | Consejo Nacional de Ciencia y Tecnología (National Science and Technology Council) |
| CONAE | Comisión Nacional de Actividades Espaciales (National Commission on Space Activities)—Argentina |
| CONIDA | Comisión Nacional de Investigación y Desarrollo Aeroespacial (National Commission for Aerospace Research and Development)—Peru |
| COPERS | European Preparatory Commission for Space Research |
| COSPAR | Committee on Space Research |
| CPC | Committee for Programme and Coordination—UN |
| CRECTEALC | Regional Centre for Space Science and Technology Education for Latin America and the Caribbean |
| CSA | Chinese Society of Astronautics |
| CSC | Colombian Space Commission |
| CSSTEAP | Centre for Space Science and Technology Education in Asia and the Pacific |
| CTU | Caribbean Telecommunications Union |
| DLR | German Aerospace Centre |
| DSSP | Data Sharing Service Platform |
| DV-30 | Asia-Pacific Regional Cooperation Organization's Development Vision 2030 |
| ECA | Economic Commission for Africa |
| ECE | Economic Commission for Europe |
| ECLA | Economic Commission for Latin America |

| | |
|---|---|
| ECLAC | Economic Commission for Latin America and the Caribbean (formerly ECLA) |
| ECOSOC | United Nations Economic and Social Council |
| ECS | European Cooperating States |
| ECSL | European Center for Space Law |
| ECU | European Currency Unit |
| EGNOS | European Geostationary Navigation Overlay Service |
| ELDO | European Organisation for the Development and Construction of Space Vehicle Launchers |
| EO | Earth Observation |
| ESA | European Space Agency |
| ESC | European Space Conference |
| ESCAP | Economic Commission for Asia and the Pacific |
| ESCWA | Economic and Social Commission for Western Asia |
| ESDAC | European Space Data Analysis Centre |
| ESO | European Southern Observatory |
| ESP | European Space Policy |
| ESRO | European Space Research Organisation |
| EU | European Union |
| EUMETSAT | European Organisation for the Exploitation of Meteorological Satellites |
| EUSP | European Union Space Policy |
| EUSPA | European Union Agency for the Space Programme |
| EXA | Agencia Espacial Civil Ecuatoriana (Ecuadorian Civil Space Agency) |
| FAE | Ecuadorian Air Force |
| GALILEO | Europe's Global Satellite Navigation Programme |
| GDP | Gross Domestic Product |
| GEERS | European Space Research Group |
| GEO | Group on Earth Observations |
| GEOSS | Global Earth Observation System of Systems |
| GIE | Grupo Internacional de Expertos (International Group of Experts) |
| GIS | Geographic Information Systems |
| GJU | GALILEO Joint Undertaking |
| GLAC | Global Space Applications Conference |
| GNI | Gross National Income |
| GNP | Gross National Product |
| GNSS | Global Navigation Satellite System |
| GOE | Grupo de Operaciones Espaciales (Space Operations Group) |
| GOVSATCOM | Governmental Satellite Communications Programme |
| GPS | Global Positioning System |
| GRSS | Geoscience and Remote Sensing Society |
| GRULAC | Group of Latin American and the Caribbean |

| | |
|---|---|
| GSA | European Global Navigation Satellite System Agency (formerly the European GNSS Advisory Agency) |
| HAS | Haiti's Space Agency |
| IAA | International Academy of Astronautics |
| IAC | International Astronautical Congress |
| IACID | Inter-American Council for Integral Development |
| IADC | Inter-Agency Space Debris Coordination Committee |
| IAF | International Astronautical Federation |
| IAIASL | Instituto Iberoamericano de Derecho Aeronáutico y del Espacio y de la Aviación Comercial (Iberian-American Institute of Air and Space Law) |
| ICG | International Committee on Global Navigation Satellite Systems |
| ICT | Information and Communications Technologies |
| IDB | Inter-American Development Bank |
| IGO | International Intergovernmental Organisation |
| IICA | Inter-American Institute for Cooperation on Agriculture |
| IIN | Inter-American Children's Institute |
| INAOE | Instituto Nacional de Astrofísica, Óptica y Electrónica (National Institute for Astrophysics, Optics and Electronics) |
| INTERSPUTNIK | Intersputnik International Organization of Space Communications |
| IRC | International Relations Committee—ESA |
| ISA | Israel Space Agency |
| ISF | International Space Forum |
| ISS | International Space Station |
| ISSI-BJ | International Space Science Institute Beijing |
| ITU | International Telecommunication Union |
| JAES | Joint Africa-European Union Strategy |
| LASA | Latin American Space Agency |
| LASP | Latin American Space Policy |
| LASPr | Latin American Space Programme |
| LIAB | UN Liability Convention |
| LSC | Legal Subcommittee—UNCOPUOS |
| MCMFA | Meeting of Consultation of Ministers of Foreign Affairs—OAS |
| MOON | UN Moon Agreement |
| MoU | Memorandum of Understanding |
| NAOC | National Astronomical Observatories of China |
| NASA | National Aeronautics and Space Administration—United States |
| NATO | North Atlantic Treaty Organization |
| NGO | Non-governmental Organization |
| NINS | National Institutes of Natural Sciences—Japan |
| NSF | United States National Science Foundation |
| NSPs | National space policies, strategies and plans |

| | |
|---|---|
| OAS | Organisation of American States |
| OAU | Organisation of Africa Unity |
| OECD | Organization for Economic Co-operation and Development (formerly OEEC) |
| OEEC | Organization for European Economic Co-operation |
| OST | UN Outer Space Treaty |
| PAHO | Pan American Health Organization |
| PAIGH | Pan American Institute of Geography and History |
| PARLACEN | Parlamento Centroamericano (Central American Parliament) |
| PCC.II | Permanent Consultative Committee II |
| PPDEC | Presidential Program for Colombian Space Development |
| PPT | Presidencia Pro Témpore (Presidency Pro Tempore) |
| PROSUR | Foro para el Progreso de América del Sur (Forum for the Progress of South America) |
| PSA | Programme on Space Applications—UN |
| PSAg | Peruvian Space Agency |
| R&D | Research and Development |
| REC | Regional Economic Community |
| REG | UN Registration Convention |
| RELACA-Espacio | Red Latinoamericana y del Caribe del Espacio (Latin American and Caribbean Space Network) |
| RSO | Regional Support Office—UN-SPIDER |
| SASA | South American Space Agency |
| SBASP | Proyecto Satelital Andino Simón Bolívar (Simón Bolívar Andean Satellite Project) |
| SCA | Conferencia Espacial de las Américas (Space Conference of the Americas) |
| SCT | Secretaría de Comunicaciones y Transportes (Ministry of Communications and Transportation)—Mexico |
| SELPER | Sociedad Latinoamericana en Percepción Remota y Sistemas de Información Espacial (Latin-American Society in Remote Sensing and Spatial Information Systems) |
| SFCG | Space Frequency Coordination Group |
| SGAC | Space Generation Advisory Council |
| SIASGE | Sistema Italo-Argentino de Satélites para la Gestión de Emergencias (Italian-Argentine Satellite System for Emergency Management) |
| SICA | Sistema de la Integración Centroamericana (Central American Integral System) |
| SIRIS | Sistema Integral Regional de Información Satelital (Regional Satellite Integrated Information System) |
| SO Standards | Standards for the Implementation and Coordination of the Provisions of the Charter Relating to the Inter-American Specialized Organisations |
| SO | Inter-American Specialized Organisation |

| | |
|---|---|
| SSAU | Ukraine Space Agency |
| STC | Scientific and Technical Subcommittee—UNCOPUOS |
| TFEU | Treaty on the Functioning of the European Union |
| U.S. | United States of America |
| UACh | Austral University of Chile |
| UN | United Nations |
| UNAM | Universidad Nacional Autónoma de México (National Autonomous University of Mexico) |
| UNASUR | Unión de Naciones Suramericanas (Union of South American Nations) |
| UNCOPUOS | United Nations Committee on the Peaceful Uses of Outer Space |
| UN-ESCAP | United Nations Economic and Social Commission for Asia and the Pacific |
| UNGA | United Nations General Assembly |
| UNISPACE 82 | Second United Nations Conference on Peaceful Uses of Outer Space |
| UNOOSA | United Nations Office for Outer Space Affairs |
| UN-RCSSTEAP | Regional Centre for Space Science and Technology Education in Asia and the Pacific (China) affiliated to the United Nations |
| UN-SPIDER | United Nations Platform for Space-based Information for Disaster Management and Emergency Response |
| UVG | University of the Valley of Guatemala |
| WMO | World Meteorological Organisation |
| WRC | World Radiocommunication Conferences |

# Chapter 1
# Latin America and the Principle of International Space Cooperation

*If we can touch the sky together, we can conquer our destiny together.*
*Ronnie Nader, Ecuadorian Cosmonaut*

**Abstract** The principle of international cooperation in the outer space field has been promoted and implemented by practically all Latin American countries since the beginning of the space era. Different reasons and interests have led these countries to collaborate between them or with international partners in a great variety of cooperative arrangements. This chapter focuses on the implementation of space cooperation by Latin American countries and is divided into two main parts: the first deals in a general manner with the principle of space cooperation, while the second presents the different forms of cooperation in the space field fostered and implemented by Latin American countries.

## 1.1 The Principle of International Space Cooperation

International cooperation in the outer space field has existed since the beginning of the space race. Great achievements in the use and exploration of outer space would hardly been possible without the joint efforts of different countries. The International Space Station (ISS) is one of the most ambitious and successful examples of such international space cooperation.[1] Moreover, there is a great array of international cooperation mechanisms that have contributed to the development of national, regional and global space capacities. People of all continents have enjoyed the benefits of space technology and its applications thanks to these cooperation mechanisms. However,

[1] National Aeronautics and Space Administration, "International Space Station, International Cooperation", www.nasa.gov/mission_pages/station/cooperation/index.html (all websites cited in this chapter were last accessed and verified on 25 February 2021).

 
A. Froehlich and D. A. Amante Soria, *A Regional Space Agency for Latin America*, Studies in Space Policy 32, https://doi.org/10.1007/978-3-030-79434-7_1

the question that arises is: what exactly does international space cooperation mean and how do Latin American countries apply it?

International cooperation is usually considered as a principle or a conduct standard with a wide moral scope and a poor legal efficiency.[2] However, the transnational character and history of space activities has made international cooperation almost mandatory for all states to the extent that these activities require coordination, mutual assistance and technology transfer.[3] This principle has been recognized in different international instruments, including UN treaties, declarations and resolutions, and is strongly promoted by several space actors.

Early instruments in which the international cooperation principle in the space field is enshrined are the United Nations General Assembly (UNGA) resolution 1348 (XIII),[4] by which UN member states recognized the importance of this principle in the study and utilisation of outer space for peaceful purposes and established an ad hoc Committee on the Peaceful Uses of Outer Space (UNCOPUOS), and UNGA resolution 1472 (XIV),[5] which transformed UNCOPUOS into a permanent body. UNCOPUOS promotes, facilitates and encourages international cooperation in the peaceful uses of outer space, encourages space research programmes, and studies legal problems arising from the exploration of outer space. UNCOPUOS produces annual resolutions on international cooperation in the peaceful uses of outer space.[6]

Another important instrument is the UNGA resolution 1962 (XVIII) called the "Declaration of Legal Principles Governing the Activities of States in the Exploration and Use of Outer Space", which recognizes international cooperation as part of the main international legal space principles.[7] International cooperation is also recognized by the Treaty on Principles Governing the Activities of States in the Exploration and Use of Outer Space, including the Moon and Other Celestial Bodies [also known as the Outer Space Treaty (OST of 1967)],[8] the main multilateral space treaty. The OST preamble highlights that the states parties to the treaty desire to contribute to broad international cooperation in the scientific and legal aspects of the exploration and use of outer space for peaceful purposes and believe that such cooperation will contribute to the development of mutual understanding and to the strengthening of friendly relations between states and peoples. Meanwhile, Articles I, III, IX, X and XI

[2] Mireille Couston, *Droit spatial*, Ellipses, Paris (2014), p. 100.

[3] Ibid.

[4] UNGA RES 1348 (XIII), "Question of the peaceful use of outer space", 13 December 1958.

[5] UNGA RES 1472 (XIV), "International co-operation in the peaceful uses of outer space", 12 December 1959.

[6] United Nations Office for Outer Space Affairs, "Committee on the Peaceful Uses of Outer Space", www.unoosa.org/oosa/en/ourwork/copuos/index.html.

[7] UNGA RES 1962 (XVIII), "Declaration of Legal Principles Governing the Activities of States in the Exploration and Use of Outer Space", 13 December 1963.

[8] UNGA RES 2222 (XXI), "Treaty on Principles Governing the Activities of States in the Exploration and Use of Outer Space, Including the Moon and other Celestial Bodies", 19 December 1966; opened for signature on 27 January 1967; entry into force on 10 October 1967.

of the OST enshrine the principle of international cooperation. These articles address different forms of international space cooperation, such as transfer of information, mutual assistance, use and exploration of outer space, possibility of observation, access to installations and equipment on celestial bodies, coordination, etc.[9] Other UN space treaties and declarations also refer to international space cooperation, such as the Preamble of the Rescue Agreement (ARRA) of 1968,[10] Articles 2 and 4 of the Moon Agreement (MOON) of 1979,[11] and section D paragraph 6 of the Principles Governing the Use by States of Artificial Earth Satellites for International Direct Television Broadcasting.[12]

This principle is also enshrined in the Declaration on International Cooperation in the Exploration and Use of Outer Space for the Benefit and in the Interest of All States, Taking into Particular Account the Needs of Developing Countries, adopted by the UNGA in 1996.[13] This instrument, known as the "Declaration of Benefits", was adopted after a significant negotiation process that considered the different views of states on the scope of the principle of international cooperation enshrined in the OST.

This Declaration highlights that international cooperation in the exploration and use of outer space for peaceful purposes shall be conducted in accordance with international law, including the UN Charter and the OST, and should be carried out for the benefit and in the interest of all states, irrespective of their degree of economic, social or scientific and technological development, and shall be the province of all mankind.[14] It also stipulates that particular account should be taken of the needs of developing countries, and that states are free to determine all aspects of their participation in international space cooperation on an equitable and mutually accepted basis.[15] The Declaration also refers to the different modes used to promote international cooperation, such as governmental and non-governmental; commercial and non-commercial; global, multilateral, regional and bilateral mechanisms.[16] Finally, it enumerates a set of goals that should be promoted and attained through international cooperation, namely the development of space science and technology and of its applications; the development of relevant and appropriate space capabilities in

[9] Couston, *Droit spatial*, p. 101.

[10] UNGA RES 2345 (XXII), "Agreement on the Rescue of Astronauts, the Return of Astronauts and the Return of Objects Launched into Outer Space", 19 December 1967; opened for signature on 22 April 1968; entry into force on 3 December 1968.

[11] UNGA RES 34/68, "Agreement Governing the Activities of States on the Moon and Other Celestial Bodies", 5 December 1979; opened for signature on 18 December 1979; entry into force on 11 July 1984.

[12] UNGA RES 37/92 of 10 December 1982. See also: preamble and principles V, VIII and XIII of the "Principles Relating to Remote Sensing of the Earth from Outer Space" (UNGA RES 41/65 of 3 December 1986), and principle 7 of the "Principles Relevant to the Use of Nuclear Power Sources in Outer Space" (UNGA RES 47/68 of 14 December 1992).

[13] UNGA Resolution 51/122 of 13 December 1996.

[14] Ibid., para. 1.

[15] Ibid., para. 3.

[16] Ibid., para. 4.

interested states, and the exchange of expertise and technology among states on a mutually acceptable basis.[17]

In conclusion, the different multilateral instruments noted above recognize the principle of international cooperation as an important catalyst for the development of space capacities for the benefit of all countries of the world. Therefore, the question arises as to how this principle has been applied by Latin American countries.

## 1.2 Fostering and Implementing Space Cooperation by Latin American Countries

Latin American countries have long participated in different space cooperation mechanisms. Their degree of participation depends on various factors, such as the character of the respective mechanism and the status of the country within that mechanism. National institutions, such as space agencies and telecommunication bodies, are the usual participants in these mechanisms. However, individuals, companies, universities, NGOs, scientific and professional groups, and other non-governmental entities from Latin America also take part in a great array of space cooperation mechanisms. Nowadays, there are four levels of space cooperation implemented by Latin American actors: global, multilateral, regional and bilateral.[18]

### *1.2.1 Global Cooperation*

Among the more relevant space related cooperation mechanisms in which Latin American countries participate or collaborate are UNCOPUOS, the International Telecommunication Union (ITU), the Group on Earth Observations (GEO), and the International Astronautical Federation (IAF).

#### 1.2.1.1 United Nations Committee on the Peaceful Uses of Outer Space

As the main global intergovernmental space forum, the United Nations Committee on the Peaceful Uses of Outer Space (UNCOPUOS) promotes international space cooperation among its members. Several Latin American countries are part of this body and participate in the works of its Scientific and Technical and Legal Subcommittees. Some countries have been members of UNCOPUOS since its inception,

---

[17] Ibid., para. 5.

[18] See further: Annette Froehlich (ed.), Space Fostering Latin American Societies, Developing the Latin American Continent through Space, Part 1, Southern Space Studies, Springer (2020); Annette Froehlich (ed.), Space Fostering Latin American Societies, Developing the Latin American Continent through Space, Part 2, Southern Space Studies, Springer (2021).

**Table 1.1** Latin America's UNCOPUOS members

| UNCOPUOS Latin American members | Year of accession |
|---|---|
| Argentina, Brazil and Mexico (founding members) | 1958 |
| Chile and Venezuela | 1973 |
| Colombia and Ecuador | 1977 |
| Uruguay | 1980 |
| Cuba, Peru and Nicaragua | 1994 |
| Bolivia | 2007 |
| Costa Rica | 2012 |
| El Salvador | 2015 |
| Paraguay | 2018 |
| Dominican Republic | 2019 |

*Source* UNOOSA

such as Argentina, Brazil and Mexico, while others have recently incorporated to it. Currently, 16 Latin American countries are UNCOPUOS members (Table 1.1; Fig. 1.1).

Latin America's participation in UNCOPUOS and its subcommittees has taken various forms. In general, Latin American countries participate in their individual capacity by making unilateral statements or proposals. However, it can be that several or all Latin American UNCOPUOS members participate through groups to make joint statements and defend common interests and points of view. Some groups are permanent, while other are created for specific purposes or meetings.

There are two main groups in which Latin American countries have participated within UNCOPUOS: The Group of 77 (currently G77 and China), and the Group of Latin American and the Caribbean (GRULAC), both permanent and independent groups.[19] All Latin American UNCOPUOS members are members of both groups. However, there are some Latin American states that are members of one of both groups but have no seat at UNCOPUOS, such as Guatemala and Honduras. Thus, the interests of these states are usually represented by one or several UNCOPUOS members.

Further groups composed exclusively of Latin American states or by Latin American states and other countries have also participated in UNCOPUOS. For example, "a group of Latin American countries" was formed in 2019 bringing together most

[19] The G77 and China is the largest intergovernmental organization of developing countries in the UN aimed at providing the means for these countries to articulate and promote their collective economic interests and enhance their joint negotiating capacity on different international topics within the UN system, and promote South-South cooperation for development, see: The Group of 77 at the United Nations, About the Group of 77, www.g77.org/doc/. GRULAC is one of the five UN regional groups made up of all Latin American and Caribbean countries. Its purpose is to dialogue and achieve non-binding consensus on regional topics, "Latin American and Caribbean Group (GRULAC)", Cancillería, Gobierno de Colombia, www.cancilleria.gov.co/en/content/latin-american-and-caribbean-group-grulac, see also: Chap. 3, Sect. 3.3.2.2.

**Fig. 1.1** Latin America's UNCOPUOS Members

Latin American UNCOPUOS members. Curiously, that year GRULAC did not take part in the sessions of UNCOPUOS[20] and its two subcommittees as the regular

[20] GRULAC's last participation in UNCOPUOS was at the fifty-fifth session of the Scientific and Technical Subcommittee held in Vienna from 20 January to 9 February 2018, see: Chap. 3, Sect. 3.4.

regional voice.[21] Other examples are smaller groups composed by two or more Latin American states to present joint initiatives or positions.

Meanwhile, Latin American countries have also cooperated with UNCOPUOS' secretariat, the Office for Outer Space Affairs (UNOOSA), which is responsible for promoting international cooperation in the peaceful use and exploration of outer space. For years, UNOOSA has assisted Latin American countries in strengthening their capacity to use space technology and applications for development.

UNOOSA also maintains the UN Register of Objects Launched into Outer Space and implements the UN Secretary-General's responsibilities under international space law. In this respect, Latin American countries have collaborated with UNOOSA according to their international obligations. For example, most Latin American countries have notified UNOOSA of the launching of their space objects into outer space[22] and the discovery of foreign space objects that have crashed in their territories.[23]

Furthermore, UNOOSA, through the UN Programme on Space Applications (PSA),[24] has supported the creation of a regional centre for space science and technology education (CRECTEALC) in Latin America and the Caribbean to promote space cooperation and development in the region.[25]

Latin American countries have also cooperated with the UN Platform for Space-based Information for Disaster Management and Emergency Response (UN-SPIDER) established in 2006 under UNOOSA. This platform develops solutions for developing countries with limited specialized technologies in managing disasters and reducing disaster risks.[26] UN-SPIDER is a catalyst for cooperation between satellite data and information providers and users such as policymakers, disaster risk managers and emergency responders.[27]

UN-SPIDER is supported in Latin America and the Caribbean by six regional support offices (RSO), which are regional or national centres of expertise that communicate and coordinate with UN-SPIDER on a regular basis, namely in the fields of dissemination and capacity-building, horizontal cooperation, and technical assistance (Fig. 1.2).[28] Since 2011, UN-SPIDER and the RSOs have jointly organized

[21] This change of formula (from "the" to "a") could be interpreted as a sign of non-conformity of points of view among some Latin American members.

[22] Annette Froehlich/Diego Alonso Amante Soria et al., *Space Supporting Latin America: Latin America's Emerging Space Middle Powers*, Springer (2020), pp. 124–127.

[23] Ibid., pp. 128–130.

[24] Created in 1971, the PSA conducts space science and technology dissemination activities and training courses to the benefit of developing countries. The PSA has helped to reduce the gap between developed and developing countries, UNOOSA, "United Nations Programme on Space Applications", www.unoosa.org/oosa/en/ourwork/psa/index.html#:~:text=Mission%20of%20the%20Programme,geographic%20regions%20of%20the%20world.

[25] See: this chapter, Sect. 1.2.3.2.

[26] UNOOSA, "United Nations Platform for Space-based Information for Disaster Management and Emergency Response (UN-SPIDER)", www.unoosa.org/oosa/en/ourwork/un-spider/index.html.

[27] Ibid.

[28] The RSOs of Argentina, Brazil, Colombia, and Mexico, the University of the West Indies—Disaster Risk Reduction Center located in Trinidad and Tobago, and the Water Centre for the

**Fig. 1.2** UN-SPIDER regional support offices in Latin America and the Caribbean. *Source* UN-SPIDER

regional expert meetings, training courses and joint efforts. The last expert meeting held virtually from 22 to 24 September 2020, which brought together some 200 disaster management stakeholders from about 70 institutions of 14 countries of the region, dealt with the topic "Space-based Solutions for Disaster Risk Reduction and Emergency Response in Latin America". This event enabled participants to discuss the progress of Latin American institutions in the use of space technologies and space-based information in risk reduction management, preparedness, recovery and disaster

Humid Tropics of Latin America and the Caribbean (CATHALAC—Centro del Agua del Trópico Húmedo para América Latina y el Caribe) located in Panama, see: UN-SPIDER Knowledge Portal, "Regional Support Offices", www.un-spider.org/network/regional-support-offices.

response, and disseminate satellite technology applications for the development of hazard maps in early warning systems and disaster response operations.[29]

A further UN-SPIDER main project in the region is the SEWS-Drought (SEWS-D) project,[30] which aims to strengthen national drought policies in Latin American and the Caribbean by using space-based information on a permanent basis.[31] Thanks to the cooperation between international, regional, and national partners in the use of space data, the SEWS-D project has supported Central American countries and Dominican Republic to strengthen their national capacities to reduce the impact of droughts in their territories.[32]

Lastly, UN-SPIDER has conducted support technical missions to various Latin American countries, such as the Technical Advisory Mission to Peru to assess the current and potential use of space-based information in all aspects of disaster management,[33] and the Institutional Strengthening Mission to Ecuador to run a training programme on the "Analysis of satellite images to monitor floods, drought and forest fires" with the aim of training participants in the use of EO data,[34] both carried out in April 2019.

#### 1.2.1.2 International Telecommunication Union

Space cooperation is also promoted by the International Telecommunication Union (ITU). International coordination and consultation are of great importance to avoid harmful interference when using Earth orbits and radio frequencies for space services, and the significant role of the ITU to this end has been largely acknowledged. All Latin American countries are ITU members and participate in the work of its organs, such

[29] The recommendations issued from this meeting were: to conduct additional webinars to continue taking note of the progress made by Latin American institutions in the use of space technologies and space-based information in risk reduction management, preparedness, recovery and disaster response; to establish a regional technical group of professionals and experts who can contribute to disaster response efforts in Latin America through the processing of satellite imagery in a coordinated fashion in case of large disasters, and to explore opportunities for cooperation to develop satellites, including for meteorology, and to take advantage of opportunities made available by UNOOSA and the space community, UN-SPIDER Knowledge Portal, "UN-SPIDER conducts virtual expert meeting for Latin America", 29 September 2020, https://un-spider.org/news-and-events/news/un-spider-conducts-virtual-expert-meeting-latin-america.

[30] In Spanish: "Fortaleciendo sistemas de alerta temprana para sequías" (FOSAT-S).

[31] UN-SPIDER Knowledge Portal, "SEWS-Drought in Latin America and the Caribbean", www.un-spider.org/projects/SEWS-D-project-caribbean.

[32] Ibid., see also: "Informaci6n de antecedentes FOSAT-S", www.un-spider.org/es/proyectos/FOSAT-S/FOSAT-S_informacion.

[33] UN-SPIDER Knowledge Portal, "UN-SPIDER conducts Technical Advisory Mission to Peru", 1 April 2019, https://un-spider.org/news-and-events/news/un-spider-tam-peru.

[34] UN-SPIDER Knowledge Portal, "UN-SPIDER conducts Institutional Strengthening Mission to Ecuador", 8 April 2019, https://un-spider.org/news-and-events/news/un-spider-conducts-institutional-strengthening-missino-ecuador.

as the Plenipotentiary Conference, the world conferences on international telecommunication, the Council,[35] and the Development, Standardization, and Radiocommunication Sectors. There are many Latin American entities that are members and associate members of one of more of these sectors.[36]

Moreover, Latin American countries and entities also participate in the World Telecommunication/ICT Policy Forums to discuss information and communications technologies (ICT) key policies and promote global policies on the matter.[37] They also participate in regional radiocommunication seminars, such as the ITU Regional Radiocommunications Seminar 2020 (RRS-20-Americas) for the Americas, an online meeting held on 13–24 July 2020 organized by the ITU in collaboration with the Caribbean Telecommunications Union (CTU).[38] In this seminar, the participants discussed future radio-frequency spectrum requirements for radiocommunication systems according to the outcome of the ITU World Radiocommunication Conference (WRC-19) held in Sharm el-Sheikh, Egypt, in 2019.[39]

#### 1.2.1.3 Group on Earth Observations

Latin American countries also participate in the Group on Earth Observations (GEO), a global network established in 2005 to coordinate Earth Observation (EO) systems and build the Global Earth Observation System of Systems (GEOSS) for the benefit of humankind. There are currently 15 Latin American countries that are members of GEO.[40] Participation of Latin America in GEO includes the 2015 GEO Ministerial

[35] There are six Latin American countries in the current ITU Council (period 2019–2022): Argentina, Brazil, Cuba, El Salvador, Mexico and Paraguay.

[36] The following Latin American entities participate in one or more ITU Sectors: Empresa Argentina de Soluciones Satelitales (AR-SAT S.A.) from Argentina; Claro S.A., and Fundação Instituto Nacional de Telecomunicações—FINATEL from Brazil; Empresa de Telecomunicaciones de Bogotá S.A. ESP from Colombia; Instituto Costarricense de Electricidad from Costa Rica; Empresa de Telecomunicaciones de Cuba (ETECSA) from Cuba; Compañía Dominicana de Teléfonos, C. por A. (CODETEL) from Dominican Republic; América Móvil, S.A.B. de C.V., and Telecomunicaciones de México (TELECOMM) from Mexico; Cable and Wireless Panamá S.A. from Panama; Compañía Paraguaya de Comunicaciones (COPACO S.A.) from Paraguay; Organismo Supervisor de Inversión Privada en Telecomunicaciones (OSIPTEL) from Peru; and Compañía Anónima Nacional Teléfonos de Venezuela (CANTV) from Venezuela; see: ITU, "List of Sector Members", www.itu.int/online/mm/scripts/gensel11?lang=fr&_memb=S.

[37] ITU, "Fifth World Telecommunication/ICT Policy Forum", www.itu.int/en/wtpf-13/Pages/default.aspx.

[38] The CTU is an inter-governmental organisation that supports the development of the Caribbean ITC sector. CTU members are all members and associated states of the Caribbean Community. Cuba is the only Latin American country that participates in CTU and has the status of associated state, see: Caribbean Telecommunications Union, www.ctu.int/.

[39] ITU, "Digital revolution spurs greater demand for limited radio-frequency spectrum in the Americas", Geneva, 27 July 2020, www.itu.int/en/mediacentre/Pages/cm04-2020-rrs-americas.aspx.

[40] Argentina, Brazil, Chile, Colombia, Costa Rica, Ecuador, El Salvador, Guatemala, Honduras, Mexico, Nicaragua, Panama, Paraguay, Peru and Uruguay.

Summit held in Mexico City, where the Mexico City Ministerial Declaration was adopted through which participants called on GEO to launch a GEO initiative to leverage EO to support the implementation, monitoring and evaluation of the 2030 Global Goals for Sustainable Development, as well as to endorse the GEO Strategic Plan 2016–2025 for the implementation of GEOSS.[41] Within GEO, there is a regional initiative for the Americas, named AmeriGEOSS. This initiative promotes collaboration and cooperation among GEO members in the continent by using EO data to the benefit of four priority areas: agriculture, disaster risk reduction, water, and biodiversity and ecosystem monitoring.[42]

#### 1.2.1.4 International Astronautical Federation

Established in 1951, the International Astronautical Federation (IAF) is an international non-governmental organization in which experts from space agencies, industry, and research gather to dialogue on space issues. In order to promote space cooperation at the international and regional levels, several Latin American governmental and non-governmental entities have actively participated in the IAF annual International Astronomical Congress (IAC) and other international and regional IAF events, such as the Global Space Applications Conference (GLAC) held in Montevideo, Uruguay, in 2018, and the International Space Forum at Ministerial Level - the Latin American and Caribbean Chapter, held in Buenos Aires in 2019.[43]

The IAF has established the Latin American and Caribbean Regional Group (IAF GRULAC),[44] which has several responsibilities, including giving advice and reporting to the IAF on the space activities and technologies of Latin America and the Caribbean; encouraging institutions, corporations and individuals of the region to participate in IAF GRULAC and IAF activities; and coordinating representatives of the hemisphere in promoting space research and technology, formulating local demands in technology and applications, defining regional interests and political priorities, and promoting proposals for the IACs.[45] In 2017, IAF GRULAC adopted "LATCOSMOS", a space development plan for Latin American and the Caribbean.[46] LATCOSMOS includes several programs, such as the "Latin Americans in Space" program, which aims at sending a crew of Latin American professionals in a suborbital space mission to carry out a science experiment and an engineering test, and

---

[41] The Group on Earth Observations (GEO), "Mexico City Declaration", Mexico City, 13 November 2015, www.earthobservations.org/documents/ministerial/mexico_city/MS3_Mexico_City_Declaration.pdf.

[42] AmeriGEOSS, "Overview", www.amerigeoss.org/amerigeoss/about/overview.

[43] International Astronautical Federation, www.iafastro.org/.

[44] Not to be confused with the Latin American and Caribbean Group (GRULAC) of the United Nations, see: Chap. 3, Sect. 3.3.2.2.

[45] LATCOSMOS, "IAF GRULAC", www.latcosmos.org/iaf-grulac.

[46] Ibid.

to experience several minutes of microgravity,[47] and the "Latin American Lunar Program", whose objective is to initiate a seed program to call for a technological development program to do research and acquire space technology that would allow regional countries, entities and individuals to contribute and participate in a future Moon Village.[48]

### *1.2.2 Multilateral Cooperation*

Multilateral cooperation between Latin American countries and other countries or international partners outside the region has existed for decades and has largely increased in recent years. One of the best examples is APSCO, an intergovernmental space organization for Asia–Pacific based in Beijing, China. Created in 2008, APSCO promotes multilateral cooperation in space science, technology and applications to facilitate capacity building of its members.[49] Peru is the only Latin American country member of APSCO. In 2015, Mexico obtained observer status, and in 2019 it was invited to join APSCO as a permanent member.[50] Peru is a beneficiary of several APSCO cooperative networks, such as the Data Sharing Service Platform (DSSP), which allows meteorological and satellite remote sensing data; the Ground-Based Space Object Observation Network (APOSOS), which is used to detect and track space objects, and identify capacity building (one of the three telescopes of the system was installed in Peru in 2015 (Fig. 1.3));[51] and the Space Technology Applications

[47] LATCOSMOS, "Latin Americans in Space", www.latcosmos.org/c. In September 2020, the first Latin American space mission was announced as part of the LATCOSMOS program. The crew, made up of representatives of Costa Rica, Ecuador, Mexico and the United States, will carry out the ESAA—01 EX SOMINUS AD ASTRA suborbital flight. This suborbital flight—together with the above-mentioned goals—will strengthen academic collaboration in Latin American for the development of space activities, see: Laura Romero, "Un puma, en la primera misión espacial latinoamericana", *Gaceta UNAM*, 14 September 2020, www.gaceta.unam.mx/un-puma-en-la-primera-mision-espacial-latinoamericana/.

[48] To implement this program, the Ecuadorian and Colombian civilian space agencies created the joint venture "The Colombo-Ecuadorian Lunar Program", see: LATCOSMOS, "Latin American Lunar Program", www.latcosmos.org/latinamerican-lunar-program.

[49] Asia–Pacific Space Cooperation Organization, "About APSCO", www.apsco.int/html/comp1/content/WhatisAPSCO/2018-06-06/33-144-1.shtml.

[50] Agencia Espacial Mexicana, "Se integra México a actividades de cooperación internacional Asia-Pacífico en materia espacial", 27 July 2015, www.gob.mx/aem/prensa/se-integra-mexico-a-actividades-de-cooperacion-internacional-asia-pacifico-en-materia-espacial-19686; Agencia Espacial Mexicana, "Invitan a AEM a ser miembro permanente de la APSCO", 10 May 2019, www.gob.mx/aem/prensa/invitan-a-aem-a-ser-miembro-permanente-de-la-apsco-199663.

[51] Two telescopes has been installed in Thailand and Iran, and the APOSOS Data Centre is located in Beijing, hosted by the National Astronomical Observatories of China (NAOC), APSCO, "Ground-Based Space Object Observation Network", www.apsco.int/html/comp1/content/APOSOS/2019-03-01/59-261-1.shtml.

**Fig. 1.3** Asia–Pacific ground-based space object observation system (APOSOS). *Source* APSCO

Network, a project aiming at establishing and evaluating ionospheric models in the Asia–Pacific region through the study of radio wave propagation and solar activity.[52]

Another example of multilateral cooperation is APRSAF, a space-related conference established in 1993 to enhance space activities in the Asia–Pacific region. National and international governmental and non-governmental entities of this region participate in APRSAF, whose activities provides opportunities to discuss international cooperation on space issues. Some Latin American institutions take part in APRSAF: INVAP—FRONTEC[53] from Argentina; the Information Centre of Natural Resources and the Ministry of Economy, Development and Tourism from Chile[54]; the Colombian Commission of Rocketry and Astronautics, and the Portean Learning Unit[55] from Colombia.[56]

---

[52] APSCO, "Cooperative Programs", www.apsco.int/html/comp1/channel/Cooperative_Programs/26.shtml.

[53] INVAP is a company devoted to the design and construction of complex technological systems, while FRONTEC is an enterprise and technological platform created by INVAP based on massive remote sensing data processing, INVAP, www.invap.com.ar/old/en/.

[54] Centro de Información de Recursos Naturales (CIREN) y Ministerio de Economía, Fomento y Turismo, respectively.

[55] Comisión Colombiana de Cohetería y Astronáutica and Unidad Porteña de Aprendizaje, respectively.

[56] Asia–Pacific Regional Space Agency Forum, "Participants", https://aprsaf.org/participants/.

**Fig. 1.4** Atacama large millimetre/submillimetre array (ALMA), Chile. *Source* ALMA, © Clem and Adri Bacri-Normier

Meanwhile, Cuba and Nicaragua are members of INTERSPUTNIK, an international organization established in 1971 aimed at leasing satellite capacity to telecommunications companies, broadcasters and corporate customers under contracts with satellite system operators [57].

Finally, it is worth mentioning the space cooperation agreement adopted in 2001 between Chile and representatives of Europe, Japan and North America for the construction and operation of the largest astronomical project in the world: the Atacama Large Millimetre/submillimetre Array (ALMA), an astronomical interferometer of 66 radio telescopes in the Atacama Desert of northern Chile.[58] This project has benefited Chile through the growth of its technical and human resources in the fields of astronomy and space technology (Fig. 1.4).[59]

[57] INTERSPUTNIK International Organization of Space Communications, www.intersputnik.com/intersputnik/countries/. In addition, the Cuban Telecommunications Company S.A. has a "signatory" status in the organization. This telecommunications entity was established by Cuba, for which the INTERSPUTNIK Operating Agreement entered into force, Ibid.

[58] ALMA is also an international partnership of the European Southern Observatory (ESO), the U.S. National Science Foundation (NSF) and the National Institutes of Natural Sciences (NINS) of Japan, together with NRC (Canada), MOST and ASIAA (Taiwan), and KASI (Republic of Korea), in cooperation with Chile, see: Atacama Large Millimetre/submillimetre Array (ALMA), www.almaobservatory.org/en/home/.

[59] ALMA, "Benefits for the Community", www.almaobservatory.org/en/about-alma-at-first-glance/alma-in-chile/benefits-for-the-community/.

## 1.2.3 *Regional Cooperation*

Latin American countries have established several regional cooperation mechanisms to discuss space topics of common interest for the region, share knowledge on space science and technology, promote space education and capacity-building, undertake joint space projects and activities, and foster the development of their space sectors. The most relevant regional space cooperation mechanisms are the Space Conference of the Americas (SCA), the Regional Centre for Space Science and Technology Education for Latin America and the Caribbean (CRECTEALC), the Latin-American Society in Remote Sensing and Spatial Information Systems (SELPER), the Latin American and Caribbean Space Network (RELACA-Espacio), the Inter-American Telecommunications Commission (CITEL), and the Andean Satellite System.

### 1.2.3.1 Space Conference of the Americas

The Space Conference of the Americas (SCA)[60] is a regional space cooperation forum created in 1990 with the support of the UN in which countries of the Americas gather to advance the development of space activities, space technology and its applications.[61] This regional forum is attended by member states and observers. The SCA designs regional strategies to promote space applications in different areas, such as environmental protection and mitigation of natural disasters.[62]

To date, seven SCAs have been organized in different countries of Latin America, each of which dealing with a specific topic (Table 1.2). The participants in the SCAs have adopted declarations, action plans and other non-binding documents to promote regional space cooperation.[63] During the Second SCA held in Santiago, Chile, in 1993, a Pro Tempore Secretariat was created to follow up the results of the SCA, and other minor bodies—a group of independent experts—were created in later SCAs to support the work of the Pro Tempore Secretariat.

---

[60] Not to be confused with the "Americas Space Conference", an intergovernmental virtual meeting of five countries of the American continent (Brazil, Chile, Colombia, Peru and the U.S., plus Canada as observer) held on 4–5 November 2020. The purpose of this conference was to gather these countries to discuss issues related to coordination, cooperation and collaboration in space research and development. The event was aligned with the U.S. Department of Defense strategy of multinational security cooperation and strategic partnership, see: U.S. Space Command Public Affairs Office, "Americas Space Conference brings together 6 nations to discuss research, development opportunities", 6 November 2020, www.spacecom.mil/News/Article-Display/Article/2408564/americas-space-conference-brings-together-5-nations-to-discuss-research-develop/.

[61] CEA-VI 2010, "Acerca de la CEA", México, www.astroscu.unam.mx/congresos/ALF/cea/acerca.html.

[62] Ibid.

[63] The history of the SCAs is examined in detail in Chap. 2.

**Table 1.2** Space Conferences of the Americas

| SCA | Seat and date | Subject | Main result |
|---|---|---|---|
| I | San José, Costa Rica, 12–16 March 1990 | Perspectives of Collaboration for Development | N/A |
| II | Santiago de Chile, 26–30 April 1993 | Cooperation, Development and Regional Integration | Santiago Declaration |
| III | Punta del Este, Uruguay, 4–8 November 1996 | Science and Technology, Sustainable Development, Environment, Education and Communications | Declaration of Punta del Este |
| IV | Cartagena de Indias, Colombia, 14–17 May 2002 | The Application of Space Science and Technology in the Americas and their Benefits for Civil Society | Declaration of Cartagena de Indias |
| V | Quito, Ecuador, 25–28 July 2006 | Regional Space Cooperation for Security and Human Development | Declaration of San Francisco de Quito |
| VI | Pachuca, Hidalgo, Mexico, 15–19 November 2010 | Space and Development: Space Applications to serve Humanity and the Development of the Americas | Pachuca Declaration |
| VII | Managua, Nicaragua, 17–19 November 2015 | Science and Technology for human development in an environment of cooperation, culture of peace and respect for international space law | Managua Declaration |

#### 1.2.3.2 Regional Centre for Space Science and Technology Education

The Regional Centre for Space Science and Technology Education (CRECTEALC) is a cooperation mechanism aimed at promoting space science and technology education in Latin America. CRECTEALC has two headquarters or campuses that were inaugurated in 2003 in Mexico and Brazil.[64] These regional centres are affiliated to the UN through cooperation agreements with the host countries. Part of CRECTEALC's work is the enhancement of the space capabilities of Latin American countries by providing postgraduate education, research and application programmes on remote sensing and geographic information systems, satellite communications and geopositioning systems, meteorological satellite applications, and space and atmospheric sciences[65] (Fig. 1.5).

---

[64] UNOOSA, "Regional Centres for Space Science and Technology Education (affiliated to the United Nations)", www.unoosa.org/oosa/en/ourwork/psa/regional-centres/index.html.

[65] UNGA A/AC.105/782, *Regional Centres for Space Science and Technology Education (affiliated to the United Nations)*, 14 March 2002.

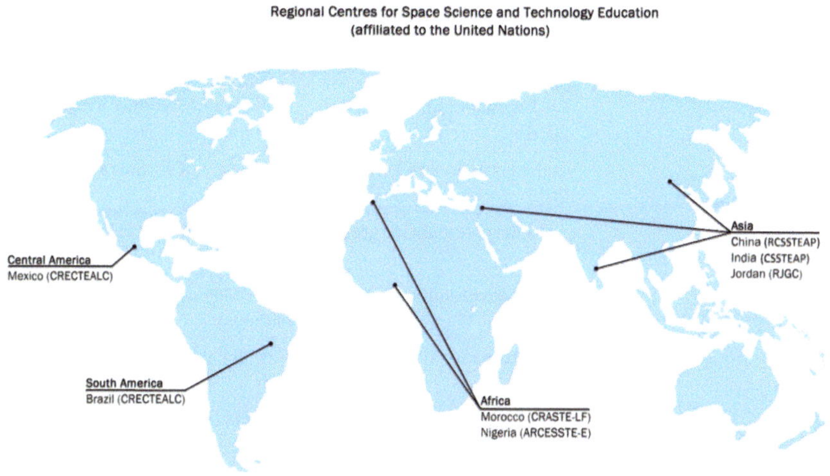


**Fig. 1.5** Regional centres for space science and technology education (affiliated to the UN). *Source* UNOOSA

#### 1.2.3.3 Latin-American Society in Remote Sensing and Spatial Information Systems

The Latin-American Society in Remote Sensing and Spatial Information Systems (SELPER)[66] is an international non-profit scientific and technical society aimed at promoting remote sensing cooperation in Ibero-America,[67] created during the First Meeting on Latin American Remote Sensing Experts held in Ecuador, in 1980. SELPER's main objectives are the promotion of remote sensing activities and improving capacity-building to benefit Latin America countries; the gathering of remote sensing experts and entities working on remote sensing research, development, applications and operations, to foster cooperation and data exchange, and the association with other scientific and technical societies working on remote sensing.[68]

SELPER is made up of national and special chapters. National chapters include professionals from Argentina, Bolivia, Brazil, Chile, Colombia, Cuba, Haiti, Mexico, Peru and Venezuela, while special chapters comprise professionals from Spain,

---

[66] Sociedad Latinoamericana en Percepción Remota y Sistemas de Información Espacial (SELPER).

[67] Latin America is SELPER's field of action, although it uses the denomination of Ibero-America to include the native American cultures and the influence of the Iberian Peninsula countries in the region, see: *Revista SELPER*, October–December 1985, p. 8.

[68] Sociedad Latinoamericana en Percepción Remota y Sistemas de Información Espacial, "¿Qué es SELPER?", https://selper.info/que-es-selper/. In 2014, SELPER and the IEEE Geoscience and Remote Sensing Society (GRSS) signed an agreement for two years to promote the exchange and dissemination of technical data to promote understanding and cooperation between them, SELPER, "Convenio SELPER and GRSS", https://selper.info/pdf/Convenio-GRSS-SELPER.pdf.

**Table 1.3** RELACA-Espacio's congresses

| RELACA-Espacio's congresses | Seat |
|---|---|
| 1st International Congress, 2016 | University of Sergio Arboleda, Colombia |
| 2nd International Congress, 2017 | University of El Salvador, Argentina |
| 3rd International Congress, 2018 | University of The Republic, Uruguay |
| 4th International Congress, 2019 | University of San Carlos, Paraguay |
| 5th International Congress, 2020 | Virtual Congress |
| 6th International Congress, 2021 | University of Applied Sciences, Peru |

Italy and France. In this regard, European countries with advanced remote sensing technology support the development of SELPER's activities.[69]

Among SELPER's activities, there are national, regional and international remote sensing and geographic information systems (GIS) seminars, courses and symposia, such as the International Symposiums on Remote Sensing and Space GIS.[70]

#### 1.2.3.4 RELACA-Espacio

The Latin American and Caribbean Space Network of universities and institutions that do research on technology, policy and law of the outer space, also known as the RELACA-Espacio Network (RELACA-Espacio) is a regional cooperation forum created in 2016 under the impulse and support of the European Centre for Space Law (ECSL) of the European Space Agency (ESA). RELACA-Espacio aims at promoting and coordinating the development of regional efforts to foster space in Latin American and Caribbean countries. To this end, it encourages knowledge and supports research activities in the space field, notably by disseminating relevant information through workshops, professional exchanges and symposia.[71]

RELACA-Espacio holds an international meeting/congress every year where international and regional participants, including government representatives, academics and experts present lectures on space science and technology, society, policy, and law (Table 1.3). This network has also supported the organization of the

[69] Ibid.

[70] Ibid.

[71] Froehlich/Amante Soria et al., *Space Supporting Latin America*, p. 136.

Latin American Manfred Lachs Space Law Moot Court Competition in the 2019 and 2020 test rounds, and the 2021 regional round.[72]

#### 1.2.3.5 Inter-American Telecommunications Commission

The Inter-American Telecommunications Commission (CITEL) is a specialized agency for telecommunications and ICTs of the Organisation of American States (OAS).[73] CITEL's mission is to facilitate and promote the integral and sustainable development of interoperable, innovative and reliable telecommunications/ICTs in the Americas, under the principles of universality, equity and affordability.[74] CITEL is also a forum for cooperation on telecommunications/ICT in the Americas[75] and one of its objectives is the promotion of the harmonization, equitable access, and efficient use of the radio spectrum among the OAS member states.[76] CITEL's functions include maintaining contact with the international governmental and non-governmental organizations working in the field of telecommunications/ICTs; suggesting recommendations to CITEL member states; taking the recommendations of the ITU and other relevant organizations, and promoting coordination of positions among CITEL member states for the different international telecommunications/ICT conferences, assemblies, and meetings.[77] For example, the Permanent Consultative Committee II (PCC.II) of CITEL develops common positions and prepares Inter-American proposals on radiocommunications to the World Radiocommunication Conferences (WRC), which is the institution responsible for reviewing and revising the ITU Radio Regulations, the international treaty governing the use of the radio-frequency spectrum and the geostationary-satellite and non-geostationary-satellite orbits.[78]

#### 1.2.3.6 Andean Satellite System

A further example of regional space cooperation in Latin America is the Andean Satellite System, which is composed of the Satellite Project Simón Bolívar

[72] Ibid., p. 135, see also: International Institute of Space Law, "Latin America", https://iislweb.org/awards-and-competitions/manfred-lachs-space-law-moot-court-competition/participating-in-the-lachs-competition/latin-america/; RELACA-Espacio, "Latin American Round of the Manfred Lachs Space Law Moot Court Competition", https://relaca.space/moot-court.

[73] See: Chap. 3, Sect. 3.3.1.1.1.

[74] Reform of the Statute of the Inter-American Telecommunication Commission (CITEL), CITEL/RES.88 (VII-18).

[75] AG/RES. 1224 (XXIII-O/93).

[76] Art. 3 objectives (i), CITEL/RES.88 (VII-18).

[77] Art. 3 functions (d), (g) and (k), respectively, CITEL/RES.88 (VII-18).

[78] Inter-American Telecommunication Commission (CITEL), "World Radiocommunication Conference (WRC)", www.citel.oas.org/en/Pages/PCCII/WRC.aspx.

(ASPSB)[79] and satellites of different operators registered in the Andean Satellite List.[80] Originally conceived in 1977 as the Condor Project, the ASPSB is a telecommunication satellite project of the Andean Community (formerly the Andean Group), an international integration and cooperation organization composed of four South American countries: Bolivia, Colombia, Ecuador and Peru.[81] The ASPSB was promoted in 1994 by the Andean Telecommunications Authorities Committee, an intergovernmental body of the Andean Community. In 2009, the Andean Community granted to the Dutch company New Skies Satellites B.V. the authorization to exploit and commercialize the orbital-spectrum resource of the Andean Community members in the 67° W position for 30 years.[82] In July 2010, the Andean Satellite Network Simón Bolívar 2 was reactivated with the position of satellite AMC 4 into the 67° W. Later, in March 2017, the Andean satellite SES-10 was successfully put into the 67° W orbital position as part of the Andean Satellite Network Simón Bolívar 2.[83] Satellite SES-10 operates in Band Ku for satellite communication and television services. Among the benefits of the Andean Satellite Network Simón Bolívar 2 are the use of satellite technology for the development of governmental social programs for the community members free of charge, social connectivity projects and other governmental objectives.[84] In addition to the ASPSB, there are around 60 satellites of twelve satellite operators located in 48 satellite orbits covering the territory of the Andean Community members, all registered in the Andean Satellite List.[85]

#### 1.2.3.7 Further Regional Space Cooperation Mechanisms and Projects

Further regional space cooperation mechanisms in Latin America are mostly academic and professional. They mainly contribute to the promotion of space disciplines and develop capacity-building in Latin America countries through the organization of international seminars, conferences and workshops, and by bringing together experts, academics, professionals and interested people in the space sector

---

79 Proyecto Satelital Andino Simón Bolívar (SBASP).

80 Secretaría General de la Comunidad Andina, "Red Satelital Andina Simón Bolívar 2", Power Point Presentation, 2017, www.itu.int/en/ITU-R/space/workshops/2017-Bariloche/Presentations/34%20-%20C%C3%A9sar%20Monta%C3%B1o%20-%20Comunidad%20Andina%20de%20Naciones%20(CAN).pdf.

81 Comunidad Andina, "Somos Comunidad Andina", www.comunidadandina.org/Seccion.aspx?id=189&tipo=QU&title=somos-comunidad-andina.

82 Decisión 725, Autorización comunitaria para la explotación y comercialización del Recurso Órbita Espectro de los Países Miembros en la posición 67° Oeste. On 5 February 2010, the General Secretariat of the Andean Community, representing the State Members, and New Skies Satellites B.V., signed the corresponding contract.

83 Comunidad Andina, "Telecomunicaciones", www.comunidadandina.org/Seccion.aspx?id=315&tipo=TE&title=telecomunicaciones.

84 Secretaría General de la Comunidad Andina, "Red Satelital Andina Simón Bolívar 2", Power Point Presentation, 2017.

85 The list is available at www.comunidadandina.org/StaticFiles/Temas/Telecom/ListaSatelites.pdf.

to discuss and share experiences and knowledge, and to increase social networks. Examples of these organizations are the Iberian-American Institute of Air and Space Law (IAIASL)[86] and the Latin-American Association of Aeronautical and Space Law (ALADA),[87] which promote the development and teaching of space law in the region.

The Space Generation Advisory Council (SGAC), a non-governmental, non-profit organisation and network that supports students and professionals interested in space to be represented to the UN, space agencies, industry and academia around the world also participates in the promotion of space cooperation in Latin America. In North, Central and South America, as well as in the Caribbean, SGAC has supported many Latin American students and young professionals to join the space community for the benefit of their countries. In this regard, several North, Central America and the Caribbean, and South American Space Generation Workshops have been held in the last years,[88] and participants from different Latin American countries have taken part in various SGAC's events, such as the SG Latin American Webinar Series in 2020.[89]

An example of a regional space cooperation project in Latin America is the Regional Satellite Integrated Information System or SIRIS, from its Spanish acronym,[90] a digital space data platform created in 2020 and partly financed by the Inter-American Development Bank (IDB). SIRIS aims at improving risk management in Argentina, Bolivia, Ecuador, Mexico, Paraguay, Peru and Uruguay in four areas: fire, health, water, and agriculture.[91] The platform also provides without cost high resolution space products to the space, agricultural and scientific related institutions of these countries.[92]

---

86 Instituto Iberoamericano de Derecho Aeronáutico y del Espacio y de la Aviación Comercial (IAIASL), located in Spain.

87 Asociación Latino Americana de Derecho Aeronáutico y Espacial (ALADA), based in Argentina.

88 The 1st South American Space Generation Workshop was held in Buenos Aires, Argentina, in 2015; the 2nd Workshop took place in Lima, Peru, in 2016; the 3rd Workshop in São Paulo, Brazil, in 2017; the 4th Workshop in Bogota, Colombia, in 2018, and the 5th Workshop in La Paz, Bolivia, in 2019. The 1st North, Central America and the Caribbean Space Generation Workshop was held in 2019, and the 2nd Workshop, to be held in Mexico City in 2020, was postponed due the global health situation caused by COVID-19.

89 Space Generation Advisory Council, "South America Region", https://spacegeneration.org/regions/south-america.

90 Sistema Integral Regional de Información Satelital (SIRIS).

91 Space Climate Observatory, "Towards a Latin American SCO", 17 November 2020, www.spaceclimateobservatory.org/towards-latin-american-sco?language_content_entity=en.

92 The participating institutions are the National Space Activities Commission (CONAE) of Argentina; the Bolivian Space Agency (ABE); the Military Geographical Institute of Ecuador; the Mexican Space Agency (AEM); the Paraguayan Space Agency (AEP) and the National Science and Technology Council (CONACYT) of Paraguay; the Peruvian Space Agency (CONIDA) and the Ministry of Agriculture and Irrigation (MINAGRI) of Peru; the National Institute of Agricultural Research (INIA) and the Julio Ricaldoni Foundation, both from Uruguay, see: Sistema Integral Regional de Información Satelital, www.sistemasiris.org/#section4, and Agencia Espacial Mexicana, "Articulan Sistema Regional Latinoamericano de Información Satelital "SIRIS"", 3 December 2020, www.gob.mx/aem/prensa/articulan-sistema-regional-latinoamericano-de-informacion-satelital-siris-258654?idiom=es.

### 1.2.4 *Bilateral Cooperation*

Bilateral space cooperation in Latin America has existed since the beginning of the space race. Countries such as Argentina and Brazil have carried out joint space programs for a long time. In the last decade, bilateral space cooperation in the region has greatly increased thanks to the creation of several national space agencies and other space and telecommunications bodies that enable the exchange of space benefits, such as satellite data and space technology and its applications, as well as the development of capacity-building. This kind of cooperation can be divided into two main types:

- bilateral cooperation between a Latin American country and a non-Latin American country or international institution (intercontinental cooperation), and
- bilateral cooperation between two Latin American countries (intracontinental cooperation).

#### 1.2.4.1 Intercontinental Bilateral Cooperation

Intercontinental bilateral cooperation includes framework agreements, cooperation agreements, implementation agreements, memorandums of understanding (MoU) and letters of intent.[93] Examples of framework agreements are the framework agreement between the Peruvian Space Agency (CONIDA)[94] and the Ukraine Space Agency (SSAU), signed in 2011;[95] the framework agreement between the Mexican Space Agency (AEM) and the Israel Space Agency (ISA), adopted in 2017,[96] and the framework agreement on peaceful space cooperation between the National Commission on Space Activities (CONAE) of Argentina and the Centre National d'Études Spatiales (CNES) of France, signed in 2019.[97] Examples of bilateral cooperation agreements are the agreement between Argentina and Italy for the creation of the Italian-Argentine Satellite System for Emergency Management (SIASGE), adopted in 2005,[98] which consists of six SAOCOM satellites provided by the space agencies

[93] See: Froehlich/Amante Soria et al., *Space Supporting Latin America: Latin America's Emerging Space Middle Powers* (2020).

[94] Comisión Nacional de Investigación y Desarrollo Espacial (CONIDA).

[95] "Perú y Ucrania firman un acuerdo de cooperación en materia espacial", Infoespacial.com, 2 June 2011, www.infoespacial.com/latam/2011/06/02/noticia-peru-y-ucrania-firman-un-acuerdo-de-cooperacion-en-materia-espacial.html.

[96] Mexican Space Agency, "Colaborarán México e Israel en materia espacial y satelital", 16 September 2017, www.gob.mx/aem/es/prensa/colaboraran-mexico-e-israel-en-materia-espacial-y-satelital-127044?idiom=es.

[97] CONAE, "Acuerdo de Cooperación con CNES de Francia", 9 May 2019, www.argentina.gob.ar/noticias/acuerdo-de-cooperacion-con-cnes-de-francia.

[98] Sistema Italo-Argentino de Satélites para la Gestión de Emergencias (SIASGE); Agenzia Spatiale Italiana (ASI), "COSMO-SKYMED", www.asi.it/scienze-della-terra/cosmo-skymed/; In 2016, cooperation on SIASGE was renewed through a letter of intent adopted between ASI and CONAE, in: Caleb Henry, "Italian and Argentine Space Agencies Renew Collaborative Agreement", Via

**Fig. 1.6** Launching of Bolivian communications satellite TKSAT-1 from Xichang, China, 20 December 2013. *Source* ABE

of both countries, and the agreement between the Brazilian Space Agency (ABE) and the German Aerospace Centre (DLR) on cooperation for the exploration and use of outer space for peaceful purposes, signed in 2002.[99] Further bilateral cooperation mechanisms include the MoU for the creation of the Túpac Katari project adopted between Bolivia and China in 2010, which put the Bolivian TKSAT-1 communication satellite into Earth orbit (Fig. 1.6),[100] and the implementing agreement between ABE and ESA for the setting up and use of telemetry and tracking facilities on Brazilian territory, signed in 2018.[101] Lastly, the letters of intent include one on space cooperation between AEM and ESA, adopted in 2018,[102] the letter of intent between

Satellite, 24 May 2016, www.satellitetoday.com/government-military/2016/05/24/italian-and-argentine-space-agencies-renew-collaborative-agreement/.

99 Acordo entre a Agência Espacial Brasileira e o Deutsches Zentrum für Luft- und Raumfahrt sobre Cooperação para a exploração e uso do Espaço exterior para fins Pacíficos, Brasilia, 14 February 2002, www.gov.br/aeb/pt-br/programa-espacial-brasileiro/cooperacao-internacional/documentos-alemanha/acordoalemanha2002.pdf.

100 Peter B. Selding, "China to Build, Launch Bolivian Telecomm Satellite", SpaceNews, 2 April 2010, https://spacenews.com/china-build-launch-bolivian-telecom-satellite/.

101 ESA, "ESA and Brazil sign Implementing Agreement for Natal tracking station", 12 December 2018, www.esa.int/About_Us/Corporate_news/ESA_and_Brazil_sign_Implementing_Arrangement_for_Natal_tracking_station.

102 Mexican Space Agency, "Current Agreements with Space Agencies and International Organizations", www.gob.mx/cms/uploads/attachment/file/613899/Current_Agreements_with_Space_Agencies_and_International_Organizations_030221.pdf.

the Venezuelan Ministry of Popular Power for University Education, Science and Technology and the China Great Wall Industry Corporation, for the commercialization of good and services derived from space applications, signed in 2018,[103] and the letter of intent between the Paraguayan Space Agency (AEP) and the Japanese Space Agency (JAXA) for the training of Paraguayan aeronautical engineers, adopted in 2021.[104]

#### 1.2.4.2 Intracontinental Bilateral Cooperation

As regards intracontinental bilateral space cooperation, the bilateral cooperation within the Latin American region is made up of framework agreements, cooperation agreements, MoUs and letters of intent. Examples include the 2019 cooperation agreement between Bolivia and Argentina for the provision of satellite services and facilities; the Joint Declaration on Bilateral Cooperation in the Peaceful Uses of Outer Space between Argentina and Brazil, adopted in 1989; the Framework Agreement on Cooperation in Peaceful Applications of Space Science and Technologies of 1996 adopted by both countries; and the MoU between the Brazilian Space Agency and CONAE signed in 2014 for the development of the SABIA-Mar Space Mission. There is also the Framework Agreement on Cooperation in the Peaceful Uses of Outer Space between Brazil and Peru, signed in 2006, and a framework agreement between the Ecuadorian Space Agency (EXA) and the Colombian Space Agency (AEC), which signed a joint venture in 2018 to implement the Colombo-Ecuadorian Lunar Program. An example of a letter of intent is the 2018 letter of intent between the Space Agency of Paraguay and AEM on peaceful space cooperation.[105]

## 1.3 Conclusion

All Latin American countries have established cooperation relations in the space and telecommunications fields with regional and international partners. This cooperation has taken multiple forms, from institutional and non-institutional cooperation mechanisms to temporary and permanent joint academic space projects, and they involve different space related areas, including space research, space technology and its applications, as well as space education and training. Moreover, while some cooperation relations constitute the first approach between certain countries and partners, others have reached a high degree of partnership. All of them have enabled Latin American

---

[103] Froehlich/Amante Soria et al., *Space Supporting Latin America* (2020), p. 440.

[104] "El Guaranisat-1 fue puesto en órbita con éxito", Embajada de la República del Paraguay en la República del Ecuador, 14 March 2021, www.mre.gov.py/embapar-ecuador/index.php/noticias/https-www-mre-gov-py-index-php-noticias-de-embajadas-y-consulados-el-guaranisat-1-fue-puesto-en-orbita-con-exito?ccm_paging_p=2.

[105] Froehlich/Amante Soria et al., *Space Supporting Latin America* (2020), p. 409.

countries to develop and strengthen their national space sectors. The large number of current cooperation relations adopted by Latin American countries demonstrates that these countries are continuously searching for options to get more knowledge and capacities in the space field for the benefit of their populations, to develop their space industries, and to have a voice in the regional and international space arenas. The rapid development of these cooperation relations through the adoption and implementation of a great array of legal, political, academic and technical instruments is an indication that Latin American countries could be ready to undertake more ambitious space cooperation projects, namely between the countries of this region, such as the establishment of a Latin American Space Agency.

# Chapter 2
# Towards a Latin American Space Agency

*The future of humanity is supported by education, science and technology.*
*It is our duty to prepare future generations for a sustainable Earth.*
Marcos Pontes, Brazilian Astronaut.

**Abstract** This chapter provides a historical insight into the different governmental proposals concerning the concept of a regional space agency in Latin America. The first section presents the historical evolution of these proposals, which has been divided for practical purposes into three periods: the first proposal, covering the years 1982 and 1983; the efforts of the Space Conference of the Americas, which goes from 1991 to 2015, and the appearance of new fora and new proposals, concerning the years 2011–2020. The second section examines this historical process through three main considerations: the rationale and objectives of the Latin American Space Agency; the form, conditions and characteristics of this entity, and the applicable region in which the agency would operate.

## 2.1 A History of Proposals for a Latin American Space Agency

The idea of the creation of a regional space agency in Latin America is not new. In the last four decades, multiple countries have proposed or supported the creation of a mechanism to promote regional space cooperation, strengthen the development of space activities and related sectors in Latin American countries, and generate common positions in the global space arena.[1] While several proposals have been abandoned or lost support, others still survive, although they have not been able to materialize in concrete actions. This chapter presents a historical analysis and some considerations on the winding process of the proposals aimed at creating a regional

[1] This section will focus on governmental proposals on the creation of a regional space agency in Latin America.

 
A. Froehlich and D. A. Amante Soria, *A Regional Space Agency for Latin America*, Studies in Space Policy 32, https://doi.org/10.1007/978-3-030-79434-7_2

space agency in Latin America. The history of proposals for a Latin American Space Agency can be divided into three parts: the first proposal (1982–1983), then the efforts around the Space Conference of the Americas (1991–2015), and finally the appearance of new fora and new proposals (2011–2020).

### *2.1.1 The First Proposal (1982–1983)*

The first proposal for a space agency for Latin America can be traced back to April 1982 during the celebration of the United Nations Regional Seminar on Space Applications in Preparation for UNISPACE 82, held in Quito, Ecuador.[2] It was Chile who proposed the creation of a South American Space Agency (SASA), a proposal that was approved by consensus by representatives of all participant countries.[3] According to this initiative, the main objective of the regional space agency was to be the development of space technology to achieve independence and self-sufficiency to improve the social and economic conditions of the countries of the region. Moreover, the importance of considering the needs of these countries when developing space technology and infrastructure to make aware their respective populations of the benefits of the use of space technology, was highlighted.[4]

In August 1982, during the Second United Nations Conference on Peaceful Uses of Outer Space (UNISPACE 82)[5] held in Vienna, Austria, Chile submitted its SASA proposal as one of the most feasible means to obtain a rational utilization of space technology. This institutional structure would enable South America to make extensive and effective use of space for peaceful purposes.[6] To this end, Chile shared a draft agreement for the creation of SASA.[7] Its first article stated that "an international

---

[2] Cynthia Jiménez Monroy, *Legal and Institutional Aspects of Latin-American Space Cooperation, AQUARELSat: The Water Monitoring Constellation* (Wöhrmann Print Service-Zutphen 2010), p. 28.

[3] Raimundo González, "Seminar on the Applicability of Space Science", 19–23 April 1982, Quito, Ecuador, *Journal of Space Law*, Vol. 10, no. 2 (1982), p. 218.

[4] Ibid.

[5] The Second United Nations Conference on the Exploration and Peaceful Uses of Outer Space, also known as UNISPACE II or UNISPACE 82, held from 9–21 August 1982 in Vienna, Austria, was a global conference focused on strengthening the role of the United Nations in promoting international cooperation to enable developing countries to benefit from the peaceful uses of space technology, United Nations Office for Outer Space Affairs, "UNISPACE Conferences", www.unoosa.org/oosa/en/aboutus/history/unispace.html (All websites cited in this chapter were last accessed and verified on 25 February 2021).

[6] "International Space Programmes and Policies: Proceedings of the Second United Nations Conference on the Exploration and Peaceful Uses of Outer Space (UNISPACE)", Vienna, Austria, August 1982, 195 (1984), noted by Jiménez, *Legal and Institutional Aspects of Latin-American Space Cooperation*, p. 28.

[7] Raimundo González (trad.), "South American Space Agency Proposal", *Journal of Space Law*, Vol. 10, no. 2 (1982), pp. 257–259.

**Fig. 2.1** Commemorative stamps of UNISPACE 82. *Sources* Old Stamps, Pinterest, Spacephila

intergovernmental body known as the South American Space Agency shall be established".[8] It also included some features of this entity, such as being constituted by the agreement and its statutes, and having legal personality and the capacity necessary for the exercise of its functions and the achievement of its objectives (Fig. 2.1).[9]

In addition, the participants in the regional seminar agreed that the Economic Commission for Latin America (ECLA),[10] with the assistance of the United Nations (UN) should, as soon as possible, carry out a technical and institutional feasibility study for the establishment of a Latin American Space Agency (LASA).[11]

---

[8] Ibid.

[9] Ibid.

[10] ECLA changed its name to ECLAC (for Economic Commission for Latin America and the Caribbean) in 1984.

[11] *The Economic Commission for Latin America and the Second United Nations Conference on the Exploration and Peaceful Uses of Outer Space (UNISPACE 82)*, E/CEPAL/L.285, 27 April 1983. ECLA's reference to a Latin American Space Agency (LASA) instead of a South American Space Agency (SASA) probably changed after the participants of a Seminar on Outer Space held in Santiago, Chile, in 1983, agreed to change South American Space Agency to Latin American Space Agency (since then, Chile's 1982 proposal of SASA is to be considered as the LASA proposal), see: A. Cocca, "El Papel de América Latina en el Derecho del Espacio Ultraterrestre", in: *Proceedings of the Thirty-First Colloquium on the Law of Outer Space 127* (1988), mentioned by Jiménez, *Legal and Institutional Aspects of Latin-American Space Cooperation*, p. 29.

In May 1983, ECLA presented the results of its study in a seminar held at Sao José dos Campos, Brazil.[12] The study mentioned that ECLA had no technical expertise in outer space matters and that it could not financially support projects or institutions related to space activities because it was not a financing institution. It also mentioned that it could not directly carry out recommendations to this end, but it could transmit the recommendations to more appropriate institutions. Notwithstanding, ECLA stated that it had considerable resources and expertise for assisting in the creation of regional institutions. Thus, the Commission could assist in the establishment of a regional space mechanism and give some preliminary ideas in this regard. Therefore, ECLA undertook conversations with the United Nations Committee on the Peaceful Uses of Outer Space (UNCOPUOS), the Chilean mission to the UN, and the Department of Technical Cooperation for Development, from which a meeting of experts could be organised to make a scientific and technical evaluation of the proposal. ECLA suggested that the meeting could be held at ECLA's headquarters later in 1983. Additionally, ECLA recommended an expert meeting on the scientific, political and economic aspects of the matter to assess the degree of interest and commitment of Latin American countries to the initiative (Fig. 2.2).[13]

In the same study, ECLA noted that a difficult question was the proposed form of the regional mechanism and considered that it was "perhaps premature to suggest specific attributes for a mechanism which has yet to be agreed upon".[14] However, it acknowledged that there should be a bare idea about this mechanism if discussions on the matter were to be undertaken. ECLA also identified that the proposition of a study about the LASA proposal implied an inter-governmental organisation similar to the model provided by the European Space Agency (ESA). Then, after summarizing the main characteristics of ESA, ECLA concluded that ESA's "basic principle of pooling resources to achieve otherwise unattainable objectives could be applied in Latin America".[15]

Finally, ECLA considered it unnecessary to further assess the LASA proposal for the moment. It would do so if additional instructions were required by ECLA member states. Nevertheless, despite ECLA's constructive analysis of the proposal for a LASA, it seems that the suggested expert meetings were not held and ECLA never again received instructions on the matter.[16]

---

[12] *The Economic Commission for Latin America and the Second United Nations Conference on the Exploration and Peaceful Uses of Outer Space (UNISPACE 82)*, E/CEPAL/L.285, 27 April 1983.

[13] Ibid., p. 3.

[14] Ibid., p. 4.

[15] Ibid., p. 5.

[16] ECLAC's digital repository does not contain information on further developments of LASA's proposal after this study. An information request was made to ECLAC, which was not answered.

UNITED NATIONS

ECONOMIC
AND
SOCIAL COUNCIL

Distr.
LIMITED

E/CEPAL/L.285
27 April 1983

ORIGINAL: ENGLISH

E C L A

Economic Commission for Latin America

United Nations Regional Seminar on Space Applications in Consideration of the Results of the Second United Nations Conference on the Exploration and Peaceful Uses of Outer Space (UNISPACE 82)

Sao José dos Campos, Brazil, 2-6 May 1983

THE ECONOMIC COMMISSION FOR LATIN AMERICA AND THE SECOND UNITED NATIONS CONFERENCE ON THE EXPLORATION AND PEACEFUL USES OF OUTER SPACE (UNISPACE 82)

83-4-639

**Fig. 2.2** Cover of ECLA's 1983 report on the recommendations of UNISPACE 82. *Source* ECLAC

## 2.1.2 *The Efforts of the Space Conference of the Americas (1991–2015)*

A decade after UNISPACE 82, the proposal for a regional space agency reappeared in a new continental forum: The Space Conference of the Americas (SCA).[17] During the First SCA held in San José, Costa Rica, in 1990, the LASA initiative was laid on

[17] See: Chapter 1 (1.2.3.1).

the table to be discussed by the representatives of several Latin American countries. In fact, the original SCA proposal did not deal with the creation of LASA but with the establishment of a Pan-American Space Agency that would include the United States (U.S.) and Canada, following the model of ESA.[18] Despite the high interest in the proposal shown by some countries of the region, Brazil opposed it and, as a result, the SCA did not formally support the initiative. According to Franklin Chang-Díaz, a National Aeronautics and Space Administration's (NASA) astronaut born in Costa Rica and a fervent supporter of LASA, the strategy of the First SCA was not to focus too much on creating a regional space organisation but more on the adoption of common projects by the countries of the region that would be catalytic to the eventual establishment of that organisation.[19]

During the Second SCA held in Santiago, Chile, in 1993, the LASA proposal was not mentioned in the Santiago Declaration, the final document adopted by the Conference. However, the participants agreed on the need for "national space programmes and their projects progressively to converge, integrating as appropriate the space activities of the Americas".[20] Similarly, the Punta del Este Declaration adopted in 1996 by the Third SCA held in Uruguay, stated that the SCA agreed "to cooperate and interact as necessary to facilitate future projects" and firmly believed "that cooperation projects pertaining to outer space will lead to the broadest possible development and application of space technology",[21] which opened the possibility of fostering space cooperation through new cooperation mechanisms such as a potential regional space agency.

In 2002, the Declaration of Cartagena de Indias issued from the Fourth SCA held in Colombia, highlighted in paragraph 17 that it was "important to establish mechanisms for effective cooperation and coordination in the region" and welcomed "the report presented by the delegation of Chile on the creation of a mechanism for regional coordination on space matters",[22] which was entitled "The Creation of a Regional Organism on Space for Latin America and the Caribbean".[23] In addition, the Plan of Action adopted together with the Declaration instructed the pro tempore secretariat[24] of the SCA to take appropriate actions to implement paragraph 17 of the Declaration, such as the identification of space capacities in all the countries of the

[18] "Reaping the Benefits of Latin American Space Cooperation, Interview with Astronaut Franklin Chang-Díaz", *21st Century Science and Technology Magazine*, 21 February 2002, http://21sci-tech.com/articles/winter01/Chang_Diaz.html.

[19] Ibid.

[20] "Santiago Declaration", Second Space Conference of the Americas, Santiago, Chile, 26–30 April 1993, para. 4.

[21] "Punta del Este Declaration", Third Space Conference of the Americas, Punta del Este, 1996, paras. 3 and 6.

[22] "Declaration of Cartagena de Indias and Plan of Action", Fourth Space Conference of the Americas, Cartagena de Indias, Colombia, 14–17 May 2002, para. 17.

[23] Mentioned by Jiménez, *Legal and Institutional Aspects of Latin-American Space Cooperation*, p. 26.

[24] Created by paragraph 8 of the Santiago Declaration, the pro tempore secretariat was responsible to follow up and give continuity to the results of the Conference.

region and the creation of a working group to determine areas of action for regional coordination.[25]

Moreover, the 2003 UNCOPUOS report to the General Assembly stated that the Committee noted "the desire of its member states in Latin America and the Caribbean to institutionalize the Space Conference of the Americas" and that the SCA had "agreed on the importance of creating effective mechanisms for cooperation and coordination in the region".[26] The 2004 UNCOPUOS report also made reference to the institutionalization of the SCA[27] and that the Committee noted the organization of a seminar held at Río Negro, Colombia, in 2004 to exchange experiences in Latin America and the Caribbean and elsewhere "on establishing a space entity in order to enhance access to the socio-economic benefits accruing from the use of space technologies".[28]

It was the Declaration of San Francisco de Quito adopted by the Fifth SCA held at Quito, Ecuador, in 2006, that explicitly indicated "the advisability of having each member state study the possibility of establishing a national space body, which would contribute to the subsequent establishment of a regional space body".[29] An analogous formula was used by the 2007 UNCOPUOS report, which mentioned that the Declaration of San Francisco de Quito invited Latin American and Caribbean States to "set up national space entities to lay the foundation for a regional entity for cooperation".[30] The 2010 UNCOPUOS report also made reference to this Declaration after noting that more states in the Latin America and Caribbean region had set up national space entities of a civilian nature.[31]

---

[25] The specific actions were: (a) Analysis of common requirements, based on a survey sent to all the countries in the region, so as to identify priorities, areas of interest, available human resources, existing research centres, projects in progress, focal points, etc.; (b) Securing of the participation and support of UNCOPUOS, the United Nations Office for Outer Space Affairs (UNOOSA) and, if necessary, other organizations at all stages of the implementation of this process; (c) Identification of sources of funding for multilateral cooperation; and (d) Creation of a working group composed of representatives of the countries of the region, designated by their respective Governments, to help determine areas of action for regional coordination; to that end, the group will work closely with the pro tempore secretariat, "Plan of Action", Fourth Space Conference of the Americas, Cartagena de Indias, Colombia, 14–17 May 2002.

[26] UNGA, Report of the COPUOS, Fifty-eighth session, UN Doc. Supplement No. 20 A/58/20 (2003), para. 34. Similarly, paragraph 88 states that "[t]he Committee also noted the desire of members States in Latin America and Caribbean region to institutionalize the Space Conference of the Americas".

[27] UNGA, Report of the COPUOS, Fifty-ninth session, UN Doc. Supplement No. 20 A/59/20 (2004), para. 55. The report refers to the United Nations General Assembly (UNGA) resolution 58/89.

[28] Ibid., para. 54.

[29] "Declaration of San Francisco de Quito", Fifth Space Conference of the Americas, Quito, Ecuador, 2006, www.unoosa.org/pdf/limited/c1/AC105_C1_2007_CRP15E.pdf, point 21.

[30] UNGA, Report of the COPUOS, Sixty-second session, UN Doc. Supplement No. 20 A/62/20 (2007), para. 27.

[31] UNGA, Report of the COPUOS, Fifty-third session (9–18 June 2010). Sixty-fifth session, UN Doc. Supplement No. 20 A/65/20 (2010), para. 28.

**Fig. 2.3** Banner of the VI SCA, Pachuca, Mexico, 15–19 November 2010

Nevertheless, the strong impetus shown in the Third, Fourth and Fifth SCAs for the creation of a regional space agency disappeared with the adoption of the Declaration of Pachuca, the final document of the Sixth SCA held in Mexico in 2010. This Declaration did not explicitly allude to any aspects relating to the future creation of a regional space body, although it mentioned other significant questions concerning space cooperation in the region, such as the promotion of effective cooperation and coordination mechanisms for the development of space activities on the continent, and the increase of national capacities, especially in countries with less space development, to integrate to regional and international space programmes.[32] In addition, the Pachuca Declaration established a space technical advisory group[33] made of representatives of Latin American government bodies responsible for space matters to provide advisory assistance to the work of the SCA and its pro tempore secretariat.[34] These achievements were highlighted by UNCOPUOS in its reports of 2011–2015.[35] Furthermore, a consultative group on space technology comprising representatives of space-related entities in the region was created in 2012 by the Pachuca Declaration (Fig. 2.3).[36]

---

[32] "Pachuca Declaration", Sixth Space Conference of the Americas, Pachuca, Mexico, 2010, paras. 5–6.

[33] Ibid., para. 24.

[34] UNCOPUOS Fifty-fourth session, 641st Meeting, 9 June 2011, Vienna, Doc. COPUOS//.641, p. 3; see also: UNGA, Report of the COPUOS, Fifty-fourth session (1–10 June 2011). Sixty-sixth session, UN Doc. Supplement No. 20 A/66/20 (2011), para. 34.

[35] UNCOPUOS Report (2011); UNGA, Report of the COPUOS, Fifty-fifth session (6–15 June 2012). Sixty-seventh session, UN Doc. Supplement No. 20 A/67/20 (2012); UNGA, Report of the COPUOS, Fifty-sixth session (12–21 June 2013). Sixty-first eighth session, UN Doc. Supplement No. 20 A/68/20 (2013); UNGA, Report of the COPUOS, Fifty-seventh session (11–20 June 2014). Sixty-first ninth session, UN Doc. Supplement No. 20 A/69/20 (2014), and UNGA, Report of the COPUOS, Fifty-eighth session (10–19 June 2015). Seventieth session, UN Doc. Supplement No. 20 A/70/20 (2015).

[36] UNCOPUOS Report (2012), para. 38. The group was formally established in 2015 by the Declaration of Managua of the VI SCA (recommendation 10).

Interestingly, the 2013 UNCOPUOS report mentioned that the Pachuca Declaration developed a "regional space policy for the near future"—terms that are not included as such in the Declaration—that may be understood as a series of recommendations to promote the space sector to be followed by the countries of the region.[37] These words were replicated in the 2014 and 2015 UNCOPUOS reports.[38] However, it is noteworthy that the 2016 UNCOPUOS report changed the words "regional space policy" for a "regional space cooperation mechanism".[39] This modification of formula could be due to the absence of consensus among the participants of the SCA in respect of the correct interpretation of the Pachuca Declaration or of the path to be followed by the SCA in subsequent meetings.

The issue of the regional space agency appeared again in 2015 with the adoption of the Managua Declaration adopted by the Seventh SCA held in Managua, Nicaragua. This declaration highlighted the importance of creating effective mechanisms for cooperation and coordination in the region and recommended to continue the examination of the viability and pertinence of the establishment of a regional space agency to foster cooperation projects of common interest for the development of space technologies and their applications.[40] In this sense, the 2016 UNCOPUOS report emphasized that the Committee noted the successful conclusion of the Seventh SCA, but gave no details about the content of the Managua Declaration or its action plan.[41] It seems that the participant countries of the SCA did not want to make any specific recommendation of the Managua Declaration in the UNCOPUOS report. This assumption is reinforced by the fact that the UNCOPUOS reports of 2017, 2018 and 2019 make no reference to any SCA, declaration or plan of action adopted by this forum. In fact, the last SCA's achievements mentioned by an UNCOPUOS report (the 2016 report) were those concerning the intention of Venezuela to host the Eight SCA, an event that has not yet materialized (Fig. 2.4).[42]

### *2.1.3 New Fora, New Proposals (2011–2020)*

Outside the SCA framework, new proposals on the creation of a regional space agency in Latin America have come up in the last decade. In 2011, during a meeting of the South American Defence Council of the Union of South American Nations (UNASUR),[43] the Argentinian Defence minister, Arturo Puricelli, proposed to the

[37] UNCOPUOS Report (2013), para. 46.

[38] UNCOPUOS Reports of 2014 and 2015, paras. 63 and 60, respectively.

[39] Report of the COPUOS, Fifty-ninth session (8–17 June 2016), UNGA, Seventy-first session, UN Doc. Supplement No. 20 A/71/20 (2016), para. 47.

[40] "Declaration of Managua", VII Space Conference of the Americas, Managua, Nicaragua, 18 November 2015, recommendation 12.

[41] UNCOPUOS Report (2016), para. 47.

[42] Ibid.

[43] Unión de Naciones Suramericanas (UNASUR). UNASUR is an international organization aimed at creating an integrated and unified area in the fields of culture, society, economy and political

**Fig. 2.4** Inauguration meeting of the VII SCA. *Source* UNOOSA

Brazilian Defence minister, Celso Amorim, the creation of a South American Space Agency within the framework of this Union in order to develop common space projects and have own satellites by 2025. Amorim considered positive and suitable this proposal while Puricelli cautioned that the initiative should be well thought out and structured.[44] Other ministers of the region joined the initiative and agreed that every country would examine the feasibility of the proposal.[45] However, with the suspension and subsequent withdrawal from UNASUR of most of its members in

between the peoples of the South American Nations. Its constitutive treaty was adopted in Brasilia, Brazil, in 2008, and entered into force in 2011. Its original members were Argentina, Bolivia, Brazil, Chile, Colombia, Ecuador, Guyana, Paraguay, Peru, Suriname, Uruguay, and Venezuela. See further in detail: Froehlich/Amante Soria et al., *Space Supporting Latin America: Latin America's Emerging Space Middle Powers*, Springer (2020), p. 29.

[44] "Argentina propõe ao Brasil criação de agência espacial sul-americana", *EFE, Último Segundo*, 30 August 2011, https://ultimosegundo.ig.com.br/ciencia/argentina-propoe-ao-brasil-criacao-de-agencia-espacial-sulamericana/n1597186026553.html, see also: "Los ministros de Defensa de Unasur plantean crear una agencia espacial conjunta", *infoespacial.com*, 13 November 2011, www.infoespacial.com/latam/2011/11/13/noticia-los-ministros-de-defensa-de-unasur-plantean-crear-una-agencia-espacial-conjunta.html.

[45] It was planned to create the regional space agency not within the South American Defence Council, but as part of the general framework of UNASUR as a tool of foreign policy, in: Daniel Blinder, "Hacia una política espacial en la Argentina", *Revista Iberoamericana de Ciencia, Tecnología y Sociedad—CTS*, vol. 10, N° 29 (2014), p. 75.

recent years, including Argentina and Brazil,[46] the materialization of the proposed regional space agency within this forum practically vanished.

Another attempt to advance the establishment of a regional space agency took place in 2013 during a meeting of representatives of Latin American space agencies held in Bogotá, Colombia. This time, the presidency of the Brazilian Space Agency (AEB) discredited all efforts aimed at reaching any formal engagements or agreements that would lead to the creation of a regional space agency, discouraging other countries of the region to support the proposal.[47] Instead, Brazil proposed the creation of an Alliance of Latin American Space Agencies (ALAS),[48] which would serve as a forum to promote and stimulate joint programs and projects for the benefit of the countries of the region.[49] Nevertheless, the ALAS proposal did not gain the expected support.

At the bilateral level, Argentina and Mexico have promoted the creation of a regional space agency on several occasions.[50] In this regard, during the celebration of the 67th International Astronautical Congress held in Guadalajara, Mexico, in 2016, both countries signed a space cooperation agreement that foresaw the possibility to create a regional space agency.[51] Interestingly, the Italian Space Agency (ASI)[52] supported this initiative. In this regard, in 2018, the heads of the Mexican Space Agency (AEM)[53] and ASI highlighted the necessity of establishing a space agency in Latin America to develop the capacities of the countries of the region,[54] and in 2019 ASI supported the proposal during the signature of a cooperation agreement

---

[46] After leaving UNASUR, several South American countries created a new regional mechanism called Forum for the Progress of South America or PROSUR (Foro para el Progreso de América del Sur), Javier Sáez Leal et al., "Sudamérica entierra a la Unasur de Chávez, Kirchner y Lula", *El País*, 22 March 2019, https://elpais.com/internacional/2019/03/22/argentina/1553281368_627367.html.

[47] Julio Ottoboni, "AEB recua e extingue criação da Agência Espacial Latino Americana", *Defesanet*, 21 May 2015, www.defesanet.com.br/space/noticia/19200/AEB-recua-e-extingue-criacao-da-Agencia-Espacial-Latino-Americana/.

[48] Alianza Latinoamericana de Agencias Espaciales (ALAS).

[49] ALAS was to start its activities with at least two programmes: (1) through the cooperation of Latin American universities for the development of useful, efficient and economic small satellites to provide services to the countries of the region, and (2) through the development of a regional system for access, distribution and use of satellite data and images for the social and economic development plans of each country, Iván Leonardi, "Brasil propone una alianza Latinoamericana de agencias espaciales", *MundoGeo*, 11 November 2013, https://mundogeo.com/es/2013/11/11/brasil-propone-una-alianza-latinoamericana-de-agencias-espaciales/.

[50] "Queremos crear una agencia espacial para América Latina", *Argentina en el Espacio Blogspot*, 28 June 2016, http://argentinaenelespacio.blogspot.com/2016/06/queremos-crear-una-agencia-espacial.html.

[51] "Argentina y México van por un NASA Latinoamericano", *El Economista*, 30 September 2016, www.asi.it/2019/12/firmato-laccordo-di-collaborazione-tra-asi-ed-iila/.

[52] Agenzia Spatiale Italiana (ASI).

[53] Agencia Espacial Mexicana (AEM).

[54] "Expertos coinciden en necesidad de Latinoamérica de impulsar alianza espacial", *EFE*, 21 May 2018, www.efe.com/efe/america/tecnologia/expertos-coinciden-en-necesidad-de-latinoamerica-impulsar-alianza-espacial/20000036-3623068.

between ASI and the Italo-Latin American Institute,[55] adding that Italy was ready to share its experience in the development of ESA as being one of its founding members.[56]

Meanwhile, relevant official statements on the matter were pronounced in the framework of the 3rd International Space Forum at the Ministerial Level—the Latin American and Caribbean Chapter—organized by the International Space Forum at Ministerial Level (ISF) in Buenos Aires, Argentina, in November 2018. In the "Buenos Aires Page",[57] one of the official documents adopted in this meeting, the participants (ministers, heads of delegations, heads of space agencies and other delegates from Latin America and the Caribbean—"the Region") agreed that one of the main objectives to be achieved in a medium-short term was "to promote an ever greater space cooperation in the Region to prepare the adequate environment for the development of a future regional space agency". This idea was reaffirmed in the final report of the Forum, in which delegates from Argentina, Mexico and Uruguay explicitly supported the creation of the regional space agency.[58] Moreover, representatives of NASA and ASI welcomed this initiative (Figs. 2.5 and 2.6).[59]

A radical development concerning the creation of a regional space agency occurred in 2020. First, in January, during the presentation of its 14 point-plan for the 2020 presidency pro-tempore of the Community of Latin American and Caribbean States (CELAC),[60] Mexico made a call to the countries of the region to foster space cooperation through the development, among others, of a Latin American and Caribbean nanosatellite.[61] Then, in July 2020, Mexico organized the "Latin American and Caribbean Space Meeting, CELAC 2020", in which Mexico reaffirmed its proposal

---

[55] The Italo-Latin American Institute is an intergovernmental organization created in 1966 aimed at promoting and strengthening relations between Italy and Latin America, see: Organizzazione internazionale italo-latino americana, "Quiénes somos", https://iila.org/es/quienes-somos/.

[56] "Firmato l'Accordo di Collaborazione tra ASI ed IILA", *Agenzia Spatiale Italiana*, December 2019, www.asi.it/2019/12/firmato-laccordo-di-collaborazione-tra-asi-ed-iila/.

[57] "The Buenos Aires Page", *3rd International Space Forum at Ministerial Level—The Latin American & Caribbean Chapter*, International Space Forum at Ministerial Level, Buenos Aires, Argentina, 1 November 2018.

[58] The Argentinian representative stated that "certainly there is no integrating place that can optimize the cooperation in this area (space) in Latin America and the Caribbean. So I think that this leads to what we, at CONAE, have been proposing as a great desire, as almost a dream, which is to have a regional space agency"; the Mexican representative stated that "Mexico is committed to integrate in Latin American space initiatives, programs and, in a mid-term, a possible Latin American space organization", and the Uruguayan delegate said "We hope that the initiative mentioned by (Argentina) and (Mexico), about creating a regional space agency, initiative presented by Chile in the 80's, become a reality", in: "Final Report", *3rd International Space Forum 2018—The Latin American and Caribbean Chapter*, Buenos Aires, Argentina, 1 November 2018.

[59] Victor Ingrassia, "Avanza el proyecto de formar una agencia espacial Latinoamericana", *Infobae*, 20 November 2018, www.infobae.com/tendencias/innovacion/2018/11/20/avanza-el-proyecto-de-formar-una-agencia-espacial-latinoamericana/.

[60] Comunidad de Estados Latinoamericanos y Caribeños (CELAC), see: Chapter 3 (3.3.2.3).

[61] "Plan de trabajo 2020, Presidencia Pro Témpore (PPT) de México en la Comunidad de Estados Latinoamericanos y Caribeños (CELAC) 2020", CELAC 2020, https://ppt-celac.org/plan-de-trabajo?fbclid=IwAR1EbpA6jQPAX0AJSPffgJAVnfyOkLbPdmj4u_zteLbNqa6qARK_vOH6LcQ.

**Fig. 2.5** Third International Space Forum 2018—The Latin American and Caribbean Chapter, 1 November 2018. *Source* IAF

**Fig. 2.6** Third International Space Forum 2018—The Latin American and Caribbean Chapter, 1 November 2018. *Source* IAF

and announced its intention to elaborate a regional space development agenda. Moreover, the participant countries signed the "Joint Declaration on the Use of Space in the Community of Latin American and Caribbean States" and presented a joint working plan to set up a Latin American and Caribbean Space Council.[62] In the same meeting, the Mexican Minister of Communications and Transportation suggested the creation of the "Bolívar System of Latin American Nanosatellites".[63] On 22 September 2020, Mexico presented a project for the foundation of a Latin American and Caribbean space agency, a long-term project whose main activities would be Earth observation (EO), exchange of satellite images and multisector dialogue.[64] On 9 October 2020, within the activities of the World Space Week and under the Mexican CELAC's presidency pro-tempore (PPT), Mexico and Argentina laid the foundations of a Latin American and Caribbean Space Agency ("ALCE" for its acronym in Spanish)[65] through the signature of the "Declaration on the Constitution of a Regional Cooperation Mechanism in the Space Field" (ALCE Declaration) (Table 2.1).[66] Furthermore, during the virtual ceremony, which had the participation of Mexican, Colombian, and Argentinian representatives,[67] the signatories of the declaration—Argentina and Mexico—committed to invite Latin American and Caribbean countries to adhere to the initiative and establish ALCE.[68] The ALCE Declaration enumerates the following programmatic actions: foster the creation of a regional space cooperation mechanism to coordinate its activities with those of the relevant national entities; give legal personality and capacities to ALCE to operate as catalyst of the regional space efforts; hold regular consultations to determine the seat, structure, legal framework, working methods, financial schemes, and types of cooperation of the agency; put the results of the consultations into ALCE's constituent instrument, and support ALCE's activities as the ideal forum to channel the space collaboration with national, regional and international governmental and non-governmental entities (Fig. 2.7).[69]

---

[62] "México impulsa una agenda de cooperación espacial en la CELAC", *Agencia Espacial Mexicana*, 2 July 2020, www.gob.mx/aem/articulos/mexico-impulsa-una-agenda-de-cooperacion-espacial-en-la-celac-247200?idiom=es.

[63] Ibid.

[64] The proposal was presented by Javier López Casarín, the honorary president of the Knowledge and Innovation Technical Council of the Mexican Agency for International Development Cooperation [Agencia Mexicana de Cooperación Internacional para el Desarrollo (AMEXCID)], "México invita a países a sumarse al proyecto para crear la Agencia Espacial Latinoamericana y Caribeña", *Sin Embargo*, 22 September 2020, www.sinembargo.mx/22-09-2020/3864234.

[65] Agencia Latinoamericana y Caribeña del Espacio (ALCE).

[66] Declaración sobre la Constitución de un Mecanismo Regional de Cooperación en el Ámbito Espacial.

[67] Colombia did not sign the declaration. The Colombian representative to the virtual meeting was the Principal of the National University of Colombia.

[68] "México y Argentina sientan las Bases para la Constitución de la Agencia Latinoamericana y Caribeña del Espacio", *Agencia Espacial Mexicana*, 9 October 2020, www.gob.mx/aem/prensa/mexico-y-argentina-sientan-las-bases-para-la-constitucion-de-la-agencia-latinoamericana-y-caribena-del-espacio-254452.

[69] ALCE's inauguration ceremony can be watched at the Facebook's official page of the Mexican Ministry of Foreign Affairs, 9 October 2020, www.facebook.com/watch/?v=3844787895554615.

**Table 2.1** Declaration on the constitution of a regional cooperation mechanism in the space field (ALCE Declaration)

| Declaration on the Constitution of a Regional Cooperation Mechanism in the Space Field (Latin American and Caribbean Space Agency - ALCE) |
|---|
| The Ministers of Foreign Affairs of the countries of Latin America and the Caribbean,<br><br>Considering space technology is an essential factor in pursuing and achieving the objectives of the information society, strengthening transport infrastructures and promoting the protection of the environment;<br><br>Encouraged by the strengthening of cooperation ties for the development of space sciences and technological applications of space;<br><br>Convinced of the importance of promoting the exchange of knowledge, the execution of projects for the construction of space infrastructure and participation in accordance with the identified needs of the region;<br><br>Desiring to increase the number of space projects by attracting the talent of Latin American and Caribbean youth, as well as the efficient use of available resources;<br><br>Aware of the need to have a permanent collaboration mechanism to strengthen capacities in the space field in order to reduce the digital divide in the region;<br><br>Determine to undertake the following programmatic actions:<br><br>1. Promote the creation of a regional cooperation mechanism in the space field in charge of coordinating activities with the relevant institutions of the Latin American and Caribbean countries to address the priorities identified in this area;<br>2. Encourage the mechanism to have the legal personality and necessary capacities to operate as a catalyst for regional efforts, giving priority to the development of projects in space matters, the results of which will support the well-being and prosperity of the region;<br>3. Hold regular consultations to determine the seat of the mechanism, its administrative structure, the rules to regulate its operation, the work methodology, the financing schemes and the different forms of cooperation;<br>4. Document the results of the consultations in the founding instrument of the mechanism;<br>5. Support the activities of the mechanism as the ideal body to channel collaboration on space matters with national, regional, international agencies, academic institutions, non-governmental organizations, civil society organizations and the private sector;<br>6. Reaffirm that the regional mechanism does not exceed the capacity of its bilateral cooperation members in the field of peaceful uses of outer space.<br><br>Signed on October 9, 2020 in Spanish, English and French,<br><br>On the part of the Argentine Republic, Felipe Carlos Solá, Minister of Foreign Relations, International Trade and Worship;<br><br>For the United Mexican States, Marcelo Luis Ebrard Casaubón, Minister of Foreign Relations |

The translation from the Spanish version was made by the author

**Fig. 2.7** Virtual meeting for the signature of the ALCE Declaration, 9 October 2020. *Source* SCT

Later, in a virtual meeting held on 16 November 2020, representatives of Bolivia, Ecuador, El Salvador, and Paraguay joined the ALCE Declaration. Colombia and Peru attended the meeting as observers.[70] Moreover, two important issues were agreed in this meeting: first, that the ALCE Declaration was a product of the agreements reached at the Latin American and Caribbean meeting held in July 2020 as part of the first point of the Mexican Working Plan (in its capacity of being CELAC's PPT), with the main purpose of promoting collaboration in the field of technology transfer to develop common projects, such as putting into orbit the nanosatellite "CELAC-SAT"[71]; and second, that ALCE would start operations in 2021.[72] Also in this meeting, the Mexican Minister of Communications and Transportation stated that with this integration of Latin American nations it would be possible to build common satellites, share space segment infrastructure, and develop ground stations and terminal equipment, with significant economies of scale.[73] Therefore, new details on ALCE and its potential members states are expected to be released in 2021.

Finally, it is relevant to mention a further recent proposal—a subregional one—consisting in the creation of a space agency in Central America and the Caribbean (AECA).[74] On 25 September 2020, the Central American Parliament

[70] "Avanza mecanismo regional para constituir la Agencia Latinoamericana y Caribeña del Espacio", *Agencia Espacial Mexicana*, 16 November 2020, www.gob.mx/aem/articulos/avanza-mecanismo-regional-para-constituir-la-agencia-latinoamericana-y-caribena-del-espacio-257272?idiom=es.

[71] Ibid.

[72] This point was made the same day of the meeting by the Mexican Minister of Foreign Relations, Mr. Marcelo Ebrard, in his Twitter account, "La Agencia iniciará operaciones en 2021", *Marcelo Ebrard*, https://twitter.com/m_ebrard/status/1328464380309061635.

[73] ALCE's inauguration ceremony, 9 October 2020.

[74] Agencia Espacial de Centroamérica y el Caribe (AECA).

(PARLACEN)[75] of the Central American Integral System (SICA)[76] approved a resolution “To promote in the Central American and Dominican Republic region the establishment of a space agency”, an initiative sponsored by the Nicaraguan MP Daniel Ortega Reyes.[77] Accordingly, the AECA should foster the scientific, political and social development of Central America and Dominican Republic through the space sector, giving special importance to the promotion of space education.[78] Moreover, PARLACEN suggested that SICA’s member states should ask the Central American Bank of Economic Integration (BCIE)[79] for a loan to finance the creation and operation of the AECA. Because PARLACEN’s decisions are not mandatory, these states must urge the Summit of Central American Heads of State and Government to promote the setting up of the AECA (Fig. 2.8; Table 2.2).[80]

## 2.2 Detailed Analysis of the Proposals

The idea of the creation of a space agency in the Americas has suffered ups and downs since its inception. Actually, this idea has been included in sets of proposals that have emerged from different sources and times and, therefore, presents significant variations. Some proposals cover the whole Latin American region while others focus on one specific subregion of the Americas; some proposals have appeared in established regional forums while others have been submitted in ad hoc meetings; and some proposals are more detailed than others concerning their objectives and contents. These inconsistencies may be preventing the concretization of a unique

[75] The Central American Parliament or PARLACEN (Parlamento Centroamericano) is the political organ of the Central American Integration System, which is composed of 126 representatives of the region: 20 representatives for each country plus the ex-presidents and ex-vice presidents of all Central American countries. PARLACEN has planning, analysis and recommendation capacities, Sistema de Integración Centroamericana, “El Parlamento Centroamericano”, www.sica.int/organos/parlacen.

[76] Sistema de la Integración Centroamericana (SICA). It is the regional institutional framework of Central America created on 13 December 1991 by the Tegucigalpa Protocol. SICA’s main goal is the integration of Central America to become a region of peace, freedom, democracy, and development. There are currently eight members: Belize, Costa Rica, Dominican Republic, El Salvador, Guatemala, Honduras, Nicaragua, and Panama, see: Sistema de Integración Centroamericana, “La integración centroamericana”, www.sica.int/integracion/proceso.

[77] The sponsors of the AECA have declared that Russia is willing to help the region to establish the agency, see: Avance en creación de Agencia Espacial de Centroamérica y el Caribe resaltan en Primer Foro de Cooperación Espacial Rusa-Latinoamérica, Parlamento Centroamericano/PARLACEN, 6 October 2020, www.facebook.com/parlacen/posts/3899356993442517/.

[78] Sistema Económico Latinoamericano y del Caribe, “Centroamérica trabaja para crear su agencia espacial”, 28 September 2020, www.sela.org/es/prensa/servicio-informativo/20200928/si/69163/centroamerica.

[79] Banco Centroamericano de Integración Económica (BCIE).

[80] José Miguel Castañeda, “Una agencia espacial centroamericana: la propuesta del Parlacen”, *Nodal*, October 2020, www.nodal.am/2020/10/el-parlacen-impulsa-la-creacion-de-una-agencia-espacial-centroamericana/.

**Fig. 2.8** New countries join the ALCE Declaration, 16 November 2020. In the picture, the Mexican Minister of Foreign Affairs, Marcelo Ebrard. *Source* SCT

**Table 2.2** Chronology of the main proposals for a regional space agency in the Americas

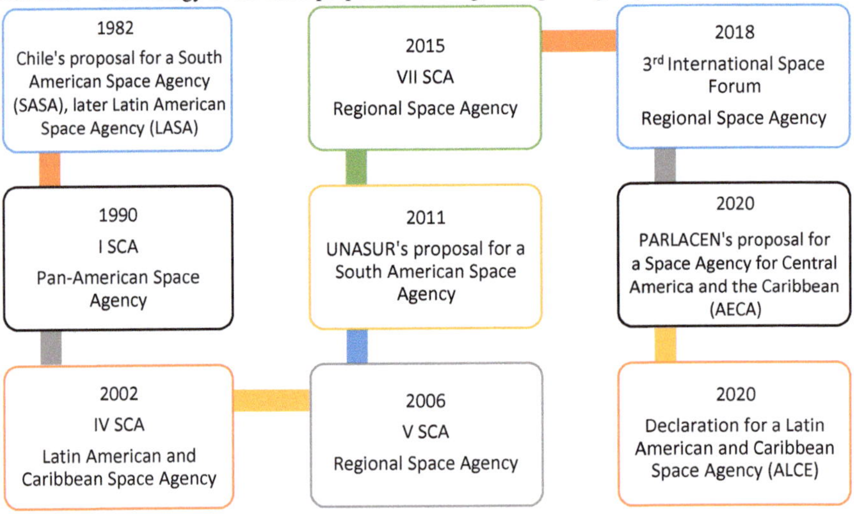

regional space agency (or several subregional space agencies). Take for example the issue of the diverse discussion forums. The SCA was for two decades the main space forum in the hemisphere, but it has lost relevance in recent years due to its lack of activity; instead, new regional bodies, such as CELAC and the IAF GRULAC have gained ground to discuss regional space issues, including the creation of LASA. The change of forum may be the result of political differences among Latin American governments or the momentum of a particular forum in Latin American integration history, as in the case of UNASUR in 2011 and CELAC nowadays. Thus, varying the regional forum may be counterproductive in giving continuity to any LASA proposal, especially if the corresponding discussions last a long time without tangible results and the participants vary among the forums.[81]

The following sections analyse some issues of the history of LASA proposals that could be helpful to advance in the establishment of a regional space agency in Latin America: the rationale and objectives of LASA, the form, conditions and features of LASA, and the applicable region.

### 2.2.1 *Rationale and Objectives of a Latin American Space Agency*

The first hints of the rationale and objectives of LASA were given in 1982 by Raimundo González, delegate of the Permanent Mission of Chile to the UN. He declared that "since Latin American countries, isolated from each other could not reach the "critical mass" required for an effective lift-off toward self-reliance, the way out is to add up the available human and material resources in a joint venture",[82] and suggested that one of LASA's first objectives should be the establishment of "the capabilities to utilize space technology applications, with the idea of progressing toward gradual technical self-reliance".[83] Furthermore, the preamble of the draft agreement of the 1982 Chile's SASA proposal—later LASA—provided that the states parties were aware that it was "necessary to establish regional machinery for co-operation and that the establishment of such machinery implies, furthermore, the elimination of any possibility of militarizing outer space in the South American region".[84] In addition, Article 1 of this agreement stated that SASA "shall channel the cooperation among the countries in the area towards a mutual elaboration, execution and financing of projects for the utilization of space technology entailing economic and

[81] There are some countries that have continuously supported the creation of LASA, including Argentina, Chile, Mexico, and Uruguay. However, Mexico could not be part of the UNASUR proposal because UNASUR's membership is restricted to South American nations. By January 2021, Chile and Uruguay had not yet expressed their intention to join the ALCE Declaration.

[82] Statement of Mr. Raimundo González, representative of Chile, "Seminar on the Applicability of Space Science", April 19–21, 1982, Quito, Ecuador, *Journal of Space Law*, Vol. 10, no. 2 (1982) p. 218.

[83] Ibid.

[84] Ibid., p. 258.

social development of the peoples", and Article Five enshrined SASA's main goals, namely "to ensure and to develop, exclusively for peaceful purposes, the cooperation among the South American countries in the fields of research and utilization of space technology".[85] In summary, the first attempts to create LASA were aimed at giving the region more technological independence through the peaceful use of space technology for the economic and social development of Latin American countries.

As to the period of great activity of the SCA, it can be observed, for example, that the Declaration of San Francisco de Quito highlighted the need to establish cooperation and coordination mechanisms for the region "for the purpose of promoting the development of space activities in the countries of the Americas, as well as for the application and peaceful use of technologies stemming from them".[86] Similarly, the Pachuca Declaration considered that these mechanisms were necessary "in order to further the development of space activities, while at the same time promoting interregional dialogue" and "expanding national capacities, particularly in countries of Latin America and the Caribbean that are less advanced in the space field, with the firm intention of supporting their incorporation into the principal regional and international space programs".[87] In the Managua Declaration, the participants agreed that LASA would "promote cooperation projects of common interest for the development of space technology and its applications".[88] In this regard, the SCA mainly focused on establishing LASA as a means to develop joint space activities to increase the capabilities of the countries of the region, use space technology and its applications, and promote interregional dialogue in the space sector.

Meanwhile, recent developments within CELAC's framework for the creation of ALCE provide some ideas of the *raison d'être* and the objectives of this mechanism. During the signature of the ALCE Declaration, the Mexican Minister of Foreign Affairs remarked that regional space cooperation was a strategic and geopolitical topic and that the cohesion of Latin America and the Caribbean was essential to achieve more autonomy and more possibilities of negotiations in the world. He also stressed that the exchange of knowledge and capacity building in the field of science and technology were essential to the economic and social development of the region, strengthening Latin American and Caribbean integration. Specifically, the Minister emphasised that CELAC did not want to create another organism, but a tool symbolizing the will and effectiveness of Latin America and the Caribbean to achieve their common objectives.[89] In turn, his Argentinian counterpart stated that the cooperation mechanism would allow the best use of the common resources to implement projects for the benefit of the region.[90] Further official statements have

---

[85] Ibid.

[86] "Declaration of San Francisco de Quito", V Space Conference of the Americas, para. 9.

[87] "Pachuca Declaration", VI Space Conference of the Americas, para. 4 and 6.

[88] "Managua Declaration", VII Space Conference of the Americas, para. 14.

[89] "Evento de la firma de la Declaración para la creación de la Agencia Latinoamericana y Caribeña del Espacio (ALCE)", *NODAL—Noticias de América Latina y el Caribe*, 9 October 2020, www.youtube.com/watch?v=u931ZdXs9gw.

[90] "México y Argentina sientan las bases para la constitución de la Agencia Latinoamericana y Caribeña del Espacio", Comunicado conjunto México—Argentina, *Mexican Ministry of Foreign*

advanced some of the objectives of ALCE, among which are the development of a regional EO nanosatellite, the exchange of satellite images, and the development of a multisector dialogue.[91] Javier López, one of the main supporters of ALCE in Mexico, elaborated that ALCE would carry out space exploration and scientific research, create governmental projects such as satellite internet access, strengthen academic cooperation in the region, and unify ALCE's activities with the activities of other space agencies such as ESA.[92]

In addition, the ALCE Declaration provides that the future regional space agency will support the construction of space infrastructure, reduce the digital divide, and attract young people interested in space. It also mentions that ALCE would serve as a catalyst for regional space projects aimed at supporting the well-being and prosperity of the region, and coordinate activities with other regional space related institutions to address "the priorities identified in this area", although it does not mention any examples of these priorities. Thus, further consultations are expected to be held to clarify this issue. Therefore, this initiative aims at achieving more autonomy and development in the region by using the space agency as the appropriate tool to carry out common projects, namely the development of a regional EO nanosatellite, the exchange of satellite images and the promotion of space capacity building.

In conclusion, the different LASA proposals include a great variety of reasons, goals, and objectives. In their fundamental aspects, they do not really differ too much from each other. Increasing autonomy, developing collaborative space projects, promoting peaceful space activities, and improving the well-being of the people of the countries of the region by using space science, technology and its applications are common visions and goals in most of the proposals. However, some proposals pay more attention to specific issues than others. For example, the 1982 Chilean proposal emphasizes the peaceful character of the regional space agency—probably because at that time Latin America did not want to be part of the ideological battle that divided the world during the Cold War, while the ALCE initiative focuses more on the importance of developing space applications for the rational use of Latin American resources and suggests the development of a regional EO satellite, a specific regional space programme (something that is absent in the rest of proposals) (Fig. 2.9).

To some extent, the existence of multiple visions, goals, and objectives contained in the different proposals is indicative of the rich variety of ideals and wishes of what Latin American countries expect of a regional space cooperation mechanism. Nevertheless, these variations may also constitute an obstacle to go further in the concretization of LASA. Due to the proposals having been made in different times and political contexts, and sometimes by diverse countries, there is a risk that any

*Affairs*, 9 October 2020, www.gob.mx/sre/prensa/mexico-y-argentina-sientan-las-bases-para-la-constitucion-de-la-agencia-latinoamericana-y-caribena-del-espacio?idiom=es.

[91] According to the 14 point-plan of the Mexican CELAC's PPT and the statement of Mexico of the CELAC meeting of July 2020.

[92] Javier López Casarín, "ALCE, una nueva etapa en la búsqueda del conocimiento en pro de la humanidad", *Forbes México*, 15 October 2020, www.forbes.com.mx/red-forbes-agencia-latinoamericana-y-caribena-del-espacio/?fbclid=IwAR1fkcreShfBv42wBcRw69zroBsQRtUKeLifKK04YVBpMZsFAXDpylNu7WM.

**Fig. 2.9** Logo of the Latin American and Caribbean Space Agency (ALCE)

current or subsequent proposition will fail if the interested countries cannot reach an agreement on the rationale, goals, and objectives of LASA. A Latin American space policy and strategy, for example, may help to solve this problem.[93]

### *2.2.2 Form, Conditions and Characteristics of the Latin American Space Agency*

What would be the form and features of LASA? And what are the conditions for setting it up? Various LASA proposals contain aspects related to these issues. First, it is important to note that there is not a single formula used by the proposals to refer to LASA. While some proposals use "regional space agency" or "Latin American (and Caribbean) space agency" others use the general formula "regional space cooperation mechanism". That does not necessarily mean that the proposals deal with two or more different ideas. Actually, both formulas are frequently used as synonyms. For example, while the ALCE Declaration provides for the creation of a "regional cooperation mechanism in the space field" without mentioning "regional space agency", official statements of Argentina and Mexico related to this declaration refer to a "Latin American and Caribbean Space Agency". However, it is also plausible that a specific proposal uses "regional space cooperation mechanism" as a broader formula than "regional space agency", which would include additional forms

[93] See: Chapter 3 (3.2.3).

of regional space cooperation mechanisms, such as forums, associations or partnerships, networks, regional projects or programmes, or regional space centres. Even considering this possibility, a regional space agency is the most common form of regional space cooperation mechanism advanced by most LASA proposals. For this reason, it is likely appropriate to consider the two terms—"regional space agency" (or LASA) and "regional space cooperation mechanism"—as interchangeable.

After this clarification, the next question is: "How is LASA conceived by the Latin American countries?" In other words, would Latin America follow a model of a regional space agency?[94] The answer is not simple because most of the proposals are not clear in this regard. Perhaps the clearest proposal is the 1982 Chilean LASA draft agreement, which foresaw LASA as an international intergovernmental body with legal personality and contractual capacity. Although its sponsor did not allude to a model for LASA, ECLA had considered that this initiative implied an entity similar to ESA. Moreover, during the first SCA, the reference model for LASA was ESA, and it is possible that the subsequent SCAs regarded ESA as the model par excellence for a future regional space agency. Conversely, the most recent proposals are silent in this respect. The Buenos Aires Page, the ALCE declaration and the respective official statements do not allude to a specific model to be used in Latin America. Is this an indication that ESA is no more the predilected model for Latin America? A possible explanation of this omission is that Latin American countries may currently differ on the form of LASA due to the appearance in recent decades of new regional space cooperation mechanisms in the world, such as the Asia–Pacific Space Cooperation Organization (APSCO) and the African Space Agency (AfSA), which may also serve as models for LASA. In sum, LASA proposals are ambiguous on the specific form of this entity and on the use of a specific model of regional space cooperation mechanism. Negotiations by Latin American countries to clarify these issues should be held to settle the building blocks of LASA.

As to the conditions for the conceptualisation of LASA and the characteristics of this entity, there are some proposals that have dealt with these issues. As noted above, the 1982 Chilean proposal encouraged some states to ask ECLA to prepare a study on the technical, institutional and financial feasibilities for the creation of LASA.[95] However, ECLA did not undertake the study because it had no technical expertise in outer space matters and no further instructions were given to it to prepare a deeper analysis. Nevertheless, this first attempt raised awareness of the importance of possessing relevant information on the space capacities of the countries of the region to advance the creation of LASA. In this regard, the identification of existing national space capabilities (for example, space facilities, academic and research institutes, space industry, and regional space organizations)[96] in Latin American countries has been considered crucial to define the characteristics of LASA. This matter was addressed by the Fourth SCA, in which the pro tempore secretariat was entrusted to identify space capacities in all countries of the region, although there is no evidence

---

[94] See: Chapter 3 (3.1).

[95] González, "Seminar on the Applicability of Space Science", *Journal of Space Law*, p. 219.

[96] Jiménez, *Legal and Institutional Aspects of Latin-American Space Cooperation*, p. 65.

that the study has ever been published. More specifically, the Declaration of San Francisco de Quito of the Fifth SCA highlighted that the establishment of national space bodies in Latin American countries would contribute to the foundation of a regional space entity.[97] Finally, the ALCE Declaration expresses the necessity to carry out regular consultations to determine ALCE's characteristics, namely legal framework, financial schemes, cooperation agreements, and working methods. A representative of the Mexican Ministry of Foreign Affairs declared that the intention of the ALCE proposal is to follow the model of ESA, which started with a handful of countries and projects, but which later grew.[98]

In brief, some LASA proposals acknowledge the necessity of identifying the conditions to establish LASA while others determine one or more conditions to be fulfilled to this end. Some proposals also mention several possible features of this entity. To advance the establishment of LASA, Latin American countries should work to identify and fulfil these conditions and define the characteristics of the space agency.

### 2.2.3 The Applicable Region

A further significant issue derived from the analysis of the proposals is the applicable region in which LASA would supposedly operate. Some proposals have foreseen the creation of a space agency only for South America, leaving aside the Caribbean countries and other Latin American states such as Mexico and the Central American nations. However, these initiatives have not been backed for a long time. Similarly, the idea of a Pan-American space agency comprising all countries of the Americas has received little, if any, support. The proposal by SICA's Parliament of a space agency for Central American and Dominican Republic is still on the negotiation table. Conversely, the proposals concerning the creation of a space agency for all the countries of the American continent, except for Canada and the U.S., which usually use the formulas "regional space agency", "space agency for Latin America" or "space agency for Latin America and the Caribbean" have received more adherents and still survive. In fact, it is possible that some may consider these proposals as being the only one. For example, a country that uses the words "regional space agency" may refer to all countries of the American continent except Canada and the U.S., while other countries may use the same words to refer exclusively to Latin American countries, without including the Caribbean states (except for Cuba, the Dominican Republic and Haiti, which are Latin American countries).

Individual statements on this issue in the diverse fora are usually uneven or unclear. SCA's documents—and related UNCOPUOS reports—usually refer to both Latin

[97] "Declaration of San Francisco de Quito", V Space Conference of the Americas, para. 21.

[98] Elías Camhaji, "ALCE, el sueño de la conquista latinoamericana del espacio", *El País*, 21 November 2020, https://elpais.com/mexico/2020-11-21/alce-el-sueno-de-la-conquista-latinoamericana-del-espacio.html.

**Fig. 2.10** Members of the Central American Integral System (SICA)

American and the Caribbean countries when talking about the creation of a multilateral space agency in the continent. Nevertheless, on some occasions these documents use the words "regional space agency" without clarifying if the notion includes all countries of the Americas or whether it comprises Latin American and Caribbean countries or only Latin American countries. It is not improbable that the SCA prefers to use "regional space agency" to avoid excluding some countries, especially because this forum has "the Americas" in its name, a denomination that comprises all nations of the Americas, including Canada and the U.S. (both participants in the SCA). Less ambiguous examples on this issue are the proposal that emerged from the 3rd International Space Forum—the Latin American and Caribbean Chapter, and the ALCE Declaration, which comprises all Latin American and Caribbean countries (Fig. 2.10).

Although the inclusion of some countries such as the Caribbean states is omitted by a few proposals, that does not strictly mean that these countries are excluded from them. Perhaps some proposals unintentionally skip these states. In any case, it is a matter of fact that the major supporters of a regional space agency in the American continent are Latin American countries. Statements in favour of a regional space agency by the Caribbean states are scarce or non-existent.[99]

This issue is important because the inclusion or not of some states or subregions of the Americas in the ultimate proposal may deeply modify the characteristics of the regional space agency and, therefore, demand a different approach to the subject.[100] Thus, to advance the establishment of a regional space agency in the continent the

[99] There are supporters of the creation of a Caribbean Space Agency, see: "The Launching of the Caribbean Space Society", *Rebuild Dominica Inc.*, 6 October 2018, https://rebuilddominica.org/2018/10/06/the-launching-of-the-caribbean-space-society/. Dominican Republic, which is both a Latin American and Caribbean country, has already manifested its intention to participate in the creation of the AECA.

[100] See: Chapter 4 (4.3.4).

supporters of this idea should be clear on the applicable region in which the agency will work. For example, in the ALCE proposal all Latin American and Caribbean countries are invited to become members of ALCE.

As to the present study, it has been considered appropriate to use the terms "Latin American Space Agency" (and its acronym "LASA") and "regional space agency" as synonyms, both terms comprising all Latin American countries without excluding the possibility of incorporating the Caribbean nations. This does not imply that this choice reflects the real sense and scope of the terms, content or intention of the statements, proposals or opinions made by other proposals. In other words, former, current, or new proposals on the creation of a regional space agency in the Americas may certainly include the Caribbean countries or other states.[101]

## 2.3 Conclusion

To date, practically all proposals have been presented more as ideal projects, regional aspirations, and political intentions than actual and concrete initiatives. None of them has reached a profound development stage. The recent ALCE initiative is changing this tendency with the formal declaration to constitute ALCE, although it remains to be seen if more practical steps are taken in the years to come. Therefore, the interested countries should agree on a unique and consistent proposal to concretize LASA. This proposal should at least consider the conditions to establish LASA, and define the applicable region, the rationale, objectives, and characteristics of LASA. The history of the LASA proposals may provide significant elements to this end.

---

[101] Nevertheless, this study will sometimes refer to the Caribbean countries as potential candidates for LASA.

# Chapter 3
# The Creation of a Space Agency in Latin America

*My dream is that a young Latin American goes to Mars.*
*Franklin Chang-Díaz, Costa Rican Astronaut*

**Abstract** For almost forty years, several countries of Latin America have suggested the creation of a regional space agency, but this entity has not yet seen the light. Going from the conception of this entity to its definite concretization may become exceedingly complex if there is not a clear idea of what kind of structure this entity should have and what should be the necessary conditions to materialize it. This chapter examines some regional space cooperation mechanisms that Latin America could use as models for its regional space agency and analyses several conditions to establish this entity. Therefore, this chapter is divided into four sections: the first section presents the potential models for a Latin American Space Agency; the second section examines the conditions for the establishment of this entity; the third section analyses the potential forums to discuss the creation of the regional space agency, and the fourth section presents a set of considerations about the precedent sections.

## 3.1 Models for a Latin American Space Agency

What would a space agency for Latin America look like? Conceptualizing a regional space agency in Latin America requires a set of elements that Latin American countries must jointly identify and define. However, in the history of the proposals for a regional space agency in the Americas,[1] almost all proposals have been vaguely formulated, making impossible to identify an agreed form or features of this entity. An exception was the 1982 Chilean proposal, which included a draft agreement for the creation of a South American Space Agency (SASA, later Latin American Space

[1] See: Chap. 2.



A. Froehlich and D. A. Amante Soria, *A Regional Space Agency for Latin America*, Studies in Space Policy 32, https://doi.org/10.1007/978-3-030-79434-7_3

Agency (LASA)). Its Article 1, for example, stated that "An international intergovernmental body known as the South American Space Agency shall be established".[2] This article also included some features of this body: it shall be constituted by that agreement and its statutes, and it shall have legal personality and the capacity necessary for the exercise of its functions and the achievement of its objectives.[3] Unfortunately, this proposal did not receive political support and passed into oblivion. Subsequent proposals have shown little development in this regard.

A possible way to set up a LASA is to adopt an existing model of regional space cooperation mechanism. For some, the ideal model is the European Space Agency (ESA) because it has been largely acknowledged as a successful example of regional space cooperation.[4] However, there are nowadays further regional space entities that may also be the inspiration for LASA. Although there are different regional cooperation mechanisms in the world, only the following models will be analysed in the present study: ESA, the Asia–Pacific Space Cooperation Organisation (APSCO), the African Space Agency (AfSA), the European Organisation for the Exploitation of Meteorological Satellites (EUMETSAT), and the European Global Navigation Satellite System Agency (European GNSS Agency or GSA). The rationale for this choice lies in the fact these models better respond to the common understanding of a "regional space agency"[5] and share several characteristics advanced by different LASA proposals: they are intergovernmental and institutional regional space cooperation mechanisms, and their existence is directly or indirectly based in international legal instruments. The exception could be EUMETSAT because it is considered more as a specialized operational organization than a regional space agency.[6] However, EUMETSAT will be examined within this study because there is at least one proposal in Latin America to create a similar organization.

This does not necessarily mean that LASA should be like these models. It is totally possible that Latin American states would consider it more suitable to use other institutional models or create a non-institutional cooperation mechanism and

---

[2] Raimundo González, "Seminar on the Applicability of Space Science", 19–23 April, 1982, Quito, Ecuador, *Journal of Space Law*, Vol. 10, no. 2 (1982), p. 258.

[3] This capacity shall include the capacity to conclude agreements with states and international organizations, employ staff, acquire and dispose of property, and file lawsuits, Ibid.

[4] Chukeat Noichim, *The Asean Space Organisation. Legal Aspects and Feasibility*, Leiden (2008), p. 121. In 1983, the United Nations Economic Commission for Latin America (ECLAC) mentioned that ESA could be considered by Latin American countries as a model for LASA, see: Chap. 2, Sect. 2.1.1.

[5] The official website of the United Nations Office of Outer Space Affairs (UNOOSA) only mentions three regional space agencies: ESA, APSCO and the GSA, see: UNOOSA, "Worldwide Space Agencies", www.unoosa.org/oosa/en/ourwork/space-agencies.html (All websites cited in this chapter were last accessed and verified on 28 March 2021).

[6] For the purpose of this study, EUMETSAT will be considered a regional space agency. EUMETSAT's official website defines EUMETSAT as "the European operational satellite agency for monitoring weather, climate and the environment from space", and the previous EUMETSAT's Strategy, adopted in June 2011, was called "EUMETSAT: a global operational satellite agency at the heart of Europe", see: www.eumetsat.int/about-us/who-we-are.

name it LASA, but this last entity would be essentially different from the above regional space agencies.

Before examining the potential models for LASA, it is, however, convenient to clarify some similarities and differences between these entities. ESA, the GSA, and EUMETSAT are from Europe, APSCO is from the Asia–Pacific region, and AfSA from Africa. ESA, APSCO, EUMETSAT and the GSA are fully active, while AfSA is currently under development. ESA, APSCO, and EUMETSAT are independent international organizations, while AfSA and the GSA are subsidiary bodies of two international intergovernmental organizations: the African Union (AU) and the European Union (EU), respectively. ESA, APSCO and EUMETSAT's constituent instruments are international conventions, AfSA's constituent instrument is the AfSA Statute, which was adopted by a resolution of the AU Assembly, and the GSA main legal framework is Regulation (EU) No 912/2010. Finally, ESA, APSCO and the AfSA are competent in various space fields, including space research and space applications, while EUMETSAT and the GSA are focused on specific space applications.

### *3.1.1 The European Space Agency*

ESA could be a model for LASA due to its successful history in promoting European space cooperation. ESA is an international intergovernmental organisation (IGO) composed of member states and a model of international cooperation in the use and exploration of outer space.[7] ESA shapes the development of Europe's space capability; its member states cooperate through ESA, and ESA cooperates with other partners.[8] ESA was created in 1975 by the ESA Convention[9] and is the result of the merger of two European institutions: the European Space Research Organisation (ESRO) and the European Organisation for the Development and Construction of Space Vehicle Launchers (ELDO),[10] both created in 1964.[11] ESA is a subject of public international law with international legal personality. Therefore, it can possess rights and duties, and it is entitled to actions and responsibilities different from those of its member states.[12] There are currently 22 ESA member states (as of 2021): Austria, Belgium, Czech Republic, Denmark, Estonia, Finland, France, Germany, Greece, Hungary, Ireland, Italy, Luxembourg, The Netherlands, Norway, Poland, Portugal, Romania, Spain, Sweden, Switzerland and the United Kingdom. Canada

---

[7] United Nations Committee on the Peaceful Uses of Outer Space (UNCOPUOS), "The European Space Agency as a mechanism and actor of international cooperation", A/AC.105/C.2/2014/CRP.28, 28 March 2014, p. 3.

[8] Ibid.

[9] Convention for the Establishment of a European Space Agency (ESA Convention), adopted on 30 May 1975, and entered into force on 30 October 1980.

[10] ELDO is commonly known as the European Launcher Development Organisation.

[11] The European Space Agency, "Key dates 1960–2018", www.esa.int/About_Us/ESA_history/Key_dates_1960-2018.

[12] UNCOPUOS, A/AC.105/C.2/2014/CRP.28, p. 4.

also sits on the Council and takes part in some projects under a Cooperation Agreement. Latvia and Slovenia are associate members.[13] In this regard, Canada, Latvia and Slovenia, based on their agreements with ESA, qualify to fully participate in the programmes of the ESA Education Office[14] (Table 3.1).

The purpose of ESA is to provide for and to promote, for exclusively peaceful purposes, cooperation among European states in space research and technology and their space applications, for scientific purposes or operational space applications systems.[15] ESA has four lines of action to achieve this purpose[16]:

a. By elaborating and implementing a long-term European space policy,
b. By elaborating and implementing activities and programmes in the space field,
c. By coordinating the European space programme and national programmes, and
d. By elaborating and implementing an appropriate industrial policy.

ESA designs and carries out the European space programme, which includes the exploration of Earth's immediate space environment, the Solar System and the Universe, the development of satellite-based technologies and services, and the promotion of European industries.[17] ESA's activities are of two kinds: mandatory and optional. The mandatory activities are those that fall under the General Budget and the Space Science programme budget, which include ESA's basic activities.[18] All member states contribute to these programmes on a scale based on their Gross National Product (GNP). In the optional programmes, ESA's member states are free to decide on their level of participation (Figs. 3.1 and 3.2).[19]

ESA's headquarters are in Paris, France, and has in addition the following sites (Fig. 3.3):

- EAC, the European Astronauts Centre in Cologne, Germany,
- ESAC, the European Space Astronomy Centre, in Villanueva de la Canada, Madrid, Spain,
- ESOC, the European Space Operations Centre, in Darmstadt, Germany,
- ESRIN, ESA's centre for Earth observation (EO), in Frascati, near Rome, Italy,
- ESTEC, the European Space Research and Technology Centre, Noordwijk, the Netherlands,
- ECSAT, the European Centre for Space Applications and Telecommunications, Harwell, Oxfordshire, United Kingdom, and
- ESEC, the European Space Security and Education Centre, Redu, Belgium.

---

[13] ESA, "Member States and Cooperating States", https://www.esa.int/About_Us/Corporate_news/Member_States_Cooperating_States.

[14] ESA, "ESA Member States, Canada, Latvia and Slovenia", www.esa.int/Education/ESA_Member_States_Canada_Latvia_and_Slovenia; see also: Chap. 4, Sect. 4.3.4.

[15] ESA Convention, art. II.

[16] Ibid.

[17] The European Space Agency, "ESA Facts", www.esa.int/About_Us/Corporate_news/ESA_facts.

[18] The European Space Agency, "Funding", www.esa.int/About_Us/Corporate_news/Funding.

[19] Ibid.

**Table 3.1** ESA's legal, political and institutional history

| | |
|---|---|
| 1960 (December) | Intergovernmental conference at Meyrin, Switzerland, setting up the European Preparatory Commission for Space Research (COPERS) |
| 1962 (March) | Signature by Belgium, France, Germany, Italy, the Netherlands, the United Kingdom and Australia (associate member) of the Convention creating ELDO, in London |
| 1962 (June) | Signature by Belgium, Denmark, France, Germany, Italy, the Netherlands, Spain, Sweden, Switzerland and the United Kingdom of the Convention creating ESRO, in Paris |
| 1963 | European Space Data Analysis Centre (ESDAC), renamed ESOC in 1967, is established in Darmstadt, Germany |
| 1964 (February) | ELDO Convention enters into force |
| 1964 (March) | ESRO Convention enters into force |
| 1965 | ESTEC is established in Noordwijk, the Netherlands |
| 1966 | ESRIN is established in Frascati, Italy |
| 1971 (December) | First Package Deal that permits ESRO to pursue application programmes comes into force |
| 1973 (July) | Second Package Deal: The European Space Conference (ESC) meeting in Brussels decides on the creation of ESA |
| 1975 (May) | Signature of the ESA Convention by Belgium, Denmark, France, Germany (Federal Republic), Italy, the Netherlands, Spain, Sweden, Switzerland and the United Kingdom |
| 1975 (December) | Signature of the ESA Convention by Ireland |
| 1980 | Arianespace is created |
| 1987 (January) | Austria and Norway become ESA member states |
| 1995 (January) | Finland becomes a member state |
| 2000 (November) | Portugal becomes an ESA member state |
| 2001 (March) | ESA Council adopts the Resolution on implementation of measures for European Cooperating States (ECS) |
| 2002 (February) | Brazil signs a Cooperation Agreement with ESA |
| 2002 (March) | Argentina signs a Cooperation Agreement with ESA |
| 2003 (November) | Signature of the Framework Agreement between ESA and the European Community in Brussels |

(continued)

**Table 3.1** (continued)

| | |
|---|---|
| 2004 (November) | First ESA/EU "Space Council" in Brussels |
| 2005 | Greece and Luxembourg become ESA member states |
| 2007 (May) | ESA/EU countries adopt a Resolution on European Space Policy |
| 2008 | Czech Republic becomes an ESA member state |
| 2009 | Cyprus signs Cooperation Agreement with ESA |
| 2011 | Romania becomes an ESA member state |
| 2011 | Israel signs Cooperation Agreement with ESA |
| 2011 | ESA's Council grants observer status to Bulgaria, Cyprus, Estonia, Hungary, Latvia, Lithuania, Malta, Poland, Slovakia and Slovenia |
| 2012 | Poland becomes an ESA member state |
| 2012 | Malta signs Cooperation Agreement with ESA |
| 2014 | Lithuania becomes an ESA ECS |
| 2014 | ESA Ministerial Council approves ESA evolution, covering the vision for ESA until 2030 |
| 2015 | Estonia and Hungary becomes ESA member states |
| 2015 | Bulgaria and Slovakia become ESA ECS |
| 2016 | Slovenia becomes an ESA associate member state |
| 2016 | ESA Ministerial Council adopts the resolution "Towards Space 4.0 for a United Space in Europe" |
| 2016 | Cyprus becomes an ESA ECS |
| 2018 | Croatia signs Cooperation Agreement with ESA |
| 2020 | Latvia becomes an ESA associate member state |

*Source* ESA

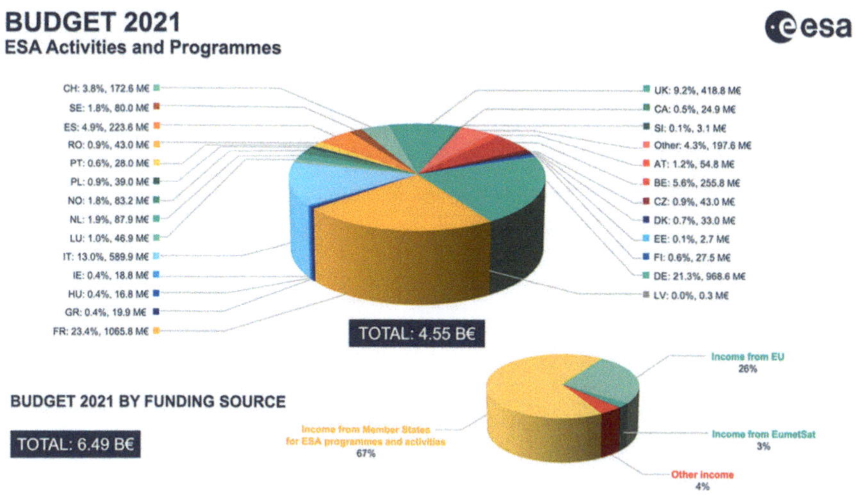


**Fig. 3.1** ESA budget 2021 by funding source. *Source* ESA

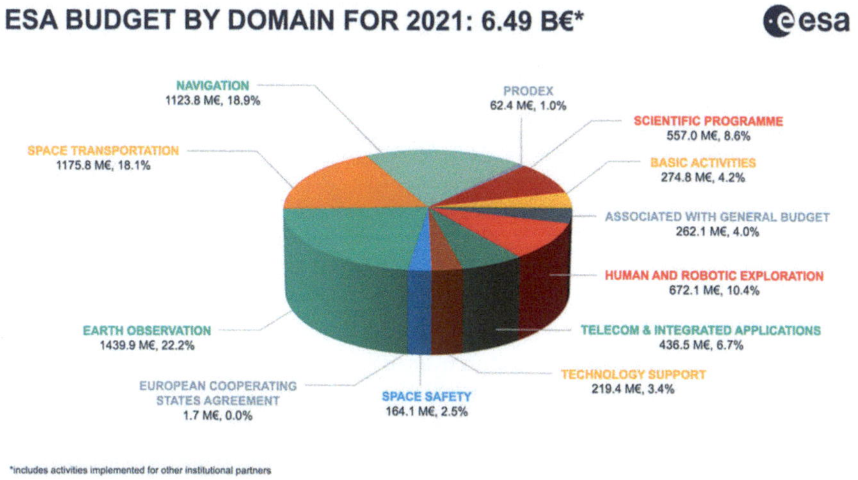


**Fig. 3.2** ESA budget by domain for 2021. *Source* ESA

ESA has liaison offices in Belgium, the U.S. and Russia; a launch base in French Guiana and ground/tracking stations in various parts of the world.[20]

ESA is empowered to establish international cooperation not only with its member states but also with governments, organisations and institutions of non-member states,

[20] See: Footnote 17.

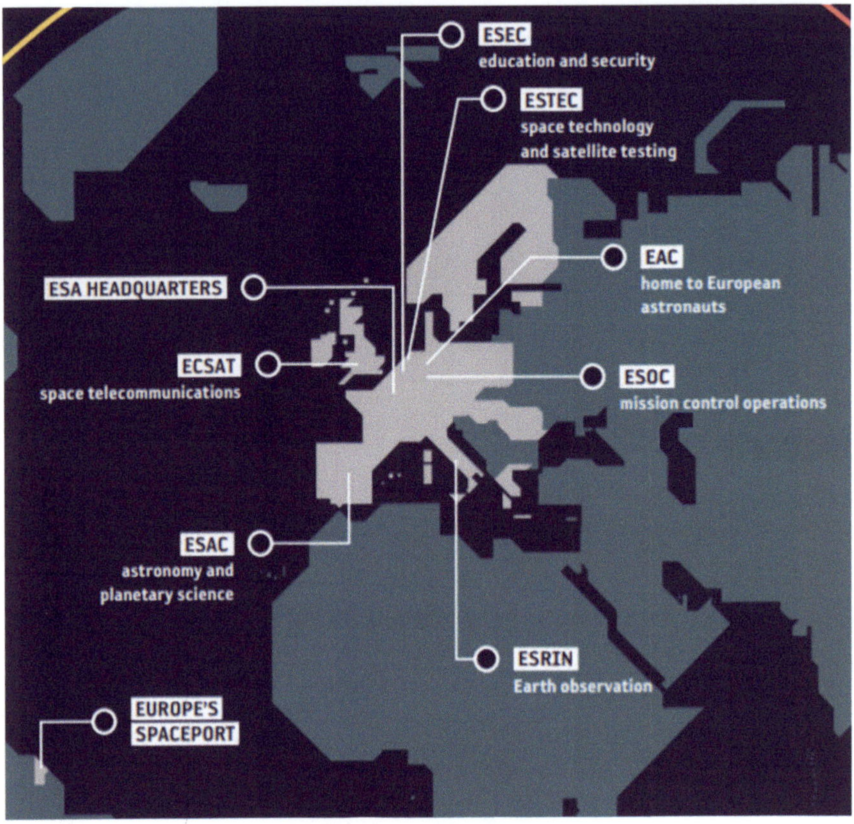


**Fig. 3.3** ESA headquarters and facilities. *Source* ESA

as well as other institutions and IGOs.[21] This cooperation is possible for both mandatory and optional programmes.[22] Moreover, ESA has treaty-making power as part of its international legal personality. In this sense, ESA may adopt a great array of legal instruments with other partners, such as cooperation agreements, other international agreements, implementing agreements, Memoranda of Understanding (MoU) (as far as they contain international obligations), and exchange of letters (as far as they contain international obligations).[23] ESA's international partners include non-member states from all regions of the world, in particular its main partners (U.S., Russia, China, Canada and Japan), and international organisations such as the European Union (EU),[24] EUMETSAT and the United Nations (UN), where

[21] UNCOPUOS, A/AC.105/C.2/2014/CRP.28, p. 12; see also: art. XIV of the ESA Convention.

[22] In 1977, the ESA Council adopted the "Resolution on the Agency and its External Relations", which provides a basis for ESA's conduct of its international cooperation activities.

[23] UNCOPUOS, A/AC.105/C.2/2014/CRP.28, p. 14.

[24] It is important to highlight that ESA and the EU are independent international organizations. However, ESA and EU have close ties thanks to a bilateral framework agreement adopted in 2004.

ESA is permanent observer of the Committee on the Peaceful Uses of Outer Space (UNCOPUOS).[25]

### 3.1.2 *The Asia–Pacific Space Cooperation Organization*

The second possible model for LASA is the Asia–Pacific Space Cooperation Organisation (APSCO), an intergovernmental regional space organization based in Beijing, China.[26] With eight member states,[27] APSCO is a non-profit independent body with full international legal status.[28] APSCO's constituent instrument is the APSCO Convention, signed in 2005, although the organization was officially inaugurated in 2008.[29] APSCO promotes multilateral cooperation in space science, technology and technology applications in the Asia–Pacific region[30] and serves as a cooperative mechanism for developing countries in the region through the peaceful use of space (Fig. 3.4).

APSCO's objectives are the promotion of collaborative space programs; the implementation of actions to assist its member states in space technological research and development (R&D), applications and training; the promotion of cooperation, joint development, and sharing of achievements among APSCO member states in space research, space technology and its applications; the enhancement of cooperation among relevant enterprises and institutions of member states and the promotion of industrialization of space technology and its applications, as well as the contribution of the peaceful uses of outer space in international space cooperative activities[31] (Table 3.2).

APSCO has established cooperation relations with different international partners.[32] APSCO is a permanent observer at UNCOPUOS, observer at the International

In addition, ESA contributes to some of the EU space programmes. Both organizations adopted a common European Space Policy in 2007, see: www.esa.int/About_Us/Corporate_news/Member_States_Cooperating_States.

[25] UNCOPUOS, A/AC.105/C.2/2014/CRP.28, p. 15.

[26] See: Chap. 1.2.2.

[27] Bangladesh, China, Iran, Mongolia, Pakistan, Peru, Thailand and Turkey.

[28] Convention for the Asia–Pacific Space Cooperation Organization (APSCO Convention), Beijing, People's Republic of China, adopted on 28 October 2005 and entered into force on 12 October 2006, art. 3.

[29] The Signing Ceremony of APSCO Convention was held in the Great Hall of the People, Beijing, on 28 October 2005. Eight countries signed the Convention in this event: Bangladesh, China, Indonesia, Iran, Mongolia, Pakistan, Peru and Thailand. In June 2006, Turkey signed the Convention. Except for Indonesia, all the countries have ratified the Convention, see: APSCO, "History Trace", www.apsco.int/html/comp1/content/historytrace/2018-06-26/21-153-1.shtml.

[30] APSCO, "About APSCO", www.apsco.int/html/comp1/content/WhatisAPSCO/2018-06-06/33-144-1.shtml.

[31] APSCO Convention, art. 4.

[32] Art. 25 of the APSCO Convention provides that APSCO "may establish cooperative partnerships with non-Member States of the Organization and other international organizations and institutions

**Fig. 3.4** APSCO training course on remote sensing application and data sharing service platform in Peru, 8–11 August 2017, Lima, Peru. *Source* APSCO

**Table 3.2** APSCO's legal, political and institutional history

| | |
|---|---|
| 1988 | China, Pakistan and Thailand conceive the idea of establishing multilateral space cooperation in the Asia–Pacific region |
| 1992 | During the Asia–Pacific Workshop on Multilateral Cooperation in Space Technology and Applications (AP-MCSTA) held in Beijing, China, the institutionalization of this mechanism is proposed, which is agreed by 16 Asia–Pacific countries through an MoU |
| 2001 | Establishment of the AP-MCSTA Secretariat in China |
| 2005 (October) | Signature of the APSCO Convention in Beijing, China, by Bangladesh, China, Indonesia, Iran, Mongolia, Pakistan, Peru and Thailand |
| 2006 | Turkey signs the APSCO convention |
| 2007 | The ASPCO Convention is registered in the UN as a multilateral international organization |
| 2008 | APSCO is inaugurated after the First Council Meeting of APSCO, held in Beijing, China |
| 2013–2017 | Actions for the standardization of APSCO cooperation activities and institutionalization of the organization |
| 2015 | Mexico becomes an observer state of APSCO |
| 2015 (October) | Adoption of the 2015-Beijing Declaration at the APSCO Development Strategic Forum with the theme "The Belt and Road Initiative for Facilitating Space Capabilities Building of the Asia Pacific Countries" |
| 2016 | Egypt becomes APSCO's associate member state |
| 2018 (November) | APSCO adopts its Development Vision 2030 |

*Sources* APSCO, UNOOSA, AEM

Committee on Global Navigation Satellite Systems (ICG) and the Group on Earth Observations (GEO), and has a working collaboration with the UN Office for Outer Space Affairs (UNOOSA), the UN Economic and Social Commission for Asia and the Pacific (UN-ESCAP), the UN Platform for Space-based Information for Disaster Management and Emergency Response (UN-SPIDER) and the Regional Centre for Space Science and Technology Education in Asia and the Pacific (China) affiliated to the UN (UN-RCSSTEAP).[33] APSCO also has relations and partnerships with the International Space Science Institute Beijing (ISSI-BJ), the Chinese Society of Astronautics (CSA), the International Academy of Astronautics (IAA), the International Astronautical Federation (IAF), Space Foundation, and ESA.[34]

### *3.1.3 The African Space Agency*

The third possible model for LASA is the African Space Agency (AfSA), one of the most recent examples of regional space cooperation mechanisms. Although the AfSA is still under development, Latin American countries may get be inspired by the AfSA Statute and the context in which this instrument was adopted.

Unlike the ESA and APSCO, which are both international organizations, AfSA is an organ of the AU. The AU is an intergovernmental organisation established in 2002 to promote the unity and solidarity of African states, to spur economic development, and to promote international cooperation.[35] It was the Assembly of the AU which, after consultations carried out by the AU Commission on the legal, structural and financial implications of the AfSA, adopted the AfSA Statute on 29 January 2018, which entered into force the same day.[36] It is expected that the AfSA will be operational by 2023.

According to AfSA Statute, the purpose of this agency will be the promotion, advice and coordination of the development and utilisation of space science and technology in Africa, and associated regulations for the benefit of Africa and the

---

in pursuit of its objectives, with the unanimous approval of the Council, for which the Council shall draw appropriate guidelines and procedure".

33 This regional centre has its headquarters at the Beihang University, Beijing. There are two additional regional centres in Asia: the Regional Centre for Space Science and Technology Education for Western Asia (RCSSTEWA), located in Amman, Jordan, and the Centre for Space Science and Technology Education in Asia and the Pacific (CSSTEAP), located at New Delhi, India, see: UNOOSA, Regional Centres for Space Science and Technology Education (affiliated to the UN), www.unoosa.org/oosa/en/ourwork/psa/regional-centres/index.html.

34 APSCO, "International cooperation", www.apsco.int/html/comp1/content/International_Cooperation/2019-02-21/17-252-1.shtml.

35 The AU replaced the Organisation of African Unity (OAU), Britannica, "African Union", www.britannica.com/topic/African-Union.

36 Statute of the African Space Agency (AfSA Statute), Thirtieth Ordinary Session of the Assembly of the African Union, Ethiopia, 29 January 2018.

world. It will also forge intra-African and international cooperation.[37] The 55 member states of the AU[38] will also be member states of AfSA.[39] AfSA will possess legal personality and capacity to enter into agreements, acquire and dispose of moveable and immovable property, and institute legal proceedings.[40] AfSA's headquarters will be in the outskirts of New Cairo, Egypt.[41]

AfSA will pursue two general objectives: (1) promoting and coordinating the implementation of the African Space Policy and Strategy, and (2) conducting activities that exploit space technologies and applications for sustainable development and improvement of the welfare of African citizens.[42] AfSA's particular objectives will comprise the following: take advantage of potential benefits of space science, technology and applications in addressing Africa's socio-economic opportunities and challenges; strengthen regional space missions to effectively use space data, services and products; develop a sustainable indigenous space market and industry; adopt good corporate governance and best practices; maximize the benefits of current and planned space activities; avoid or minimize duplication of resources and efforts; establish Communities of Practice to channel user needs on space services, and promote an African-led space agenda through reciprocal partnerships.[43]

AfSA's main function[44] will be the implementation of the African Space Policy and Strategy.[45] Further functions include the promotion and coordination of programmes and activities approved by the African Space Council; address user needs; support member states and Regional Economic Communities (RECs)[46] in building their space programmes; coordinate space efforts in Africa; enhance and

---

[37] Ibid., art. 2.

[38] AU member states are: Algeria, Angola, Benin, Botswana, Burkina Faso, Burundi, Cameroon, Cape Verde, Central African Republic, Chad, Comoros, Democratic Republic of the Congo, Republic of the Congo, Djibouti, Egypt, Equatorial Guinea, Eritrea, Eswatini, Ethiopia, Gabon, Gambia, Ghana, Guinea, Guinea-Bissau, Ivory Coast, Kenya, Lesotho, Liberia, Libya, Madagascar, Malawi, Mali, Mauritania, Mauritius, Morocco, Mozambique, Namibia, Niger, Nigeria, Rwanda, Sahrawi Arab Democratic Republic (Western Sahara), São Tomé and Príncipe, Senegal, Seychelles, Sierra Leone, Somalia, South Africa, South Sudan, Sudan, Tanzania, Togo, Tunisia, Uganda, Zambia and Zimbabwe.

[39] AfSA Statute, art. 1.

[40] Ibid., art. 3.

[41] Nour Eltigani, "Egypt to Establish African Space Agency in New Cairo", *Egyptian Streets*, 24 February 2019, https://egyptianstreets.com/2019/02/24/egypt-to-establish-african-space-agency-in-new-cairo/, see further: Annette Froehlich and André Siebrits, *Space Supporting Africa. Volume 1: A Primary Needs Approach and Africa's Emerging Space Middle Powers*, Springer (2021).

[42] AfSA Statute, art. 4.

[43] Ibid.

[44] Ibid., art. 5.

[45] See: this chapter, Sect. 3.2.3.1.

[46] African RECs are eight sub regional bodies which are the building blocks of the African Economic Community established in the 1991 Abuja Treaty, which provides the framework for continental economic integration. The RECs are: The Arab Maghreb Union (AMU/UMA), the Economic Community of West African States (ECOWAS), the East African Community (EAC), the Intergovernmental Authority on Development (IGAD), the Southern African Development Community (SADC), the Common Market for Eastern and Southern African (COMESA), the Economic

**Table 3.3** AfSA's legal, political and institutional history

| | |
|---|---|
| 2013 | AU adopts decisions and recommendations on the need for Africa to develop an African Space Policy and Strategy |
| 2016 | AU adopts the African Space Policy and Strategy in Addis Ababa, Ethiopia, to formalize an AU Agenda 2063 Outer-Space Flagship Programme |
| 2018 | Adoption of AfSA Statute in Addis Ababa, Ethiopia |
| 2019 | AU choses Egypt to host AfSA headquarters |

*Source* AfSA Statute

facilitate access to space resources and services; support member states and RECs in building critical infrastructure; develop, upgrade and operate cutting-edge African space infrastructure; coordinate space capacity-building in the continent; foster regional coordination and collaboration; promote strategic African and international partnerships and promote African participation in international efforts; strengthen research, development and innovation in space science and technology, and raise awareness of the benefits of space programmes for Africa [47] (Table 3.3).

### 3.1.4 *The European Organisation for the Exploitation of Meteorological Satellites*

The fourth model for LASA is the European Organisation for the Exploitation of Meteorological Satellites (EUMETSAT). EUMETSAT, headquartered in Darmstadt, Germany, is an intergovernmental organisation and a user-governed operational satellite agency for monitoring weather, climate and the environment from the space. EUMETSAT has 30 member states[48] and is governed by the Convention for the Establishment of EUMETSAT adopted in 1984, in force since 1986.[49] This Convention states EUMETSAT's primary objective: the establishment, maintenance and exploitation of European systems of operational meteorological satellites, taking into account as far as possible the recommendations of the World Meteorological

Community for Central African States (ECCAS), and the Community of Sahel-Saharan States (CENSAD), see: Office of the Special Adviser on Africa, The Regional Economic Communities (RECs) of the African Union, www.un.org/en/africa/osaa/peace/recs.shtml.

[47] AfSA Statute, art. 5.

[48] Austria, Belgium, Bulgaria, Croatia, Czech Republic, Denmark, Estonia, Finland, France, Germany, Greece, Hungary, Iceland, Ireland, Italy, Latvia, Lithuania, Luxembourg, Netherlands, Norway, Poland, Portugal, Romania, Slovakia, Slovenia, Spain, Sweden, Switzerland, Turkey and the United Kingdom.

[49] Convention for the Establishment of a European Organization for the Exploitation of Meteorological Satellites (EUMETSAT), adopted on 24 May 1983; entered into force on 19 June 1986 (EUMETSAT Convention).

**Fig. 3.5** EUMETSAT polar system in Spitsbergen, Svalbard, Norway. *Source* EUMETSAT

Organization (WMO).[50] A further objective is to contribute to the operational monitoring of the climate and the detection of global climatic changes.[51] In this regard, EUMETSAT supplies weather and climate-related satellite data, images and products to the National Meteorological Services of its member states,[52] as well as other users,[53] helping meteorologists to identify and monitor potential dangerous weather situations and, thus, protect human life and property. This data also contributes to the safety of air travel, shipping and road traffic, and facilitates farming, construction and other industries.[54]

International cooperation of EUMETSAT includes a collaboration with the EU to exploit the EU four Sentinel missions of the Copernicus space component aimed at monitoring the atmosphere, ocean and climate on its behalf. EUMETSAT has also established cooperation with operators of EO satellites from Europe, China, India, Japan, Russia, South Korea and the U.S.[55] (Fig. 3.5).

[50] Ibid., art. 2.1.

[51] Ibid.

[52] See: Footnote 48.

[53] EUMETSAT, "Who we are", www.eumetsat.int/about-us/who-we-are.

[54] EUMETSAT, "What we do", www.eumetsat.int/about-us/what-we-do.

[55] See: Footnote 53.

### 3.1.5 *The European Global Navigation Satellite Systems Agency*

Finally, a further potential model for LASA is the European GNSS Agency or GSA, the EU entity responsible for the operations and service provision of Europe's Global Satellite Navigation Programme (GALILEO) and the European Geostationary Navigation Overlay Service (EGNOS) programmes—Europe's independent satellite navigation and positioning programmes.[56] Similar to AfSA, the GSA is a subsidiary body of an international organization, in this case, the EU. Thus, all EU member states benefit from GSA's services.[57] The GSA was formally created as an agency of the EU by Regulation (EU) No. 912/2010,[58] which entered into force on 9 November 2010, and was subsequently amended by Regulation (EU) No. 512/2014[59] of 16 April 2014 (Table 3.4).[60] Apart from these regulations, the legal framework of the GSA includes several EU decisions and regulations on legal, technical and financial issues, as well as cooperation agreements with international partners for the promotion and development of civil GNSS and the participation in the European GNSS programmes.[61] The GSA has legal personality and all EU member states[62] and the Commission have a seat on GSA's Administrative Board.[63] GSA is based in Prague, Czech Republic.

[56] These programmes are managed by the European Commission on behalf of the EU member states. GALILEO is Europe's GNSS, which provides improved positioning and timing information with significant positive implications for many European services and users. EGNOS is Europe's regional satellite-based augmentation system that is used to improve the performance of GNSSs, such as the U.S.'s NAVSTAR Global Positioning System (GPS) and GALILEO. More information about these programmes is available at www.gsa.europa.eu/.

[57] EU member states are the following 27 countries: Austria, Belgium, Bulgaria, Croatia, Cyprus, Czech Republic, Denmark, Estonia, Finland, France, Germany, Greece, Hungary, Ireland, Italy, Latvia, Lithuania, Luxembourg, Malta, The Netherlands, Poland, Portugal, Romania, Slovakia, Slovenia, Spain, Sweden.

[58] Regulation (EU) No 912/2010 of the European Parliament and of the Council, 22 September 2010.

[59] Regulation (EU) No 512/2014 of the European Parliament and of the Council of 16 April 2014.

[60] European GNSS Agency, "About GSA", www.gsa.europa.eu/gsa/about-gsa.

[61] Ibid.

[62] The GSA does not have "member states" as such, but EU member states have a role in the operation of the GSA, which mainly consists of the transmission of information to the GSA Security Accreditation Board for the purposes of security accreditation, and other related tasks, see: Regulation (EU) No 912/2010 of the European Parliament and of the Council, 22 September 2010, art. 12.

[63] This organ is also comprised of four representatives appointed by the EU Commission and one non-voting representative appointed by the European Parliament, Regulation (EU) No 912/2010 of the European Parliament and of the Council, 22 September 2010, arts. 4 and 5.

**Table 3.4** European GNSS agency's legal, political and institutional history

| | |
|---|---|
| 2002 | Creation of the GALILEO Joint Undertaking (GJU) by the European Community and ESA |
| 2004 | Establishment of the European GNSS Supervisory Agency (GSA) by Council Regulation (EC) 1321/2004 |
| 2006 | GSA changed its status by Council Regulation (EC) No. 1942/2006 |
| 2007 | The GSA officially takes over all tasks assigned to the GJU |
| 2010 | GSA is restructured as an agency of the EU called the European GNSS Agency by Regulation (EU) No. 912/2010, which entered into force on 9 November 2010 |
| 2013 | Adoption of Regulation (EU) No. 1285/2013 on the implementation and exploitation of European satellite navigation systems |
| 2014 | Amendment of Regulation (EU) No. 912/2010 by Regulation (EU) No. 512/2014 |
| 2014 | The Council of the EU adopts Decision 2014/496/CFSP on aspects of the deployment, operation and use of the European GNSS affecting the security of the EU |
| 2018 | The European Commission submitted a regulation proposal to establish a European Space Programme for the years 2021 to 2027, and replace the GSA by the European Union Agency for the Space Programme |
| 2020 | The EU Council and the European Parliament reach a provisional political agreement on the Commission's 2018 regulation proposal |

*Source* GSA, EU

GSA's mission[64] is to serve as the essential link between space technology and user needs through the translation of GALILEO and EGNOS signals into valuable and reliable services in Europe and around the world.[65] More specifically, the GSA supports EU objectives and achieves the highest return on European GNSS investment, in terms of benefits to users and economic growth and competitiveness, by:

- Designing and enabling services that fully respond to user needs, while continuously improving the European GNSS services and infrastructure,
- Managing the provision of quality services that ensure user satisfaction in the most cost-efficient manner,
- Engaging market stockholders to develop innovative and effective applications, value-added services and user technologies that promote the achievement of full European GNSS adoption, and
- Ensuring that European GNSS services and operations are thoroughly secure, safe and accessible.

[64] European GNSS Agency, "About GSA", www.gsa.europa.eu/gsa/about-gsa; see also: art. 14 (The role of the European GNSS Agency) of Regulation (EU) No. 1285/2013 of the European Parliament and of the Council of 11 December 2013.

[65] European GNSS Agency, "What we do", www.gsa.europa.eu/about/what-we-do.

Moreover, the GSA performs multiple tasks delegated by the European Commission.[66] In addition, due to the large capacities of the European GNSS and the importance of compatibility of space systems, the GSA facilitates international cooperation with multiple international partners. This cooperation includes the promotion of international industrial cooperation and interconnectivity with other space systems; the funding of R&D initiatives inside and outside Europe; the development of technical solutions and the contribution to setting international standards, and the support of non-EU partner countries in developing a favourable ecosystem for GNSS market uptake. In Latin America, for example, the GSA contributes to the activities of the Galileo Information Centres established in Brazil and Chile, namely through market development information and market intelligence.[67]

Lastly, it is important to mention that the GSA will be soon replaced and succeeded by the "European Union Agency for the Space Programme" (EUSPA) through a new EU regulation.[68] The aim of this regulation is to establish a unified system of governance for all components of the European Space Programme and give EUSPA competence on security accreditation as well as market and downstream applications development.[69]Accordingly, the new EUSPA will manage not only the GALILEO and EGNOS programmes, but also the Copernicus EO system. Moreover, it will prepare the Governmental Satellite Communications (GOVSATCOM) programme and concentrate EU capacities to monitor the Earth's near surroundings.[70] In addition, the new EU Regulation aims at providing a clear distribution of tasks and responsibilities between the entities involved in the implementation of the European Space Programme, namely the EU member states, the Commission, EUSPA, ESA and EUMETSAT.

---

[66] The delegation agreements in place to cater for those specific activities are the PRS delegation agreement, signed in 2011; the EGNOS Exploitation delegation agreement, signed in 2014; the Galileo Exploitation delegation agreement, signed in 2014, and the Horizon 2020 delegation agreement, signed in 2014.

[67] European GNSS Agency, "International Co-operation", www.gsa.europa.eu/galileo/international-co-operation.

[68] In 2018, the EU Commission submitted its *Proposal for a Regulation of the European Parliament and the Council establishing the space programme of the Union and the European Union Agency for the Space Programme and repealing Regulations (EU) No 912/2010, (EU) No 1285/2013, (EU) No 337/2014 and Decision 541/2014/EU*, (COM(2018) 447 final, Brussels, 6 June 2018). In December 2020, the EU Council presidency and the European Parliament adopted a provisional political agreement on the EU Space Programme for the years 2021 to 2027. The proposal regulation is expected to be ready for a second reading by the EU Council and the Parliament in 2021, see: European Council, Council of the European Union, "EU Space Programme: Council presidency reaches political agreement with the European Parliament", 16 December 2020, www.consilium.europa.eu/en/press/press-releases/2020/12/16/eu-space-programme-council-presidency-reaches-political-agreement-with-the-european-parliament/.

[69] *Proposal for a Regulation adopted by the Permanent Representatives Committee on 18 December 2020*, Council of the European Union, Doc. 9898/18 + ADD 1, General Secretariat of the Council, Interinstitutional File: 2018/0236(COD), Brussels, 18 December 2020, paras. 28 and 87.

[70] "EU Agency for the Space Programme to replace GSA in 2021", *IG Inside GNSS*, 26 December 2019, https://insidegnss.com/eu-agency-for-the-space-program-to-replace-gsa-in-2021/.

In this regard, if Latin American states consider the GSA as a model for LASA, they must take into account that the GSA is part of a system in which the agency coordinates its work with other European partners, without which it would not be possible to achieve its goals. The GSA model would probably be more suitable if LASA is created as a subsidiary organ of the Organisation of American States (OAS) or another international organization, and its responsibilities be limited to the coordination of space systems or programmes technically developed by other entities (such as its own member states). The GSA model could also be used in the Latin American and Caribbean Space Agency (ALCE) proposal if this agency is mainly envisaged to coordinate regional programmes such as the CELAC-SAT satellite, which aims at providing EO services to Latin American countries.[71]

## 3.2 Conditions for Establishing a Latin American Space Agency

Apart from considering the use of a model of regional space agency for LASA, there are several conditions that Latin American states may deem necessary before creating this entity. As analysed in Chap. 2, the different LASA proposals indicate various conditions, such as the preparation of a study on the technical, institutional and financial feasibilities of LASA, the identification of space capacities of Latin American countries, and the necessity of regular consultations for the discussion of LASA's features.[72] Moreover, these conditions have been confirmed by academic sources. For example, during the Fifth International Congress of the Latin American and Caribbean Space Network (RELACA-Espacio), Marta Gaggero pointed out that the establishment of LASA should be followed by a dialogue between the interested parties, the consideration of technological capacities and financial resources, the idea of creating a project to the benefit of the smaller countries, and the importance of sharing scientific knowledge between the interested countries.[73] Fermín Romero, former Pro Tempore Secretary of the VI Space Conference of the Americas (SCA), mentions that the creation of LASA should be preceded by three stages: the definition of a regional space agenda, the formulation of a regional space policy, and the

[71] The CELAC-SAT satellite is currently designed by the Mexican Space Agency. It is expected that other Latin American institutions will participate in the development of the satellite through a collaboration agreement with Mexico, Interview with Carlos Duarte Muñoz, *Café Espacial*, directed by Fermín Romero Vázquez, 11 Cadena Global, 26 February 2021, www.facebook.com/watch/live/?v=459678345449528&ref=watch_permalink; see also: Chap. 2, Sect. 2.1.3.

[72] See: Chap. 2, Sect. 2.2.2.

[73] Gaggero Marta, "La creación de la agencia especial latinoamericana", V International Meeting of the Latin American and the Caribbean Space Network (RELACA-Espacio), Asuncion, Paraguay, May 2019.

integration of a strategic plan for regional space development.[74] Cynthia Jiménez, in turn, presents the following conditions for setting up LASA[75]:

- Establishment of a database of national space facilities, academic and research institutes, space industry, and the regional organizations involved in space science and technology, and space applications;
- Definition of strategies of coordination among the regional resources identified in the database;
- Definition of the first LASA space programme, which would include drafting the rules for the contribution schemes, and defining the funding sources for the space programme and the daily operations of LASA;
- Definition of a long-term LASA space policy;
- Negotiations on the location of the LASA headquarters and the Latin American space facilities;
- Legal drafting of the LASA Convention;
- Designing of strategies to boost space industry and capacity building in the region;
- Implementation of rules to select and hire LASA staff, and
- Preparation of a roadmap to encourage science and technology in the region.

The enumerated conditions may be summarized as follows: the creation of a regional space database, the establishment of national space agencies, the formulation of a regional space policy and strategy, the elaboration of a regional space programme, official discussions on the creation of LASA, and the adoption of LASA's constituent instrument. The first five conditions will be analysed in this chapter, while LASA's constituent instrument will be examined in the final chapter.

### *3.2.1 Regional Space Database*

Having an overall knowledge of the priorities, needs and capacities of Latin American states is paramount to conceptualize an effective, cohesive and permanent regional space cooperation mechanism that benefit all participant countries. A regional space database would allow Latin American countries to offer their expertise in specific fields, such as component manufacturing and applications implementation.[76] Since the first LASA proposal of 1982, the creation of a database of regional space capacities was considered as a previous step to the creation of this entity, and the Fourth SCA

---

[74] Fermín Romero Vázquez, "Política espacial de México", Mesa 2. Política y Derecho espacial, Secretaría Pro Témpore, Conferencia Espacial de las Américas, https://swfound.org/media/78906/7_politica%20espacial%20de%20mexico.pdf.

[75] Cynthia Jiménez Monroy, *Legal and Institutional Aspects of Latin-American Space Cooperation, AQUARELSat: The Water Monitoring Constellation*, Wöhrmann Print Service-Zutphen (2010), p. 65.

[76] Mariano Imbert, "A Latin American and Caribbean Space Organization to be Delivered in the Space 2030 Agenda", IAC-20-E3.1, 71st International Astronautical Congress—The CyberSpace Edition, 12–14 October 2020, p. 9.

was entrusted to identify space capacities in Latin American countries.[77] However, there are no signs of the creation of regional space databases derived from these proposals. Instead, different national and international initiatives or institutions—governmental,[78] academic,[79] journalistic[80]—have created databases on Latin American space capacities. However, these databases are sometimes outdated or imprecise, and most of them are limited to specific space fields. Therefore, Latin American states should decide on the establishment of a regional database to know the national space capacities and the degree of development of the overall space sector in the region, and what Latin America needs to conceive the best possible collective space agency with the available resources. The construction and management of the database could be handled by an expert group or a commission made up of representatives of the Latin American countries, or each country could provide information about their national space capacities during the negotiations on LASA.[81] A further option is that the two campuses of the regional Centre for Space Science and Technology education for Latin American and the Caribbean (CRECTEALC) affiliated to the UN serve as point of contact to gather and manage the data about regional space capacities.

[77] See: Footnote 72.

[78] One of the most important space databases is the UN Register of Objects Launched into Outer Space managed by UNOOSA, which includes Latin American registration submissions on their space objects, notifications on the establishment of their national registries of objects launched into outer space, and data on the implementation of the Space Treaties by Latin American countries. The UNOOSA Online Index of Objects Launched into Outer Space is available at www.unoosa.org/oosa/osoindex/search-ng.jspx?lf_id= ; further institutional space databases are found on the official websites of the national space related entities of Latin American countries, such as the Brazilian Space Industry Catalogue published by the Brazilian Space Agency (AEB), and the Space Education Portal of the Mexican Space Agency (AEM).

[79] For example, see: Annette Froehlich/Diego Alonso Amante Soria et al., *Space Supporting Latin America: Latin America's Emerging Space Middle Powers*, Springer (2020); Annette Froehlich (ed.), *Space Fostering Latin American Societies, Developing the Latin American Continent through Space, Part 1*, Southern Space Studies, Springer (2020); Annette Froehlich (ed.), *Space Fostering Latin American Societies, Developing the Latin American Continent through Space, Part 2*, Southern Space Studies, Springer (2021); Bruno Victorino Sarli et al., "Review of Space Activities in South America", *Journal of Aeronautical History* (2018); and Johanna Mendelson et al., *Toward the Heavens, Latin America's Emerging Space Programs*, Centre for Strategic and International Studies (2009).

[80] For instance, the magazine LATAM Satelital provides news on Latin American satellite and space related capacities, LATAM Satelital, http://latamsatelital.com/acceso-al-espacio/.

[81] This option was chosen by the European delegates to the debates on the creation of ESRO, in: J. Krige and A. Russo, *A History of the European Space Agency, 1958–1987* (*Vol. 1–ESRO and ELDO, 1958–1973*), European Space Agency (2000), p. 18.

### 3.2.2 National Space Agencies

Although international space cooperation without specialized national space bodies is possible,[82] Latin American countries could improve their cooperation relations in the space field through national space entities. As seen in Chap. 2, the Declaration of San Francisco de Quito of the Fifth SCA stated that the establishment of national space agencies in Latin American countries is an essential step to the foundation of a regional space entity. In ESA's history, all European countries wishing to participate in the joint space project established national space commissions and agencies as soon as the negotiations on ESRO started in order to be in a more appropriate position to defend their interests and coordinate their positions. Thus, it may be appropriate that all Latin American countries interested in participating in the creation of LASA have national space bodies. To date, almost all Latin American emerging space middle powers[83] possess a national space entity (Table 3.5).[84] Nevertheless, some Latin American countries have civilian (non-governmental) space entities and most of the small countries of the region have not yet created a national space body. This could hinder their participation in the intergovernmental dialogue for the preparation of LASA, especially if this agency is planned to be ready in a short time. For example, in the case of the ALCE proposal submitted by Mexico and Argentina in 2020, the bid to set up this entity for 2021 without giving Latin American small countries sufficient time to create their national space bodies may put these countries in a disadvantageous position at the negotiation table (Fig. 3.6).

[82] Many countries do not possess national space entities. However, they manage to adopt international cooperation relations on space issues through different national entities, such as the ministries of foreign relations, communications, transportation, defence, and science and technology, as well as national universities and space research centres.

[83] See: Froehlich/Amante Soria et al., *Space Supporting Latin America: Latin America's Emerging Space Middle Powers*, Springer (2020).

[84] On 18 February 2021, the Costa Rican Assembly approved the creation of the Costa Rican Space Agency (Agencia Espacial Costarricense (AEC)), and on 21 March 2021 President Carlos Alvarado signed the *Law Creating the Costa Rican Space Agency*. The headquarters of the AEC will be located at the Costa Rican capital, San José, in: José Alfaro, "Costa Rica tendrá Agencia y Centro Espacial, diputados aprueban ley de creación", *AR*, 18 February 2021, www.ameliarueda.com/nota/se-creara-agencia-centro-espacial-aprueban-ley-noticias-costa-rica; Wendy Pérez, "Alvarado firma Ley de Creación de la Agencia Espacial Costarricense", Elmundo.cr, 21 March 2021, www.elmundo.cr/costa-rica/alvarado-firma-ley-de-creacion-de-la-agencia-espacial-costarricense/; see also: Oscar Zelaya, "Costa Rica—Creación de la Agencia Espacial Costarricence (AEC)", *Central Law*, 15 March 2021, https://central-law.com/costa-rica-creacion-de-la-agencia-espacial-costarricense-aec/. In 2018, the Global Startup Ecosystem announced its plans to launch the Haiti's Space Agency (HSA), an independence agency of Haiti with government and private sector partners led by SpaceChain Foundation. However, there are no new developments in this initiative, see: "Haiti Tech Summit's 2nd Annual Program concludes with 105 million media impressions", *Meventum*, 25 June 2018, https://meventum.com/haiti-tech-summit-news/haiti-tech-summits-2nd-annual-program-concludes-with-105-million-media-impressions/.

**Table 3.5** National space agencies and entities in Latin America

| Country | Space agency or entity | Governmental/non-governmental | Year of creation |
|---|---|---|---|
| Argentina | National Commission on Space Activities (CONAE) | Governmental | 1991 |
| Bolivia | Bolivian Space Agency (ABE) | Governmental | 2010 |
| Brazil | Brazilian Space Agency (AEB) | Governmental | 1994 |
| Chile | Chile's Space Agency (ACE) ceased to exist in 2011. In its place, the following institutions took part of its responsibilities: the Space Operations Group (GOE) of Chile's Air Force—Ministry of National Defence, the Ministry of Transportation and Telecommunications, the Ministry of Science, Technology, Knowledge and Innovation, and the Council of Ministers for Space Development (CMSD) | Governmental | 2001–2011 (ACE)<br>2014 (CMSD) |
| Colombia | Colombian Space Commission (CSC), Presidential Program for Colombian Space Development (PPDEC), and Colombian Space Agency (AEC) | Governmental (CSC, PPDEC)/non-governmental (AEC) | 2006 (CSC)<br>2016 (PPDEC)<br>2017 (AEC) |
| Costa Rica | Costa Rican Space Agency (AECR) | Governmental | 2021 |
| Ecuador | Ecuadorian Air Force (FAE) and Ecuadorian Civilian Space Agency (EXA) | Governmental (FAE)/non-governmental (EXA) | 2007 (EXA) |
| Mexico | Mexican Space Agency (AEM) and Ministry of Communications and Transportation (SCT) | Governmental | 2010 (AEM) |
| Paraguay | Paraguayan Space Agency (AEP) | Governmental | 2012 |
| Peru | National Commission for Aerospace Research and Development (CONIDA)—Peruvian Space Agency (PSAg) | Governmental | 1974 (in 2007, CONIDA obtained the status of the PSAg) |

(continued)

**Table 3.5** (continued)

| Country | Space agency or entity | Governmental/non-governmental | Year of creation |
|---|---|---|---|
| Venezuela | Bolivarian Agency for Space Activities (ABAE) under the Ministry of Popular Power for Education, Science and Technology | Governmental | 2008 |

**Fig. 3.6** Latin American Countries with governmental and non-governmental space agencies or entities (2021)

### *3.2.3 Latin American Space Policy, Strategy and Vision*

Some consider that an essential condition for a proper functioning of LASA is the existence of a Latin American Space Policy (LASP), which would serve as a regional political guide for the implementation of joint space programmes that benefit Latin American countries.[85] According to Camilo Guzmán, a LASP would facilitate synergies and collaboration by Latin American states and give the region the possibility to become a major international space actor.[86] For him, there are three fundamental elements to formulate a LASP: clear objectives, the identification of needs and capacities, and appropriate organization of the interested countries.[87] Guzmán also considers that the LASP should be guided by three core principles: international cooperation, variable geometry and institutional flexibility.[88] Therefore, if Latin American countries wish to adopt a LASP, they must agree on its content, principles and objectives. In addition, they could adopt a regional vision or space strategy to complement the LASP. To facilitate the definition of a LASP, regional vision and space strategy, Latin American countries could become inspired by the space policies, visions and strategies of other regions of the world,[89] and consider local experiences in this regard.

#### 3.2.3.1 Regional Models

The first model of a regional space policy is the European Space Policy (ESP), which represents the common political space framework for Europe.[90] The legal basis of this ESP is Article 189 of the Treaty on the Functioning of the European Union

[85] At the governmental level, the subject has been dealt on rare occasions. For example, in May 2010, the Mexican campus of the Regional Centre for Space Science and Technology Education for Latin America and the Caribbean—affiliated to the UN—(CRECTEALC) participated with the topic "Advances of the development of a space policy at the regional level and its line up with the international space legislation" during a seminar-workshop on International Space Policy and Legislation (Climate Change and Food Safety) held at Quito, Ecuador. The VI SCA discussed the possibility of having a regional space policy, see: *Informe de Autoevaluación del Ejercicio Enero-Diciembre de 2010*, H. Junta de Gobierno, Primera Sesión Ordinaria 2011, Instituto Nacional de Astrofísica, Óptica y Electrónica, p. 33; Camilo Guzmán, *The Creation of Policy for Latin America Area, Myth or Reality?*, International Astronautical Congress, IAC-11.E3.1.11, p. 1.

[86] Guzmán, *The Creation of Policy for Latin America Area, Myth or Reality?*, IAC-11.E3.1.11, p. 1.

[87] Guzmán mentions three possibilities to organize Latin American countries: through the creation of LASA, by means of a non-institutional regional forum, or through the implementation of regional space policies by the pro tempore secretariat of the SCA with the support of CRECTEALC. For him, the regional forum is the most suitable option because it allows only interested countries to participate in the common effort, has greater flexibility to foster cooperation, is appropriate to put in practice the principle of variable geometry, less expensive, and allows progression to higher forms of institutional organization, Ibid., pp. 3–4.

[88] International cooperation implies that the countries of the region should avoid their political differences and start to collaborate in the space field through cooperation mechanisms; the variable geometry consists in the participation of the interested countries in common projects in a flexible manner, allowing some countries to go further in specific projects with respect to the others; and the institutional flexibility implies that only Latin American countries wishing to participate in a LASP should do it, without requiring specific financial contributions, Ibid., pp. 3–4.

[89] Guzmán suggests that the LASP could be copied from other regional models, not a specific one, but a combination of them, Ibid., p. 2.

[90] ESA, "European Space Policy", www.esa.int/About_Us/Corporate_news/European_Space_Policy.

**Table 3.6** Strategic mission of the European space policy

| |
|---|
| To develop and exploit space applications serving Europe's public policy objectives and the needs of European enterprises and citizens, including in the field of environment, development and global climate change |
| To meet Europe's security and defence needs as regards space |
| To ensure a strong and competitive space industry which fosters innovation, growth and the development and delivery of sustainable, high-quality, cost-effective services |
| To contribute to the knowledge-based society by investing strongly in space-based science, and playing a significant role in the international exploitation endeavour |
| To secure unrestricted access to new and critical technologies, systems and capabilities in order to ensure independent European space applications |

(TFEU),[91] which provides that the EU shall draw up an ESP to promote scientific and technical progress, industrial competitiveness and the implementation of its policies. To this end, the EU may promote joint initiatives, support research and technological development and coordinate the efforts needed for the exploration and exploitation of space. Moreover, the same article states that the EU shall establish appropriate relations with ESA.

Accordingly, in 2007, the Space Council of ESA and EU ministers adopted the ESP, which was drafted by the then Director General of ESA, Jean-Jacques Dordain, and the European Commission.[92] The ESP is a strategic choice for Europe, which aims to "exert global leadership in selected policy areas in accordance with European interests and values",[93] and should allow the EU, ESA and their member states "to increase coordination of their activities and programmes, and organise their respective roles relating to space, providing a more flexible framework to facilitate Community investment in space activities".[94] Through the ESP, Europe pursues an independent access to space capabilities and responds to several challenges through a strategic mission included in the ESP (Table 3.6). To achieve this mission, the EU, ESA and their member states agreed on a European Space Programme and the coordination of national and European space activities, with a user-led focus; the increase of synergy between defence and civil space programmes and technologies, and the development of a joint international relations strategy in space.[95]

A second model for a LASP is the EU Space Policy (EUSP). Although the EU is an essential partner of the ESP, it possesses its own space policy aimed at facing current challenges, supporting technological innovation, and providing socio-economic benefits to EU citizens.[96] The EUSP also aims to foster the development

[91] Consolidated versions of the Treaty on European Union and the Treaty on the Functioning of the European Union, OJ C 326, 26 October 2012.

[92] *Resolution on the European Space Policy*, ESA Director General's Proposal for the European Space Policy (2007).

[93] Ibid., p. 21.

[94] Ibid., p. 19.

[95] Ibid., p. 21.

[96] European Commission, "Space", https://ec.europa.eu/growth/sectors/space_en.

of EU space programmes[97] to deliver services to millions of people and support the implementation of EU policies through meeting key societal challenges (such as sustainable consumption of natural resources, safety and security, and climate change), promoting the creation of jobs and industrial growth, and ensuring EU autonomy, including security, defence and strategic autonomy.[98] Apart from the EUSP, in 2016 the EU Commission adopted a "Space Strategy for Europe",[99] which has four strategic goals: maximising the benefits of space for society and the EU economy; fostering a globally competitive and innovative European space sector; reinforcing Europe's autonomy in accessing and using space in a secure and safe environment, and strengthening Europe's role as a global actor and promoting international cooperation. Furthermore, this strategy promotes partnerships between the Commission, the EU member states, ESA, the GSA, EUMETSAT, industry, research, stakeholders and user communities.[100]

Lastly, it should be highlighted that EUMETSAT, which also participates in the ESP, has its own strategy. In 2016, EUMETSAT released the "EUMETSAT Strategy. Challenge 2025", which provides the direction and scope of the organisation for the coming years.[101] The strategy aims at implementing EUMETSAT's mandatory, optional and third-party programmes[102] for the benefit of its member states and the EU. The strategy also enshrines EUMETSAT's vision, policy principles, priorities[103] and strategic objectives, some of which are implemented together with the EU and ESA, such as the establishment and exploitation of the EU Copernicus programme.[104]

Outside Europe, the African Space Policy (AfSP)[105] may also be a model for Latin America. The AfSP, adopted by African heads of states and governments in

---

[97] The three flagship programmes of the EU are Copernicus (EO programme), Galileo (Europe's global satellite navigation programme) and EGNOS (a satellite navigation programme providing services to aviation, maritime and land-based users in Europe), see: Chap. 4, Sect. 4.3.6.

[98] See: Footnote 96.

[99] *Communication from the Commission to the European Parliament, the Council, the European Economic and Social Committee and the Committee of the Regions, "Space Strategy for Europe"*, European Commission, 26 October 2016, COM (2016) 705 final. In 2017, the EU Commission started to implement this strategy.

[100] Ibid., p. 12.

[101] *EUMETSAT Strategy. Challenge 2025*, June 2016, www-cdn.eumetsat.int/files/2020–04/pdf_br_cor02sum_en.pdf.

[102] These programmes are MTG, EPS-SG, Jason-C5, Sentinel-3, and Copernicus, see: EUMETSAT Programmes, 8 July 2020, www-cdn.eumetsat.int/files/2020–07/pdf_leg_programmes.pdf.

[103] EUMETSAT has two priorities: (1) to fulfil, through its own satellite programmes and in the most effective manner, the essential requirements of its member states for observations and data services for operational weather and Earth system monitoring and forecasting, and for climate services, and (2) to establish additional capabilities in partnership with the EU and other satellite operators to achieve synergy with its own satellite missions for the benefit of its member states and partners.

[104] *EUMETSAT Strategy. Challenge 2025*, September 2016, p. 17.

[105] *African Space Policy, Towards Social, Political and Economic Integration (African Space Policy)*, African Union, Second Ordinary Session for the Specialized Technical Committee Meeting on Education, Science and Technology, 21–23 October 2017, Cairo, Egypt.

**Table 3.7** African space policy: objectives and principles

| |
|---|
| Addressing user needs: to harness the potential benefits of space science and technology in addressing Africa's socio-economic opportunities and challenges |
| Accessing space services: to strengthen space mission technology on the continent in order to ensure optional access to space-derived data, information services and products |
| Developing the regional market: to develop a sustainable and vibrant indigenous space industry that responds to the needs of the African continent |
| Adopting good governance and management: to adopt good corporate governance and best practices for the coordinated management of continental space activities |
| Coordinating the African space arena: to maximise the benefit of current and planned space activities, and avoid or minimise the duplication of resources and efforts |
| Promoting intra-African and other international cooperation: to implement the African-led space agenda through mutually beneficial partnerships |

January 2016[106] and whose title includes the words "Towards social, political and economic integration", comprises a set of guiding principles for a sustainable and fully effective space programme that will enable Africa "to develop and exploit its space resources in a more coordinated and systematic manner, with the overarching objective of contributing to Africa's socio-economic development".[107] The AfSP comprises two high-level policy goals: to create a well-coordinated and integrated African space programme that is responsive to the social, economic, political and environmental needs of the continent, as well as being globally competitive; and to develop a regulatory framework that supports an African space programme and ensures that Africa is a responsible and peaceful user of outer space.[108] In particular, the AfSP aims at fostering space capacities on EO systems, navigation and positioning, satellite communication, and space science and exploration.[109] In addition, the AfSP enumerates a set of principles and objectives to adhere to and achieve during the implementation of the African space programme (Table 3.7). To implement the AfSP, several studies are being taken to understand the needs, capacities, challenges, and strengths of the African continent to develop regional space programmes.[110]

Finally, the AfSP is complemented by the African Space Strategy (AfSS) and associated implementation plans, and governance structure, all of which are intended

[106] Decision Assembly/AU/Dec.589(XXVI), 2016.

[107] *African Space Policy*, p. 3.

[108] Ibid., p. 8.

[109] "African Space Policy and Strategy: Redefining, Satellite Navigation and Positioning in Africa", *Space in Africa*, 8 September 2020, https://africanews.space/african-space-policy-strategy-redefining-satellite-navigation-and-positioning-in-africa/.

[110] For example, in 2020 a survey and gap analysis were initiated on satellite navigation, positioning infrastructure and technologies in Africa on sectors such as agriculture, transportation, and science environment and weather. Development of satellite navigation and positioning systems in Africa through the Joint Africa-EU Strategy (JAES) partnership is a priority of the African Agenda 2063, see: "African Space Policy and Strategy: Redefining, Satellite Navigation and Positioning in Africa", *Space in Africa*, 8 September 2020, https://africanews.space/african-space-policy-strategy-redefining-satellite-navigation-and-positioning-in-africa/.

to support the Science, Technology Innovation Strategy for Africa 2024 and other relevant continental strategies and contribute to the African Agenda 2063. The AfSS, also adopted in 2016, "is an expression of the key intent and programmes of action that are needed to give effect to the identified goals and strategic objectives, so that maximum impact can be made in leveraging the benefits of space science and technology as a tool for informing solutions to" African "political, economic, social and environmental challenges".[111]

In the Asia–Pacific region, there is no regional space policy implemented by APSCO. However, this organisation has adopted a "vision" that serves as a regional guide for APSCO member states and that resembles to some extent a regional space policy. In November 2018, APSCO member states (and Mexico, as an observer state) adopted the APSCO's Development Vision 2030 (DV-2030),[112] which provides a general vision statement according to which APSCO shall enhance capability within its member states in particular, and the Asia–Pacific region in general, in peaceful uses of outer space, and in the domain of space science, space technology and its applications, through voluntary sharing of financial, technological, and human resources.

The DV-2030 also mentions that APSCO will contribute to the collective effort of the international space community towards space governance and long-term sustainability of outer space activities. The DV-2030 also contains goals, priorities, principles, objectives and commitments to be followed by APSCO member states in conformity with their obligations under the APSCO Convention (Table 3.8).

#### 3.2.3.2 Local Experiences

Apart from taking inspiration from the space policies, visions and strategies of other regions of the world, Latin American countries could consider their own regional discussions, experiences and national space instruments to assess the necessity and define the content of their own regional space policy, strategy and vision.

The SCA is one of the main places in which Latin American countries have discussed regional space issues. The documents adopted in the different SCAs, such as declarations and plans of action, keep record of some ideals, goals, objectives, and priorities that the participant countries have identified and acknowledged as appropriate for the development of the space sector in the Americas. For example, the Pachuca Declaration of the VI SCA (2010) recognized that the application and peaceful use of space technologies contributes to the economic, social, environmental and human development of the countries of the region; the importance of the long-term sustainability of activities in outer space; and the convenience of adopting

[111] *African Space Strategy, Towards Social, Political and Economic Integration*, African Union, Second Ordinary Session for the Specialized Technical Committee Meeting on Education, Science and Technology, 21–23 October 2017, Cairo, Egypt, p. 25.

[112] *Development Vision 2030 of the Asia–Pacific Space Cooperation Organization (APSCO)*, APSCO 14 November 2018, Beijing, China.

**Table 3.8** APSCO's Development Vision 2030: goals, objectives and commitments

| |
|---|
| *Goals* |
| • Emphasize the perpetual promotion of resource-sharing, capacity-building, talent-cultivation and organization-development<br>• Achieve common development by closer practical cooperation and mutual help<br>• Maintain and strengthen vigorous and vital multilateral cooperation system and promote organization's contribution to the global governance of outer space activities |
| *Objectives* |
| • Build capacity in the research and development of satellites to narrow down the gap in the development of space infrastructure<br>• Build capacity in space-based applications to enhance the acquisition and sharing of space technology benefits<br>• Build capacity in the professional talents' training to promote space research and development<br>• Build capacity in the organizational development to enhance the impact of the organization on the capability building of its members |
| *Commitments* |
| • Member states pledge to consistently support APSCO's development and make concerted efforts to accelerate its development<br>• Member states pledge to further open up their respective space resources and constantly increase their space capacity, sharing services capability, quick response capability, industry driving capability and information inter-connection<br>• Member states will foster the cooperative partnerships and open wider, increase cooperation and achieve common development through international cooperation on the basis of equality and mutual benefit<br>• APSCO will keep exploring the development path and development patterns that suit its features; strengthen policy coordination and exchange of experience while maintaining its own independence to foster a sound environment for the diverse and common development of its member states |

The overview is an adapted version

policies for the popularization of space agenda topics among society to understand the relevance of space technologies for sustainable development. This declaration also stated the necessity to foster regional cooperation programmes in areas such as tele-education, tele-health, prevention and mitigation of disasters caused by natural and anthropogenic causes, conservation of the environment, and the protection of the natural and cultural heritage.[113] Similarly, in the Declaration of Managua of the VII SCA (2015), the participants recognized that the exploration and use of outer space should be for the benefit and in the interests of all states without discrimination but with equal access and freedom; the benefit of using space technology for economic, social, environmental and human development of the region; the urgency of promoting education in space science and technology; and the importance of regional coordination towards a scientific space technology integration to achieve sustainable development in the continent.[114]

[113] "Pachuca Declaration", Sixth Space Conference of the Americas, Pachuca, Mexico, 2010.

[114] "Declaration of Managua", Seventh Space Conference of the Americas, Managua, Nicaragua, 2015.

Thus, the SCAs' results could be useful to define the content of a LASP, strategy or vision, and circumventing the duplication of efforts made by dozens of representatives of the countries of the Americas in this forum during the past three decades. However, caution should be taken before considering the transference of the objectives, ideas or results of the SCAs to a LASP, strategy or vision because the SCA is open not only to Latin American countries, but also to Canada, the U.S. and the Caribbean countries, whose needs and priorities may not necessarily coincide with the interests, priorities and intentions of Latin American states.

The Group of Latin American and Caribbean Countries (GRULAC)[115] is a further forum in which the countries of the region have agreed for many years on a great array of space topics to promote and defend their common interests and opinions as a unique voice at the regional and international level, namely at UNCOPUOS and its subcommittees.[116] In this regard, when defining a collective space policy or instrument, interested Latin American countries could adopt some GRULAC's positions and participate together as a further regional voice in the international space fora.[117] Nevertheless, attention should be paid to coordinate GRULAC's positions and the positions of the countries that adopt the LASP.

An additional forum in which Latin American countries have given some ideas of future collective objectives, interests and priorities was the Third International Space Forum (ISF) at Ministerial Level—The Latin American and Caribbean Chapter, organized by the International Astronautical Federation (IAF), in which Latin American and Caribbean participating countries decided on the following objectives to be pursued in the medium-short term[118]:

- Increase and deepen networking in space cooperation activities among Latin American and Caribbean scientific and academic institutions, and with space-faring countries, in order to facilitate capacity building and technology transfer,
- Consider the existing space centres and facilities in the region to build up a space network of infrastructures to develop a sustainable roadmap for a challenging regional Capacity Building Program linked to the global IAF community,
- Consider the opportunities offered by CRECTEALC,
- Among the space education institutions, the Mario Gulich Institute in Space Advance Studies, located in Cordoba, Argentina, at the Teófilo Tabanera Space Centre of CONAE (Argentina), is a unique centre of excellence in the region for EO data use, training, teaching processing and information environment for the development of a future regional space agency, and

[115] See: Chap. 1, Sect. 1.2.3.

[116] See: Froehlich/Amante Soria et al., *Space Supporting Latin America: Latin America's Emerging Space Middle Powers*, Springer (2020), Chapter 5.

[117] ESA and APSCO are observers in UNCOPUOS and represent their respective member states in this global space forum.

[118] "The Buenos Aires Page", *3rd International Space Forum at Ministerial Level—The Latin American & Caribbean Chapter*, International Space Forum at Ministerial Level, Buenos Aires, Argentina, 1 November 2018.

**Table 3.9** National space policies, strategies and plans in Latin America

| Country | Space policy, strategy and plan | Publication year | Duration |
|---|---|---|---|
| Argentina | National Space Plan (also called Strategic Policy for Space Activities) | N/A | 2016–2027 |
| Bolivia | Bolivian Space Agency's Strategic Plan | 2016 | 2016–2020 |
| Brazil | National Policy for the Development of Space Activities | 1994 | Indefinite |
| Chile | National Space Policy | 2013 | 2014–2020 |
| Colombia | Policy of Space Development | 2020 | 2020–2021 |
| Mexico | General Guidelines of the Mexican Space Policy (1), and Satellite Policy of the Federal Government (2) | 2011 (1)<br>2018 (2) | Indefinite |
| Paraguay | Institutional Strategic Plan | 2017 | 2018–2022 |

*Source* Froehlich/Amante Soria et al., *Space Supporting Latin America: Latin America's Emerging Space Middle Powers*, Springer, 2020

- Promote the peaceful use of outer space for the benefit of the present and future generation of men and women and as a contribution to the achievement of the goals of the 2030 Agenda of the UN.

Lastly, further sources of inspiration to adopt a LASP, space strategy or vision are the national space policies, strategies and plans (NSPs) of Latin American countries (Table 3.9). In general, these instruments provide the scope and direction for Latin American countries to develop their respective space programs. They contain reasons, missions, visions, goals, priorities, objectives, commitments and strategic actions that could be extrapolated to the regional level through a LASP, strategy or vision, namely those elements that are common in all NSPs. Moreover, the experiences of Latin American countries in developing and implementing their NSPs may be helpful when elaborating a regional space policy and strategy.

### *3.2.4 Latin American Space Program*

A Latin American space cooperation mechanism would be strengthened if there was an agreement on the implementation of a regional space program (LASPr). To formulate a LASPr, Latin American countries should find common problems or needs that space can meet through applications or research and development.[119] Mariano Imbert gives some examples of priority fields where challenges are common in the countries of the region, including food security, health, education, infrastructure and

[119] Imbert, "A Latin American and Caribbean Space Organization to be Delivered in the Space 2030 Agenda", p. 8. This author includes the Caribbean countries in his proposal for a regional space agency in the Americas and suggests that the space agency should be created under the aegis of the Community of Latin American and Caribbean States (CELAC).

energy.[120] He points out that many Latin American countries have already developed space capacities in these field and, therefore, discussion and coordination would be required for the development of a regional space program. In this regard, the author suggests several goals of the LASPr to be achieved between 2020 and 2030[121]:

- Space applications development and joint implementation: regional precision agriculture program, regional natural resources assessment, monitoring and prospection program (oil, gas, minerals, urban planning, etc.),
- Regional space applications and technology education and training program,
- Regional nano and micro satellite constellation program for telecommunications,
- Regional nano and micro satellite constellation program for remote sensing, and
- Regional meteorological satellite system program.

These space-based programs are only a few of the multiple possibilities that Latin America could integrate into a LASPr.[122] Imbert also considers the LASPr should be flexible in order to satisfy some or all countries of the region. For this, the capacity building of each state, the development of its actual space activities, its available space technologies and human resources should be taken into account.[123] Finally, he suggests that countries that do not yet have a national space body should participate in the discussions on the LASPr through preliminary contacts with the existing space bodies in other countries to understand how space projects may benefit them[124] (Fig. 3.7)

[120] Ibid.

[121] Ibid.

[122] In the EU, the proposed components of the European Space Programme for the years 2021–2027 are: an autonomous civil GNSS under civil control (GALILEO); a civil regional satellite navigation system under civil control (European Geostationary Navigation Overlay Service or EGNOS); an operational, autonomous, user-driven, civil EO system under civil control, building on the existing national and European capacities (COPERNICUS); a space surveillance and tracking system (Space Situational Awareness or SSA); a satellite communications service under civil and governmental control (GOVSATCOM), and other possible additional measures for ensuring efficient and autonomous access to space for the Programme and for fostering an innovative European space sector, upstream and downstream, strengthening the Union's space ecosystem and reinforcing the Union as a global player, see: art. 3 of the *Proposal for a Regulation of the European Parliament and of the Council establishing the space programme of the Union and the European Union Agency for the Space Programme and repealing Regulations (EU) No 912/2010, (EU) No 1285/2013, (EU) No 377/2014 and Decision 541/2014/EU*, Council of the European Union, Doc. 9898/18 + ADD 1, General Secretariat of the Council, Interinstitutional File: 2018/0236(COD), Brussels, 18 December 2020.

[123] Imbert, "A Latin American and Caribbean Space Organization to be Delivered in the Space 2030 Agenda", p. 8.

[124] Ibid., p. 9.

**Fig. 3.7** Venezuela's first remote sensing satellite, VRSS-1, also known as Miranda, launched from Xichang, China, 2012. *Source* ABAE

## 3.3 The Discussion Forum

As explain in Chap. 2, the proposals for the creation of a regional space agency in Latin America have been put forward in different fora, from the UNISPACE 82 preparatory regional seminar, where Chile submitted a proposal for a South American Space Agency (SASA—later LASA), to the IAF International Space Forum of 2018, in which some countries favoured LASA's future creation, going through the Space Conferences of the Americas (SCA), the Union of South American Nations (UNASUR), the Latin American and Caribbean Space Network (RELACA-Espacio) and the Community of Latin American and Caribbean States (CELAC). The fact that the creation of a regional space agency in Latin America has been suggested in all these fora without tangible progress could be the expression of a lack of political consensus on the matter as well as the inconsistent character of some of these fora. Without choosing a definitive place to discuss and study the establishment of a regional space agency, it will be extremely difficult to materialise this project. Therefore, Latin American countries should determine a unique place to advance the discussions and negotiations of LASA. In this sense, the potential candidate fora can be divided into two kinds: institutional options and non-institutional options.

### 3.3.1 *The Institutional Options*

Two institutional organizations are suitable candidates to discuss and prepare the creation of LASA, one regional and the other international: The Organization of American States (OAS) and the UN.

#### 3.3.1.1 The Organization of American States

The establishment of a regional space agency in the Americas within the framework of the Organization of American States (OAS) or under its sponsorship could be an interesting option thanks to the experience of this hemispheric organization in promoting international cooperation among the American countries and setting out technical intergovernmental cooperation bodies.

OAS is one of the most longstanding regional intergovernmental organizations in the world.[125] Although its origins can be traced back to the nineteenth century, its current form was formally created in 1948 with the adoption of the OAS Charter, its constituency instrument, in Bogota, Colombia.[126] The OAS, whose members are the 35 countries[127] of the Americas, is the main intergovernmental political, legal, and social forum of the region.[128] International cooperation among OAS member states is promoted in different areas such as human rights, trade, governance, elections, development, and natural disaster mitigation. OAS headquarters are in Washington D.C., U.S., and some of its main organs are the General Assembly (the supreme and decision-making body), the Meeting of Consultation of Ministers of Foreign Affairs (MCMFA, an advisory body for urgent issues), the General Secretariat, the Councils (the Permanent Council and the Inter-American Council for Integral Development, which make recommendations on matters within their authority), the Specialized Conferences, and the Specialized Organizations (Fig. 3.8).

The creation of a regional space agency could be envisaged through the work of the following OAS organs: The General Assembly, the Inter-American Council for

[125] Froehlich/Amante Soria et al., *Space Supporting Latin America: Latin America's Emerging Space Middle Powers*, Springer (2020), pp. 14–16.

[126] Charter of the Organisation of American States (OAS Charter), signed in Bogota in 1948 and amended by the Protocol of Buenos Aires in 1967, by the Protocol of Cartagena de Indias in 1985, by the Protocol of Washington in 1992, and by the Protocol of Managua in 1993.

[127] The 35 countries of the Americas have ratified the OAS Charter. In 2009, the Ministers of Foreign Affairs of the Americas resolved that the 1962 resolution, which excluded the Government of Cuba from participation in the inter-American system, ceased to have effect in the OAS. The 2009 resolution provides that the participation of Cuba in the OAS will be the result of a process of dialogue initiated at the request of Cuba, and in accordance with the practices, purposes, and principles of the OAS, see: OAS, "Member States", www.oas.org/en/member_states/default.asp# Cuba.

[128] Organización de los Estados Americanos, "Quiénes somos", www.oas.org/es/acerca/quienes_s omos.asp.

**Fig. 3.8** Hall of Heroes at the OAS headquarters. *Source* OAS

Integral Development, the Specialized Conferences, the Specialized Organizations, the Inter-American Juridical Committee, and the General Secretariat.

The General Assembly

Among the principal powers of the General Assembly are the powers to decide on the general action and policy of the Organization, to determine the structure and functions of its organs, and to consider any matter related to friendly relations among the American states.[129] To this end, the General Assembly has created different subsidiary organs on several technical topics, from justice to natural disaster reduction, strengthening the integral development of the continent and fostering international cooperation. Moreover, the work of some of these organs has been improved over time giving them a significant institutional maturity to the benefit of the Inter-American system. The Inter-American Telecommunications Commission (CITEL) is a good example of this institutional maturity.[130] CITEL, a technical and autonomous body created by the General Assembly under article 53 of the OAS Charter, has facilitated and promoted the development of telecommunications/ICT in the American continent for many decades. CITEL has its own legal framework (statutes, regulations and OAS General Assembly resolutions), objectives and functions, structure (five main

[129] OAS Charter, art. 54, (a).

[130] See: Chap. 1, Sect. 1.2.3.5.

organs and other minor bodies), strategic plan (currently the CITEL Strategic Plan for 2018–2022), membership (members—all OAS member states—and associated members), observers, cooperation agreements with regional and international organizations (20 instruments signed to date), capacity building activities and dissemination resources.[131]

In this sense, it could be possible that the General Assembly decides on the establishment of a subsidiary organ like CITEL concerning the space sector. Then, the new body should be consistent with the OAS Charter and formally established by a General Assembly resolution. Furthermore, because some of CITEL's objectives and functions are related to space (namely the activities related to the efficient use of the radio spectrum for space services by the member states), the potential "Inter-American Space Commission" would narrowly coordinate with CITEL to avoid duplication of efforts and function overlapping, to protect frequency assignments for remote sensing services and avoid harmful interference.[132]

Other solutions could be the transfer of CITEL's space-related functions to the new space body or the integration in CITEL of an internal organ in charge of space issues (and changing CITEL's name to CISTEL—"Inter-American Space and Telecommunication Commission", for example).[133]

### The Inter-American Council for Integral Development

The Inter-American Council for Integral Development (IACID) promotes international cooperation among American states in the economic, social, educational, cultural, scientific, and technological fields, to achieve integral development.[134] In the specific area of technical cooperation, the IACID formulates and recommends to the OAS General Assembly strategic plans with policies, programs, and courses of action on cooperation for integral development, and establishes cooperative relations with the corresponding UN bodies and with other national and international agencies for the coordination of inter-American technical cooperation programs.[135] In this regard, the establishment of a regional space cooperation mechanism could be promoted by the IACID as long as this mechanism aims to achieve integral development in the continent. On one hand, the IACID could prepare and recommend a

[131] OAS, "Inter-American Telecommunications Commission (CITEL)", www.citel.oas.org/en/Pages/default.aspx.

[132] Jiménez, *Legal and Institutional Aspects of Latin-American Space Cooperation*, p. 180.

[133] In her PhD research, Jiménez mentions that she had originally proposed the creation of an ad hoc working group within CITEL's Permanent Consultative Committee II: Radiocommunication (PCC II), which would be responsible for a Latin American space programme of a constellation of small satellites. However, she later considered that CITEL's mandate was focused on telecommunications and that an ad hoc group within this body could not coordinate space cooperation to design, construct, deploy and operate a small satellite constellation because this task is beyond its faculties and functions, Ibid., p. 183.

[134] OAS Charter, art. 94.

[135] Ibid., art. 95.

strategic plan to the General Assembly for the creation of this mechanism (as illustrated above) that includes a space policy and program for the region, and at the same time search for opportunities for technical cooperation on space matters with UN space-related bodies, in particular UNOOSA and the International Telecommunication Union (ITU), international organizations and institutions such as ESA, the Group on Earth Observations (GEO) and the Committee on Space Research (COSPAR), as well as national space agencies. On the other hand, IACID could call for a "Specialized Conference" to discuss the establishment of a regional space agency that could eventually adopt an international convention on the matter (as discussed below).

### The Specialized Conferences

The Specialized Conferences are intergovernmental meetings that deal with special technical matters or develop specific aspects of inter-American cooperation. They are held by initiative of the General Assembly or the MCMFA or at the request of one of the Councils or Specialized Organizations on matters within their respective competences.[136] Thus, a meeting of intergovernmental representatives may be called by one of these organs to discuss the development of a regional space agency or other similar body. In addition, the General Assembly, the IACID and the governments of the OAS member states can present studies, proposals or even the draft of a regional space agency's international treaty to a specialized conference.[137] Then, the specialized conference may adopt the corresponding instrument, which shall be taken into the custody of the OAS General Secretariat.[138]

### The Specialized Organizations

A regional space agency could also be established by means of a Specialized Organization (SO). These bodies are intergovernmental organizations established by multilateral agreements that have specific functions with respect to technical matters of common interest to the American states.[139] They are part of the inter-American

[136] OAS Charter, art. 122. However, article 3 of the *Standards for the Inter-American Specialized Conferences* ("SC Standards") adopted by the General Assembly (Res. 85 (II-0/72)) does not mention the specialized organizations as the competent bodies responsible for convoking the specialized conferences (conversely, articles 7 and 8 of the same instrument foresees this possibility). In addition, art. 4 (c) of the SC Standards provides that each Council may decide to hold an Inter-American Specialized Conference "on its own initiative, in urgent cases and on matters within its competence, after consulting with the member states". The SC Standards are available at www.oas.org/legal/english/Models/Models2.htm. There is also a document adopted by the Permanent Council called *Model Rules of Procedures for Inter-American Specialized Conferences* (CP/RES. 76 (84/72), which facilitates the organization of these mechanisms, available at www.oas.org/legal/english/Models/Models3.htm.

[137] *Standards for Inter-American Specialized Conferences*, arts. 20 and 21.

[138] Ibid., art. 26.

[139] OAS Charter, art. 124.

system and enjoy the fullest technical autonomy. However, they must consider the recommendations of the OAS General Assembly and the Councils.[140] Relations between an SO and the OAS are established through agreements concluded between the SO and the Secretary General of the OAS, with the authorization of the General Assembly.[141] There are currently five SOs: the Pan American Health Organization (PAHO), the Inter-American Children's Institute (IIN),[142] the Inter-American Commission of Women (CIM), the Pan American Institute of Geography and History (PAIGH), and the Inter-American Institute for Cooperation on Agriculture (IICA). Each SO has different characteristics, members and relations with the OAS and other international entities. For example, PAHO is part of the inter-American system concerning health matters and at the same time is the World Health Organization's Regional Office for the Americas (AMRO/WHO).[143] It is composed of states, territories and regional centres. Meanwhile, the CIM is an OAS advisory body on issues related to women in the continent and the principal forum generating hemispheric policy to promote the rights of women and gender equality and equity, and whose members are all American states, with the exception of Cuba.[144]

Therefore, if countries of the Americas wish to create a regional space agency with the status of an SO and member of the inter-American system, they must first adopt a multilateral agreement establishing the space agency and give it legal personality to have the capacity to sign a bilateral agreement with the OAS. This agreement must be in conformity with the provisions of the OAS Charter (namely Chap. XVIII) and the Standards for the Implementation and Coordination of the Provisions of the Charter Relating to the Inter-American Specialized Organizations ("SO Standards").[145] Some important provisions concerning the SO are the following: the structure and functions of the SO shall be determined by the instruments establishing them; member states of the OAS have the right to be members of the inter-American specialized organizations, but their admission and participation may be subject to certain conditions; the location of the SO headquarters and other offices shall be determined after considering the principle of equitable geographical distribution and the location of already-existing SOs; the programs and activities of the SO shall be carried out

---

[140] Ibid., art. 126. The SOs can establish cooperative relations with world agencies of similar character to coordinate their activities (art. 127). In addition, in determining the location of the SOs consideration shall be given to the interest of all member states and to the desirability of selecting the seats of these organizations on the basis of a geographic representation as equitable as possible (art. 130).

[141] Ibid., art. 128.

[142] The IIN was created in 1927 under the name of the International American Institute for the Protection of Children. In 1949, the IIN joined the OAS as an SO.

[143] PAHO's predecessor was the Pan American Sanitary Bureau, which became AMRO/WHO in 1949, joining the UN System. In 1950, PAHO signed a formal agreement with the OAS to serve as the specialized health agency of the inter-American system, in: PAHO, "PAHO celebrates 110th anniversary", 2 December 2012, www.paho.org/en/news/2-12-2012-paho-celebrates-110th-anniversary.

[144] OAS, "Specialized Organizations", www.oas.org/en/about/specialized_organizations.asp.

[145] Standards adopted by the General Assembly by resolution AG/RES.87 (II-0/72) in 1972.

**Table 3.10** OAS specialized organisations

| OAS specialized organization | Creation | Agreement with OAS | No. of members |
|---|---|---|---|
| Pan American Health Organization (PAHO) | 1902 | 1950 | 35 |
| Inter-American Children's Institute (IIN) | 1927 | 1949 | 35 |
| Pan American Institute of Geography and History (PAIGM) | 1928 | 1949 | 21 |
| Inter-American Commission of Women (CIM) | 1928 | 1978 | 34 |
| Inter-American Institute for Cooperation on Agriculture (IICA) | 1942 | 1948 | 34 |

*Source* OAS

through a system that will avoid the duplication of effort or of expenditures and will facilitate the performance of the SO and other OAS organs; conferences and meetings of the SO shall have the status of inter-American specialized conferences when they are intergovernmental meetings to deal with special technical matters or to develop certain aspects of inter-American cooperation, and each SO shall send an annual report on its activities and budgets to the General Assembly.[146]

Finally, it is important to note that the creation of a space agency by the states of the region shall be preceded to its formalisation as an SO of the OAS (Table 3.10).

### The Inter-American Juridical Committee

The Inter-American Juridical Committee (CJI)[147] serves the OAS as an advisory body on juridical matters; promotes the progressive development and the codification of international law, and studies juridical problems related to the integration of the developing countries of the hemisphere and the possibility of attaining uniformity in their legislation.[148] It also undertakes studies and preparatory work at the request of the General Assembly, the MCMFA, or the Councils, or by its own initiative as it considers advisable.[149] In this regard, the CJI may give advice to the competent organs of the OAS on the legal issues related to the establishment of LASA within the OAS framework, such as questions concerning the constituent instrument of the space agency and its legal relations with other organs of the OAS or with national and international organizations.[150] Similarly, the CJI may undertake a legal study on LASA on its own initiative.

[146] SO Standards, arts. 7, 9, 11, 17, 22 and 26, respectively.

[147] Comité Jurídico Interamericano (CJI).

[148] OAS Charter, art. 99.

[149] Ibid., art. 100.

[150] The Department of International Law of the Secretariat of Legal Affairs, which serves as the Technical Secretariat of the CJI, may give legal advice on these issues.

The General Secretariat

The General Secretariat is the central and permanent organ of the OAS. It carries out the duties entrusted to it by the General Assembly, the MCMFA or the Councils. Moreover, it has some specific functions, such as the following: advise other organs in the preparation of agenda and rules of procedure; provide secretariat services for the General Assembly and other organs; prepare the proposed program-budget of the OAS; serve as depository of inter-American treaties and agreements, and establish cooperation relations, in accordance with decisions reached by the General Assembly or the Councils, with the SO and other national and international organizations.[151] As to the idea of a regional space agency within the OAS framework, the General Secretariat could support the establishment of this entity by providing technical studies and legal advisory services at the request of the competent organ.[152] For example, it could support the follow-up mechanism for a LASA convention that would be part of the inter-American system. In addition, the Secretariat could establish relations of cooperation with international bodies and organizations dealing with space matters, such as UNCOPUOS and its secretariat UNOOSA, ESA and APSCO to receive technical support.[153]

#### 3.3.1.2 The United Nations

Within the UN framework, there are two entities that could foster discussions on LASA: the United Nations Committee on the Peaceful Uses of Outer Space (UNCOPUOS) and the Economic Commission for Latin America and the Caribbean (ECLAC).[154]

The United Nations Committee on the Peaceful Uses of Outer Space

As the main global intergovernmental space forum, UNCOPUOS could function as a leverage to foster discussions on a space agency for Latin America. As stated by

[151] OAS Charter, arts. 107 and 112.

[152] For instance, the Department of Legal Services of the Secretariat for Legal Affairs (one of the seven Secretariats of the General Secretariat) provides legal services to CITEL.

[153] There is a OAS General Assembly resolution on the matter called *Standards on cooperative relations between the Organization of American States and the United Nations, its Specialized Agencies, and other National and International Organizations*, AG/RES. 57 (I-O/71), 23 April 1971, www.oas.org/legal/english/CoopRelations/CoopRelations1.htm.

[154] Due to its specialized scope on telecommunications, the ITU might not be suitable to initiate discussions on LASA. However, the ITU, and more specifically the ITU Regional Development Forum for the Americas region, could be helpful in the elaboration of a regional spectrum-management plan concerning the establishment of a Latin American satellite system, ITU, "ITU Regional Development Forums", www.itu.int/en/ITU-D/Pages/itu_rdfs.aspx; ITU, "the Americas Regional Initiatives of the Buenos Aires Action Plan 2018–2021, Brochure ITU", October 2018, www.itu.int/en/ITU-D/Documents/Regional_Initiaitves_AMERICAS-E-2.pdf.

UNGA resolution 1472, UNCOPUOS has competence to review the area of international cooperation in the peaceful uses of outer space.[155] In this regard, UNCOPUOS, its subcommittees and secretariat—UNOOSA—work to promote international cooperation among its members, not only at the international level, but also at the regional one.[156] Latin American space cooperation has been supported by UNCOPUOS in multiple ways. First, UNCOPUOS has welcomed over the years the participation during its sessions of groups of Latin American and Caribbean countries, such as GRULAC and other subregional groups.[157] Second, UNCOPUOS has supported the creation and evolution of CRECTEALC, the regional centre for space science and technology education for the Latin America and Caribbean region, which is affiliated to the UN through UNOOSA.[158] Finally, the Committee has significant experience in fostering the development of space capacities in Latin American countries through multiple activities and initiatives, such as the PSA, UN-SPIDER, and the organization of workshops in the region.[159]

Therefore, UNCOPUOS could be a feasible forum to discuss the creation of LASA.[160] This could be done, for instance, through informal meetings organized by UNOOSA at the request of one or more Latin American countries on the margins of the UNCOPUOS sessions in which all UNCOPUOS Latin American members (and maybe other parties, such as the director of UNOOSA, the chairs of UNCOPUOS and its subcommittees, and the representatives of some UNCOPUOS observers, such as ESA and APSCO) participate, or through the establishment by UNCOPUOS of a group of experts responsible for discussing and preparing a study on LASA, with a clear mandate and schedule and with the support of UNOOSA.

#### The Economic Commission for Latin America and the Caribbean

The second UN body that could promote the creation of LASA is the Economic Commission for Latin America and the Caribbean (ECLAC).[161] ECLAC is one of

---

[155] UNGA resolution 1472 (XIV), *International co-operation in the peaceful uses of outer space*, 1959, para. 1.

[156] UNOOSA, "Committee on the Peaceful Uses of Outer Space and its Subcommittees", www.unoosa.org/oosa/en/ourwork/copuos/comm-subcomms.html.

[157] Froehlich/Amante Soria et al., *Space Supporting Latin America: Latin America's Emerging Space Middle Powers*, pp. 102–105.

[158] See: Chap. 1, Sect. 1.2.3.2.

[159] Such as the UN/Argentina Workshop on Space Law "Contribution of Space Law to Economic and Social Development", held in Buenos Aires, Argentina, in 2012, www.unoosa.org/pdf/reports/ac105/AC105_1037E.pdf, and the Third UN/U.S. Workshop on the "Use of Global Navigation Satellite Systems, for the benefit of Latin America and the Caribbean", held at Santiago, Chile, in 2002, www.unoosa.org/pdf/reports/ac105/AC105_795E.pdf.

[160] UNCOPUOS participated in the drafting meetings on the APSCO Convention, "Charter for Proposed Asia–Pacific Space Group Passed in Beijing", *Xinhua News Agency*, 13 November 2003, www.china.org.cn/english/international/79920.htm.

[161] Comisión Económica para América Latina y el Caribe (CEPAL).

the five UN regional commissions.[162] Its purpose is to contribute to the economic development of Latin America and the Caribbean, coordinate actions to achieve this goal, and reinforce economic ties among ECLAC members and other countries of the world. It also contributes to the social development of the region.[163] ECLAC was established in 1948 by the UN Economic and Social Council (ECOSOC)[164] and is based in Santiago, Chile, and its subregional headquarters are in Mexico City, Mexico, and Port-of-Spain, Trinidad and Tobago.[165] ECLAC's membership is made up of 46 member states: the 33 Latin American and Caribbean countries, as well as several Asian, European and North American countries that have historical, economic and cultural ties with the region.[166] ECLAC's associate members are 14 non-independent territories in the Caribbean.[167]

To achieve its purpose, ECLAC functions as an intergovernmental platform for policy advice and dialogue, acts as a think tank for devising analysis and policy recommendations and provides technical cooperation and normative and capacity building support to its member states in several areas.[168] To this end, ECLAC undertakes studies and research, provides advisory services, and formulates, organizes and implements technical cooperation programmes at the request of its member states. It also organizes conferences and intergovernmental and expert group meetings, and sponsors training workshops, symposia and seminars.

Concerning the creation of LASA, ECLAC could undertake studies or research, or provide advisory services on the subject at the request of its member states.[169]

---

[162] The other four are the Economic Commission for Africa (ECA), the Economic Commission for Europe (ECE), the Economic Commission for Asia and the Pacific (ESCAP), and the Economic and Social Commission for Western Asia (ESCWA).

[163] ECLAC, "About ECLAC", www.cepal.org/en/about-eclac-0.

[164] ECOSOC's Resolution 106 (VI) of 25 February 1948. ECLAC's former name was ECLA (for the "Economic Commission for Latin America"). In 1984, the Commission included the Caribbean countries and changed its name to its current acronym, see: ECLAC, "About ECLAC", www.cepal.org/en/about-eclac-0.

[165] ECLAC also maintains country offices in Buenos Aires, Brasilia, Montevideo and Bogotá, and a liaison office in Washington, D.C.

[166] ECLAC associate members are 14 non-independent territories in the Caribbean: Anguilla, Aruba, Bermuda, British Virgin Islands, Cayman Islands, Curaçao, Guadeloupe, Martinique, Montserrat, Puerto Rico, Sint Marteen, Turks and Caicos Islands, United States Virgin Islands, and French Guiana.

[167] ECLAC, "Member states and associate members", www.cepal.org/en/estados-miembros.

[168] ECLAC's current work areas include international trade and cooperation, economic development, gender affairs, natural resources, statistics, the implementation of the 2030 Agenda for sustainable development, social development, planning for development, as well as production, productivity and management, ECLAC, "Work Areas", www.cepal.org/en/work-areas.

[169] Every two years, ECLAC member states determine the strategic framework of the Commission, a document that includes the programme structure and priorities of this entity for the corresponding biennium. It also sets outs ECLAC's objectives and expected results of its programmes and subprogrammes. After consultation of ECLAC's governing body, the strategic framework is reviewed by some UNGA's intergovernmental bodies, such as the Committee for Programme and Coordination (CPC) and the Fifth Committee, before adoption by UNGA, in: ECLAC, "Strategy and legal framework", www.cepal.org/en/ambito-estrategico-normativo.

**Fig. 3.9** ECLAC headquarters in Santiago, Chile. *Source* ECLAC

ECLAC does not focus on space matters,[170] altough it has dealt with space topics on rare occasions.[171] For instance, in 1983 ECLAC was requested to prepare a study on the technical, institutional, and financial feasibilities concerning the creation of a Latin American space organisation, for which it was considered imperative that a group of multidisciplinary experts support ECLAC.[172] Although ECLAC mentioned in its study that it had no experience in space matters, it stated that it would be willing to do additional analysis of the subject at the request of ECLAC member states. Thus, ECLAC could update its study on LASA by taking into account the new space developments in Latin American and the Caribbean (Fig. 3.9).

Another advantage of ECLAC is its capacity to promote and support regional and subregional integration and cooperation processes and organizations.[173] In its study of 1983, ECLAC stated that its resources and experience in supporting the creation

[170] However, ECLAC deals with innovation, science, technology, telemedicine, and ICTs.

[171] As part of the regional preparation seminars for the celebration of UNISPACE 82, ECLAC made several recommendations to its member states on remote sensing applications and satellite communications for education and development, see: *The Economic Commission for Latin America and the Second United Nations Conference on the Exploration and Peaceful Uses of Outer Space (UNISPACE 82)*, E/CEPAL/L.285, 27 April 1983. In 1985, ECLAC elaborated a document called *Activities of Latin American and Caribbean Organizations Relating to the Peaceful Uses of Outer Space: a Basis for Developing Horizontal Cooperation*, United Nations Economic Commission for Latin America and the Caribbean, Doc. LC/G.1360, 18 December 1985.

[172] See: Chap. 2, Sect. 2.1.1.

[173] The *Draft programme of work of the ECLAC System, 2020, in its subprogramme 13: support for regional and subregional integration and cooperation processes and organizations*, states that "the subprogramme's work will provide support to subregional and regional organizations, promoting coordination, cooperation, complementarity and synergy and contributing to convergence processes when the Commission's participation is required. It will also make technical and substantive contributions to facilitate debate and the construction of intraregional agreements, as well as to strengthen the interests and the positioning of Latin America and the Caribbean for participation in interregional and global political dialogues. The efforts of the subprogramme will also strengthen the regional

of regional institutions could be useful to establish a regional space organisation. One possibility to put ECLAC's experience into practice is that the Commission supports the proposal and efforts made by other regional cooperation or integration mechanisms such as the OAS or CELAC to establish LASA under their auspices.[174] An additional possibility is that ECLAC supports an independent initiative (unrelated to any regional cooperation or integration mechanism) to create LASA by facilitating dialogue and assisting states in the elaboration of the LASA convention or by providing technical and logistical support, undertaking studies and research, establishing ad hoc expert groups, and fostering political dialogue with regional and extra-regional stakeholders and third parties.

## *3.3.2 The Non-institutional Options*

Among the more appropriate non-institutional candidates to discuss the establishment of LASA are: The Space Conference of the Americas (SCA), the Group of Latin America and the Caribbean (GRULAC), the Community of Latin American and Caribbean States (CELAC), the Latin American and Caribbean Space Network (RELACA-Espacio), and an independent forum.

### 3.3.2.1 The Space Conference of the Americas

The SCA is one of the potential regional forums to discuss and launch LASA. This specialized hemispheric forum on space matters has already considered the implementation of effective cooperation mechanisms in the region and general proposals have been made on the establishment of a regional space entity.[175] Furthermore, the institutionalization of the SCA has also been proposed by the forum itself and the initiative has been welcomed by UNCOPUOS on several occasions.

In its different meetings, the SCA has identified multiple needs, interests and wishes of the countries of the region concerning the development of their space capacities and the promotion of inter-American coordination and cooperation in several fields of the space sector, such as space science and technology and its applications, natural resources and environment, natural disasters mitigation, space law and space education. Moreover, the work of the SCA's secretariats pro tempore has

---

capacity for implementation of the 2030 Agenda", *Draft programme of work of the ECLAC System, 2020*, ECLAC, https://repositorio.cepal.org/bitstream/handle/11362/43570/S1800093_en.pdf?.

[174] For example, ECLAC has recently supported CELAC with a study on the economic impact of COVID-19 in the region, see: "ECLAC presents to the Community of Latin American and Caribbean States a Study on the Economic Impact of COVID-19 that Includes and Observatory on Measures and Instruments along with Recommendations and Proposals for Confronting the Disease", *ECLAC*, 28 May 2020, www.cepal.org/en/pressreleases/eclac-presents-community-latin-american-and-caribbean-states-study-economic-impact.

[175] See: Chap. 1, Sect. 1.2.3.1 and Chap. 2, Sect. 2.1.2.

largely contributed to fulfil some of the provisions of SCA's declarations and plans of actions through the development of a great array of space activities that have benefited various countries of the region. The SCA has also created small groups of experts on space matters to provide advice to the pro tempore secretariats, such as the International Group of Experts (GIE).[176] Thus, the creation of LASA could be more easily discussed by the SCA than other fora less specialized and experienced in space issues. Furthermore, the SCA could create a working group of experts to prepare studies or a LASA convention draft.

#### 3.3.2.2 The Latin American and Caribbean Group

The Latin American and Caribbean Group, or GRULAC, is a further potential forum to discuss a LASA proposal. GRULAC is a non-binding consensus and dialogue group comprising all Latin American and Caribbean countries aimed at achieving consensus on different issues of the region.[177] Within the UN framework, GRULAC is one of the five UN regional groups of member states.[178] The group regularly meets in Geneva to exchange opinions, share documents, build common positions and prepare joint statements on the different international agenda topics such as telecommunications and space.[179] For many decades, GRULAC has submitted to UNCOPUOS and its subcommittees joint statements and positions on their respective numerous agenda items, including space and climate change,[180] and capacity-building in space law.[181] This has allowed all Latin American and Caribbean countries to have a unique and stronger voice on space related matters at the global level that would probably

---

[176] Grupo Internacional de Expertos (GIE), see: Jaime Barbéris Martínez, "Presente y futuro de la Conferencia Espacial de las Américas", AFESE, Vol. 50, Quito, April 2009, p. 93, https://afese.com/img/revistas/revista50/presfutesp.pdf.

[177] "Latin American and Caribbean Group (GRULAC)", Cancillería, Gobierno de Colombia, 2014, www.cancilleria.gov.co/en/content/latin-american-and-caribbean-group-grulac. It is important to note that the number of Latin American and Caribbean countries that are represented by GRULAC varies depending on the forum. For example, within the UN system the 33 countries of the region are part of GRULAC, but in the Inter-Parliamentary Union and in the Internet Governance Forum the Group is made of 25 and 20 countries, respectively.

[178] The other groups are the African Group, the Asia–Pacific Group, the Eastern European Group, and the Western European and Others Group, in: UN, "United Nations Regional Groups of Member States", www.un.org/depts/DGACM/RegionalGroups.shtml.

[179] GRULAC has two offices in Rome, Italy, one that deals with bilateral issues and other with multilateral issues, particularly those of the UN organizations located in Rome. GRULAC in Vienna decides mostly on candidate members for different UN bodies, and works as a link for other groups such as the G77 + China and the Non-Aligned Movement. At the UN Mission in New York, GRULAC deals with candidacies and other non-thematic aspects, see: "Latin American and Caribbean Group (GRULAC)", Cancillería, Gobierno de Colombia, 2014.

[180] UNGA, *Report of the Committee on the Peaceful Uses of Outer Space, Fifty-seventh session (11–20 June 2014)*, Doc. A/69/20, p. 45, www.unoosa.org/pdf/gadocs/A_69_20E.pdf.

[181] UNCOPUOS, *Report of the Legal Subcommittee on its fifty-second session*, held in Vienna from 8 to 19 April 2013, Doc. A/AC.105/1045, p. 18, www.unoosa.org/pdf/reports/ac105/AC105_1045E.pdf.

have had less impact if they had been separately submitted by each individual state. In addition, all GRULAC members not having a seat on UNCOPUOS are usually represented by an UNCOPUOS member of Latin America and the Caribbean on many topics of common interest, turning GRULAC into a significant representative of regional positions.

Thus, the long-standing GRULAC experience in coordinating, discussing and preparing scientific, technical, legal and political positions on space (UNCOPUOS' framework) and telecommunications (ITU's framework) in representation of the Latin American and Caribbean region is undoubtedly an important asset for the creation of LASA. Accordingly, a LASA proposal could be considered at a high-level event of GRULAC (known as the "Ambassadors meeting") or a regular meeting called by GRULAC's coordinator or president.[182] Then, representatives of GRULAC members states could exchange opinions, share draft proposals, and prepare official joint statements, positions or documents (for instance, a declaration of regional space cooperation through an institutional mechanism) that would eventually pave the way for a plenipotentiary conference of Latin American and Caribbean countries to adopt LASA's legal instrument.

#### 3.3.2.3 The Community of Latin American and Caribbean States

Although less known by the space community, CELAC is another possible forum to formally discuss, negotiate and prepare LASA. CELAC is an intergovernmental mechanism for dialogue and political agreement between all the 33 Latin American and Caribbean countries. Created in 2011,[183] CELAC takes joint decisions for the development of regional integration programs.[184] It has fostered political dialogue on different areas, such as social development, education, nuclear disarmament, family farming, culture, finance, energy, and the environment.[185] CELAC takes its decisions by consensus and each year a presidency pro tempore (PPT) is chosen by CELAC members to coordinate and implement the decisions adopted during CELAC's summits (Table 3.11).[186]

Even though CELAC has no experience in implementing regional space programs, recent promising steps have been taken by the Community in this regard.[187] In January 2020, during the Mexico City ministerial meeting of CELAC, Mexico, the PPT for 2020, presented a work plan composed of 14 points aimed at making CELAC the

[182] "Latin American and Caribbean Group (GRULAC)", Cancillería, Gobierno de Colombia, 2014.

[183] CELAC is the successor of the Rio Group and the Summit of Latin America and the Caribbean on Integration and Development (CALC), see: Declaración de Caracas "En el Bicentenario de la Lucha por la Independencia Hacia el Camino de Nuestros Libertadores", Caracas, Venezuela, 3 December 2011, https://ppt-celac.org/antecedentes.

[184] CELAC aims to complement the already existing regional architecture to avoid duplication of efforts.

[185] Community of Latin American and Caribbean States, http://celacinternational.org/celac-2-2/.

[186] Ibid.

[187] See: Chap. 2, Sect. 2.1.3.

**Table 3.11** CELAC's summits

| CELAC summit | Location | Date |
|---|---|---|
| Foundational summit | Venezuela | 2–3 December 2011 |
| I CELAC summit | Chile | 28 January 2013 |
| I CELAC-EU summit | Chile | 26–27 January 2013 |
| II CELAC summit | Cuba | 29 January 2014 |
| III CELAC summit | Costa Rica | 29 January 2015 |
| II CELAC-EU summit | Belgium | 10–11 June 2015 |
| IV CELAC summit | Ecuador | 27 January 2016 |
| V CELAC summit | Dominican Republic | 25 January 2017 |

*Source* CELAC

leading group in Latin America and the Caribbean region.[188] The first point of the plan dealt with aerospace and aeronautical cooperation.[189] Its objectives were linking aerospace agencies of CELAC members to foster technological and scientific cooperation; promoting cooperation on capacity-building and transfer of technology and applications, and developing a program to launch a Latin American and Caribbean nanosatellite. Specific projects included the organization of an aerospace forum in Mexico, the regional declaration of the peaceful use of outer space, and the exchange of satellite images to promote resilience against disasters.[190]

Five months later, the Mexican Ministry of Foreign Affairs (SRE)[191] and the Mexican Space Agency (AEM)[192] organized the "Latin American and Caribbean Space Meeting, CELAC 2020", in which delegates of different countries of the region participated.[193] On one side, Mexico proposed the development of regional space

[188] The Mexican foreign minister stated that CELAC's main goal is to create "the most powerful instrument of cooperation in Latin America and the Caribbean", in: "Foreign Secretary Ebrard Presents Mexico's Work Plan as CELAC President Pro Tempore", *Gobierno de México*, 9 January 2020, www.gob.mx/sre/prensa/foreign-secretary-ebrard-presents-mexico-s-work-plan-as-celac-president-pro-tempore?idiom=en.

[189] Ibid.

[190] "Plan de trabajo 2020", Presidencia Pro Témpore (PPT) de México en la Comunidad de Estados Latinoamericanos y Caribeños (CELAC) 2020, CELAC 2020, https://ppt-celac.org/plan-de-trabajo?fbclid=IwAR1EbpA6jQPAX0AJSPffgJAVnfyOkLbPdmj4u_zteLbNqa6qARK_vOH6LcQ.

[191] Secretaría de Relaciones Exteriores (SRE).

[192] Agencia Espacial Mexicana (AEM).

[193] Authorities of 28 Latin American and Caribbean countries participated in the meeting, including representatives of the space agencies of Argentina, Bolivia, Chile, Colombia, Mexico, Peru, Paraguay, Uruguay and Venezuela. There were also participants from the National Autonomous University of Mexico (UNAM), and the Universities of Buenos Aires (Argentina) and São Paulo (Brazil). Three of the eight Latin American astronauts and cosmonauts took part in the meeting: Astronauts Rodolfo Neri Vela (Mexico), Ronnie Nader (Ecuador) and Arnaldo Tamayo (Cuba). The

cooperation to build a new generation nanosatellite through the "Bolívar System of Latin American Nanosatellites", a satellite system created in honour of the American Liberator Simón Bolívar.[194] Mexico also declared that it was searching for the elaboration of a regional space development agenda that would include the launch of a call to create technology and connectivity with national capacities. On the other side, the participants presented a joint work plan to create the Latin American and Caribbean Space Council, which would be made up of public and private entities of CELAC countries. Finally, the event was concluded by the adoption of the "Joint Declaration on the Use of Space in the Community of Latin American and Caribbean States".[195] The outstanding breakthrough, however, appeared in September 2020 when Mexico, in its role as CELAC's PPT, announced a proposal to establish a Latin American and Caribbean Space Agency (ALCE), a proposal that was later formalized with Argentina a month later through the signature of the Declaration on the Constitution of a Regional Cooperation Mechanism in the Space Field[196] (Figs. 3.10 and 3.11).

With these developments, it is likely that CELAC will play a major role in the space field in Latin America and the Caribbean in the coming years. Even without details about the characteristics of these projects and their possible relation to CELAC, there is no doubt that the new impulse given by CELAC to the space field is a great opportunity to foster the development of space cooperation in the region in a concrete and lasting manner, namely with the recent ALCE proposal.

Although CELAC has no experience in dealing with space matters, the forum has multiple strengths that could be helpful to overcome this disadvantage. First, CELAC promotes dialogue not only with Latin American and Caribbean countries but with countries of other regions, such as China, Japan and Russia, as well as with international organizations and institutions, such as the EU[197] and the Cooperation Council for the Arab States of the Gulf. Thus, CELAC could form international partnerships

---

other four Latin American astronauts and cosmonauts are Fernando "Frank" Caldeiro (Argentina), Marcos Pontes (Brazil), Franklin Ramón Chang-Díaz (Costa Rica), Carlos I. Noriega (Perú) and José Armando López Falcón (Cuba), see: Tania Chacón, "Ocho astronautas latinoamericanos que han llegado al espacio", *Distintas Latitudes*, 14 August 2019, https://distintaslatitudes.net/oportunidades/ocho-astronautas-latinoamericanos-que-han-llegado-al-espacio.

[194] Agencia Espacial Mexicana, "México impulsa una agenda de cooperación espacial en la CELAC", 2 July 2020, www.gob.mx/aem/articulos/mexico-impulsa-una-agenda-de-cooperacion-espacial-en-la-celac-247200?idiom=es.

[195] Ibid.

[196] Agencia Espacial Mexicana, "México y Argentina sientan las Bases para la Constitución de la Agencia Latinoamericana y Caribeña del Espacio", 9 October 2020, www.gob.mx/aem/prensa/mexico-y-argentina-sientan-las-bases-para-la-constitucion-de-la-agencia-latinoamericana-y-caribena-del-espacio-254452.

[197] The EU and CELAC have been working jointly on research and innovation since 2010, when the *Joint Initiative on Research and Innovation* was established to help advance the bi-regional dialogue. To foster this relationship, the Spanish Foundation for Science and Technology supports and maintains the EU-CELAC Platform, which aims at providing information and facilitating communication for funding agencies, universities, research centres, enterprises and individuals interested in the bi-regional cooperation on research and innovation. The Platform also serves as a meeting point of the EU-CELAC Interest Group, which promotes cooperation between both regions in science, technology and innovation, see: Group of Interest EU-LAC, "About us", www.eucelac-platform.eu/.

**Fig. 3.10** CELAC's logo

CELAC
Comunidad de Estados
Latinoamericanos y Caribeños

**Fig. 3.11** II CELAC-EU summit held at Brussels, Belgium (2015). *Source* EU

on space matters to improve Latin American and Caribbean space capacities. Second, CELAC fosters the development of science and technology, the transfer of technology and the establishment of academic and research exchanges between its members. It is possible that these initiatives will cover the space field with the proposed Latin American satellite system, which would increase capacity-building and the development of indigenous space technology for the benefit of the region. Third, it has been suggested that CELAC could be the hemispheric voice in multilateral fora. To this end, CELAC could search for consensual positions in these places to promote the interests of the region on global topics. Partnerships between CELAC and UNOOSA, ITU, COSPAR or GEO, for example, could be established to achieve this goal.[198] Finally, CELAC is seeking to become a more institutionalized forum in the coming years by defining a rotating mechanism to determine its PPT and creating an online platform for the monitoring and registration of CELAC's decisions.[199] This evolution could be positive to give transparency to CELAC's activities and enhance confidence among its members to carry out complex programmes such as the proposed regional nanosatellite system or ALCE.

#### 3.3.2.4 The RELACA-Espacio Network

The RELACA-Espacio Network[200] also has the potential to become an appropriate forum for discussion on LASA. Despite its recent creation, this network has been a place of open academic dialogue on space issues and is achieving a higher presence in Latin America and the Caribbean thanks to its multidisciplinary and multilateral character. In this regard, an academic LASA proposal could arise from this regional network before involving governmental participation. In ESA's history, for example, it was the European scientific community that firstly proposed the creation of ESRO before European governments were invited to join the initiative. Thus, RELACA-Espacio could be the starting point to establish LASA. Moreover, the fact that RELACA-Espacio congresses have already received contributions from government representatives could accelerate this process by directly facilitating the dialogue on LASA between the academic and governmental sectors (and perhaps with the industrial sector too). Finally, an advantage of this network is that its activities are highly promoted by ESA through the European Centre for Space Law (ECSL), whose support could be invaluable for the discussions on LASA (Fig. 3.12).

[198] To avoid duplication of efforts, CELAC should carefully consider the regional mechanisms that have already established partnerships with some of these actors, such as CITEL with the ITU, and GRULAC with UNCOPUOS.

[199] Community of Latin American and Caribbean States, http://celacinternational.org/celac-2-2/; CELAC, "Plan de trabajo 2020", https://ppt-celac.org/plan-de-trabajo.

[200] See: Chap. 1, Sect. 1.2.3.4.

**Fig. 3.12** IV RELACA-Espacio meeting at Asuncion, Paraguay (2019). *Source* Sari G., RELACA-Espacio

#### 3.3.2.5 The Independent Forum

Apart from the previous non-institutional options, it is possible that some Latin American countries prefer to discuss the LASA proposal in an independent forum specifically prepared to this end. This could be done, for example, through an ad hoc regional conference or international seminar organized by one or more Latin American countries. The host country would be responsible for inviting governments and other interested parties such as universities and research institutes, technical and legal experts, aerospace industries, and regional or international organizations and institutions, to participate in the forum. The regional conference could also ask for technical and scientific support from regional or international institutions with experience in space matters and the formation of regional cooperation mechanisms, such as UNCOPUOS, ECLAC, ESA and the EU.

## 3.4 Considerations on the Conditions for a Latin American Space Agency

As examined above, there are different regional models for a Latin American space agency: independent international organisations or subsidiary bodies, general or specialized, with long trajectories or relatively new entities. But what model is the most suitable for Latin America? Considering its long history of successful space programmes and its wide international recognition, it is not improbable that ESA will be regarded as the ideal model for Latin America.[201] ESA's long-lasting experience in promoting space cooperation and coordination among its members and international partners, in designing and implementing a great array of space activities, in participating in multilateral space programmes, and in fostering the industrial space sector in Europe, are valuable features that other regions of the world would like to imitate. The Asia–Pacific region, for example, took ESA as its archetype in establishing APSCO, and the EUMETSAT Convention is largely inspired by the ESA Convention.[202] Thus, considering ESA as model for LASA could be appropriate. Nevertheless, a simple reproduction of this space agency in Latin America could bring unexpected results if the regional context and the capacities, needs and interests of the countries of Latin America are not duly considered. The same argument could be extrapolated to the other regional models. However, there are some models for Latin America that may be more appropriate than others.

ESA's success in promoting the development of strong European space programmes is undoubtedly attractive to other regions of the world. But ESA was not built from one day to the next. It took many decades and difficult political experiences to become the renowned entity that everybody knows today. In the 1970s two European space organisations, ESRO and ELDO, after difficult institutional and political failures, disappeared to give birth to ESA, a more ambitious European space cooperation mechanism. Thus, multilateral space cooperation in Europe was already institutionalized before the creation of ESA and the experience of ESRO and ELDO was important for ESA to give continuity to the European space effort. In this sense, elements such as a regional space programme, European space facilities, a European space industry, and a common interest in establishing a European space power were already present before the consolidation of ESA as an institutional European space entity.[203] Moreover, the European integration process and the development of joint European projects such as the European Organization for Nuclear Research (CERN) are further elements that may have contributed to the consolidation of ESA. In this regard, Latin America hardly gathers all the elements that Europe had in its beginnings to create a regional space agency. Even if these elements emerge, the next step would be to constitute LASA in the image of ESA. For example, part of ESA's

[201] Italy, a founding ESA member state, has supported the creation of LASA on several occasions, see: Chap. 2, Sect. 2.1.3.

[202] In its study about LASA in 1983, ECLAC stated that "The recommendations made at Quito, proposing a study of the feasibility of a Latin American Space Agency, imply an inter-governmental organization similar to the model provided by the European Space Agency", *The Economic Commission for Latin America and the Second United Nations Conference on the Exploitation and Peaceful Uses of Outer Space*, E/CEPAL/L.285, 27 April 1983, para. 16.

[203] Jiménez, *Legal and Institutional Aspects of Latin-American Space Cooperation*, p. 188. Jiménez is of the view that LASA should not be the first approach to space cooperation in Latin America. However, she does not discard the possibility of a future regional space agency in Latin America. She puts forward these conditions as elements that should be considered by an eventual working group of experts established under the auspices of the SCA with the aim of preparing a LASA proposal.

success is the result of the flexible approach of the European space programme, and the consideration of the differences and interests among ESA member states, offering them the possibility to participate in optional programmes and contribute to the mandatory activities on the basis of the national income of each member state.[204] Moreover, the geographic distribution of ESA contracts among its member states according to the principle of "just return" is considered crucial to ESA's success.[205]

Fulfilling all these conditions may be difficult, if not impossible, to create LASA in the exact image of ESA, at least in the short term. Even APSCO, whose convention is largely based on the ESA Convention, had to take a different approach after considering the differences between Europe and the Asia–Pacific region.

Thus, Latin America could bear in mind other models for LASA, such as APSCO. According to Mariano Imbert from the Bolivarian Agency of Space Activities (Venezuela),[206] APSCO could be a more appropriate model for Latin America than ESA not only because there are Latin American countries participating in its activities (Peru as a member state and Mexico as an observer), but also because APSCO member states are developing countries, they cover a large geographic area, and their space programs are somehow closer to the Latin American and Caribbean context (sometimes with insufficient funding from the central governments, with some advanced players like China and Iran, and other moderate developing countries such as Bangladesh, Mongolia and Peru).[207] He also believes that APSCO's pragmatic and flexible approach, as well as its goals and objectives are similar to, or the same as, what is needed in Latin America and the Caribbean.[208] Nevertheless, it should be noted that in the case of APSCO, China has a pivotal role in the activities of the organisation, not only because APSCO headquarters are based in Beijing, but also because China is the main financial contributor to the organisation and leads the decision making process of APSCO.[209] Moreover, there is a large asymmetry between China's space capabilities and those of the other APSCO members.[210] In Latin America, there is no country with space capabilities similar to those of China, and it would be difficult to imagine a sole country leading the decision making process of LASA and contributing in a huge proportion to its budget. In the case of ALCE, for example, Argentina and Mexico, the sponsor countries, could hardly lead by themselves the development and operation of the space agency without the political, financial and technical support of other Latin American countries. Thus,

---

[204] Ibid., p. 188.

[205] Ibid., p. 65; see also: Chap. 4, Sect. 4.3.6.

[206] Agencia Bolivariana de Actividades Espaciales (ABAE).

[207] Imbert, "A Latin American and Caribbean Space Organization to be Delivered in the Space 2030 Agenda", p. 2.

[208] Imbert proposes a regional space agency in which not only Latin American countries, but also the Caribbean countries may become member states, Ibid., pp. 2–3.

[209] Marco Aliberti, "Regionalisation of Space Activities in Asia?", *ESPI Perspectives 66*, European Space Policy Institute, February 2013.

[210] Ibid., p. 3.

although APSCO might be a more suitable model than ESA, the former issues must be carefully considered by Latin American countries.

Although the third model for LASA, the AfSA, is currently under development, Latin American countries could be inspired by the adoption procedure of the AfSA Statute. On the one hand, because AfSA is an organ of the AU, all African countries, regardless of their level of development, are parties to the AfSA Statute. This implies that the different interests, needs and capabilities of all African countries are considered, and that the purposes and objectives of the AfSA largely correspond to the African context. Moreover, gathering all African countries to negotiate the conception of the AfSA within the AU framework could have facilitated the adoption of the AfSA Statute because there was a specific mandate and procedure to carry out this initiative. On the other hand, the African space policy and strategy paved the way for the adoption of the AfSA Statute, so that the activities of this entity were in conformity with these regional policy instruments.

Thus, Latin American countries may use the African model if they aspire to establish a LASA under the aegis of a regional international organisation, such as the OAS. In this regard, all Latin American countries (and the other countries of the Americas) would be *ipso facto* participants in the discussions on LASA, which would be facilitated by the logistics apparatus of the organisation. A regional space policy and strategy should be also considered during the negotiations on LASA to coordinate the objectives and priorities of all countries of the region. Nevertheless, in using the African model, Latin America should pay particular attention to the current problems that Africa is facing concerning the establishment of the AfSA to avoid their replication in Latin America or to find solutions if similar problems appear. In this regard, the AU has acknowledged that one main challenge is the delay in determining the structural and financing implications of the AfSA.[211] To overcome these obstacles, the AU has considered taking the next steps: facilitate accelerated consideration of structural and financial implications of the AfSA; mobilise resources, including from the host country (Egypt), for launching and subsequently implementing the AfSA, and support member states, RECs and other institutions to operationalise the AfSA, including capacity building in areas such as EO, satellite communication, navigation and positioning, and space science and astronomy.[212]

Similar to AfSA in terms of its legal status, the GSA, as an organ of the EU, may be a model for LASA if Latin American countries decide to create a specialized space agency with legal personality within the framework of a regional intergovernmental organization such as the OAS. However, this agency would not necessarily have to carry out similar activities to those of the GSA, especially because there is currently no plan to develop a Latin American satellite navigation and positioning system. For example, LASA could specialize in EO or in space science, two areas of interest of several Latin American countries. Thus, some features of the GSA such as its

---

[211] AU, 4th Specialized Technical Committee on Finance, Monetary Affairs, Economic Planning and Integration, Experts Meeting, 9–11 March 2020, Accra, Ghana, Eco/STC/MAEPI(IV)/EXP/8.

[212] African Union Development Agency, "African Outer Space Programme", www.nepad.org/agenda-2063/flagship-project/african-outer-space-programme.

administrative and management structure, budgetary and financial provisions, role of member states, human resources, and international relations may be considered by Latin American states to create LASA in accordance with the institutional rules in which this agency would operate. In any case, it is vital that Latin America be aware of the intricated institutional and regulatory system in which the GSA operates,[213] and that the GSA will be succeeded by EUASP in the short term. In this regard, it would be prudent for Latin American countries to avoid analogous complex institutional and regulatory frameworks when considering the creation of LASA.

The final model, EUMETSAT, could be an appropriate option for LASA if Latin American countries decide to create a specialized space international organization, preferably, but not exclusively, for the exploitation of meteorological satellites. Within the CELAC framework, there is the proposal to create a Latin American EO nanosatellite and even an EO constellation satellite system, which could be used to monitor weather and prevent natural disasters, among other functions. Furthermore, the ALCE initiative, whose relationship with CELAC is not yet defined, could be a suitable entity to develop and operate this satellite system. Thus, ALCE could follow the EUMETSAT model if a regional EO satellite system is intended to be the main space project of Latin American countries. Thus, a potential "Latin American Agency for the Exploitation of Meteorological Satellites" may have some of the features of EUMETSAT.

In summary, Latin American countries should evaluate which regional space agency models are more suitable for LASA. They could even decide not to use a specific model and just take some objectives and characteristics of one or more models that could be replicated in Latin America. For example, ECLAC concluded in 1983 that ESA's "basic principle of pooling resources to achieve otherwise unattainable objectives could be applied in Latin America".[214] Meanwhile, Latin American countries could consider other models of regional space cooperation mechanisms, including non-institutional models. In any case, they should be aware that it is neither possible nor advisable to copy a full model due to the specific features of Latin America. In other words, Latin American countries should not only conceptualize a regional space agency, but also contextualize it. This conclusion is not new. Africa and the Asia–Pacific region, after assessing ESA as a model for their space agencies, established AfSA and APSCO by modifying or adding features they believed more appropriate to introduce into their respective regions. Finally, although some models could ideally be more adequate for Latin America, in the current regional political context it is possible that only a few models would be considered to set up LASA due to the characteristics of the forum in which the discussions on this agency occur.

Independent from assessing the use of a model for a regional space agency in Latin America, the desirable conditions to establish this agency—a regional space

---

[213] For information: the EU, the EU member states, ESA (this agency contributes to the technical and operational issues of the GALILEO and EGNOS programmes), EUMETSAT, users and other stakeholders contribute to the joint European space effort.

[214] *The Economic Commission for Latin America and the Second United Nations Conference on the Exploitation and Peaceful Uses of Outer Space*, E/CEPAL/L.285, 27 April 1983, p. 5.

database, national space agencies, a Latin American space policy, strategy or vision, a regional space programme—should be established as soon as possible, and with the participation of a significant number of Latin American countries. Even if one or more conditions are not totally fulfilled or are not fulfilled in time, LASA's features could begin to be discussed by the appropriate forum. Although none of these conditions are essential (for example, the Asia–Pacific (APSCO) has not adopted a regional space policy, and many African countries do not possess national space agencies), it is possible that the absence of one or more of these conditions could decrease the quality of the debates and slow down the process of creating the agency. It is possible, however, that some conditions may be achieved during the discussions on LASA. For instance, the formulation of the LASP, space strategy and vision and the elaboration of a regional space programme could be followed by the definition of the principles, goals and objectives of LASA, and participants in both discussions could be the same to achieve more coherent and reconciled instruments.

The question of the appropriate forum to discuss the creation of LASA is equally important because choosing a particular forum could ultimately determine the character and composition of LASA. This means, for instance, that if Latin American countries discuss the foundation of LASA within the framework of a regional institutional organisation such as the OAS, it is not improbable that the resultant space agency will be a subsidiary organ of that organisation or have a close relation with it as a specialized organization. That is the case of the AfSA in Africa, in which discussions for creation of this entity were undertaken under the aegis of the AU, which gave AfSA the status of an internal body of this organisation.[215]

On the contrary, if Latin American countries choose a non-institutional forum to discuss the creation of LASA, this space agency could take the form of an independent international entity, such as ESA and APSCO, whose creation was discussed in non-institutional fora. These organizations operate outside the framework of other organisations.

In Latin America, all institutional and non-institutional options analysed in this chapter have some potential to become the discussion forum on LASA. Furthermore, to some extent, all options could undertake or ask other organs or groups to undertake studies on the feasibility of a regional space agency in Latin America. To some degree, the institutional options could be more effective due to their experience, financial and technical resources, professional staff, and specific rules for setting up and monitoring subsidiary bodies. These options may also receive support in an efficient manner from other organs or organisations of their respective institutional systems. Within the OAS framework, there is a palette of possibilities not only to propose and discuss the creation of LASA, but also to elaborate scientific, technical and legal studies on the matter. Within the UN framework,[216] both UNCOPUOS and ECLAC could support a LASA initiative: UNCOPUOS with its long experience in

[215] Annette Froehlich, André Siebrits, *Space Supporting Africa. Volume 1: A Primary Needs Approach and Africa's Emerging Space Middle Powers*, Springer (2021).

[216] One of the recommendations of UNISPACE 82 stated "It is urgent to encourage countries to set up appropriate regional mechanisms designed to achieve international co-operation among them for the purpose of joint preparation, implementation and financing of space technology, research and

promoting the peaceful uses of outer space at the international, regional and national levels, and ECLAC with its endless efforts in fostering inter-American integration and cooperation mechanisms and processes.

As for non-institutional options, these forums are usually more flexible to discuss topics of regional interest and invite partners to the debates without following strict rules and administrative procedures. Moreover, some of the non-institutional options deal with space issues, such as the SCA and RELACA-Espacio, and even GRULAC has significant experience in representing Latin America and the Caribbean before UNCOPUOS and its subcommittees. This characteristic is significantly different from institutional fora such as the OAS and ECLAC, which do not deal with space matters.

Although each institutional and non-institutional option may become the suitable discussion forum on LASA, and while some options are technically or practically more suitable than others, the strength of some candidates may change when considering the political perspective around each forum.

In the case of the OAS, even though the 35 countries of the Americas are parties to the OAS Charter, it is likely that various Latin American countries would not be interested in creating or participating in the project of a regional space agency established under the OAS framework. OAS legitimacy has been questioned by different governments of the continent in the last decades, who argue that the OAS is too favourable to the U.S., a country that contributes 60% of the OAS budget and is the seat of this organisation.[217] Avoiding U.S. hegemony on the continent is one of the main reasons why alternative regional political fora, such as UNASUR and CELAC, have been created,[218] and it may explain why some countries prefer to deal with regional space matters in fora other than the OAS. A further aspect to consider is that the OAS is an "inter-American organisation", so that the creation of a "Latin American" space agency (or a Latin American and Caribbean space agency) within the OAS framework will need to meet specific conditions (apart from its name, that may be something like the "Inter-American Space Agency", independently of the participation of Canada and the U.S.). One condition (probably imposed by the U.S.) might be an obligation for OAS member states to avoid space technology transfer to certain countries or organizations, even if some OAS member states do not want to take part in the regional space agency. In addition, if OAS member states decide to establish a specialized space organisation within the inter-American system, the organisation must fulfil the conditions determined in the SO Standards of the OAS.

Concerning the SCA, there are some obstacles that could compromise the eventual creation of LASA under its aegis. First, references to the creation of a regional space agency by the SCA have disappeared in official documents in recent years.

---

application projects. The United Nations should promote initiatives aimed at establishing regional mechanisms and should encourage regional economic bodies to carry out studies that will facilitate their establishment", UN, *Report of the Second United Nations Conference on the exploration and Peaceful Uses of Outer Space*, Vienna, 9–21 August 1982, A/CONF.101/10, para. 353.

[217] Guillaume Long, "Le ministère des colonies américaines", *Le Monde diplomatique*, May 2020.

[218] Ibid.

The LASA proposal of the first decade of this century has been replaced by other initiatives since the VI SCA, such as the formulation of a regional space policy or the development of multilateral space cooperation programmes. Moreover, the LASA proposal under the SCA was very general and abstract. It seems that most of the SCA participant countries preferred to undertake formal discussions on the creation of LASA once the region is sufficiently prepared for it, but there are no criteria concerning the appropriate time to seriously consider this proposal. Second, the SCA is an inconsistent forum. The last SCA (the VII SCA) was held at Managua, Nicaragua, in 2015 and since then there has been no news about the VIII SCA, which is supposed to be held in Venezuela.[219] UNCOPUOS reports of the last five years have not even referred to former or current developments of the SCA, which is not a positive sign. The problem of this inconsistency is exacerbated by the fact that the SCA does not have a permanent secretariat or seat. Its pro tempore secretariat constantly rotates among the Latin American states. Third, despite the theoretical wide representation of the SCA, the forum does not currently receive strong support from a great majority of the countries of the region. This trend, in fact, has been highly perceptible in the last decade. In 2015, for example, only representatives of ten of the 35 countries of the Americas participated in the VII SCA.[220] The lack of participation of some regional countries with space capacities such as Bolivia, Brazil and Peru could diminish the legitimacy of this forum to reach a consensus on the creation of LASA. Thus, it is possible that the SCA is not currently the most appropriate forum to lead the discussions on LASA. Political will to strengthen this forum has considerably decreased in recent years.

Similarly, GRULAC is currently suffering a lack of political support in the space arena. Latest developments under the UNCOPUOS framework seem to indicate that GRULAC is no longer the regional voice on space matters. Until 2018, this group had submitted regular statements during the sessions of UNCOPUOS and its subcommittees.[221] In February 2019, GRULAC participated in the session of the Scientific and Technical Subcommittee (STC),[222] but not in the sessions of the Legal

---

[219] According to paragraph 17 of the "Declaration of San Francisco de Quito" of the V SCA, the participant countries had decided that the SCA should be held every three years, a term that has not been respected since the last SCA. Venezuela's current situation and the Covid-19 pandemic could indefinitely delay the celebration of the VIII SCA. However, an online-SCA could be envisaged as it has been done for other international events of the same character. There is also the option to change the country host of the SCA. For example, the VI SCA was held in Pachuca, Mexico, in 2010 after Guatemala was unable to organize it the previous year.

[220] Argentina, Canada, Chile, Cuba, Mexico, Nicaragua, Panama, Uruguay, the U.S. and Venezuela, see: VII SCA, "Plan de acción", Managua, 2015, p. 3.

[221] UN, *Report of the Committee on the Peaceful Uses of Outer Space*, Sixty-first session, 20–29 June 2018, A/73/20, https://cms.unov.org/dcpms2/api/finaldocuments?Language=en&Symbol=A/73/20.

[222] UN, *Report of the Scientific and Technical Subcommittee on its fifty-fifth session*, held in Vienna from 29 January to 9 February 2018, A/AC.105/1167, 14 February 2018, and UN, *Report of the Legal Subcommittee on its fifty-seventh session*, held in Vienna from 9 to 20 April 2018, A/AC.105/1177, 30 April 2018, where GRULAC is mentioned on several occasions; see also: UN, *Report of the Scientific and Technical Subcommittee on its fifty-sixth session*, held in Vienna from 11 to 22 February

Subcommittee (LSC) and UNCOPUOS of April and June 2019, respectively. In 2020, the group did not present statements to the STC.[223] Conversely, since 2019, GRULAC statements have been replaced by individual statements of Latin American countries or by other regional ad hoc groups. For example, during the 2019 LSC session, a group called "A Group of Latin American Countries"—and not "The Latin American and Caribbean Group (GRULAC)"—made several oral statements in the name of thirteen countries of the region.[224] One or more political reasons may be behind this change. If the trend continues, it is less likely that GRULAC can be the suitable forum to discuss a LASA proposal.

Concerning RELACA-Espacio, its increasing activity in recent years in promoting space related topics suggests that this regional forum could be a suitable place to start the discussions on LASA. The Latin American academic and professional space sector may support RELACA-Espacio with ideas, proposals and technical expertise to prepare the first debates on LASA before inviting representatives of Latin American governments to carry out intergovernmental negotiations on the matter. In Europe, for example, the first discussions for the establishment of ESRO in the 1960s were undertaken by the scientific community before the participation of European governments. However, some obstacles that RELACA-Espacio could face are the lack of governmental funding and logistical support to carry out the discussions on LASA due to the non-governmental character of this network. If another forum is chosen to discuss LASA, RELACA-Espacio could provide support and establish communication channels with space experts from all Latin America.

Finally, CELAC is probably the most suitable option to establish LASA due to the recent developments undertaken by this forum. The wide support given to the Mexican proposal for the development of a regional nanosatellite system confirms the wish of the majority of CELAC member states to carry out collaborative space programs. Although the creation of the proposed ALCE by Argentina and Mexico has not been yet properly discussed by CELAC as a forum, some indications of the relationship between CELAC and the ALCE proposal were mentioned during the announcement of the constitution of ALCE. Moreover, the CELAC-SAT satellite

---

2019, A/AC.10/1202, 28 February 2019; UN, *Report of the Legal Subcommittee on its fifty-eighth session*, held in Vienna from 1 to 12 April 2019, A/AC.105/1203, 18 April 2019, and UN, *Report of the Committee on the Peaceful Uses of Outer Space*, Sixty-second session (12–21 June 2019), A/74/20.

[223] UN, *Report of the Scientific and Technical Subcommittee on its fifty-seventh session*, held in Vienna from 3 to 14 February 2020, A/AC.105/1224, 19 February 2020. The LSC fifty-ninth session and the UNCOPUOS sixty-third session to be held in March and June 2020, respectively, were postponed due to the COVID-19 situation.

[224] Argentina, Brazil, Bolivia, Chile, Costa Rica, Cuba, Dominican Republic, Ecuador, El Salvador, Mexico, Paraguay, Uruguay and Venezuela. Colombia, Nicaragua and Peru, who are both GRULAC and UNCOPUOS members, did not join this ad hoc group; see: Froehlich/Amante Soria et al., *Space Supporting Latin America: Latin America's Emerging Space Middle Powers*, pp. 109–123.

proposed by Latin American representatives during an online meeting on the evolution of the ALCE proposal is indicative of such a relationship.[225] Thus, it is likely that the next CELAC summits or meetings will consider this issue. Nevertheless, a potential obstacle for CELAC to reach this goal is the lack of political will by some countries of the region, namely Brazil, to participate in CELAC's activities. This country suspended its participation in CELAC arguing that this forum has failed in protecting democracy and has become a stage for authoritarian states.[226] Thus, the absence of Brazil in CELAC's work could diminish the legitimacy of this forum to carry out comprehensive regional space projects. In addition, it should be clarified whether ALCE and the CELAC-SAT satellite project will contribute to the launching of the Latin American nanosatellite system—the Regional Bolívar Nanosatellite System—proposed by Mexico under CELAC's framework in July 2020, or if they will be independent projects.

Thus, according to the preceding considerations, some candidates would meet additional obstacles when considering the question of LASA. The analysis shows that some years ago certain fora were more appropriate to undertake the discussions on the matter, but they are no longer legitimate to deal with this. That is the case of the SCA and GRULAC. As to the regional institutional options, they may not presently be appropriate to advance LASA for political and technical reasons. It is difficult to imagine that the OAS or ECLAC would consider the creation of LASA if they did not have the support of an important number of countries of the region, including non-Latin American countries. Outside of the telecommunications sector within the OAS framework and a few studies made by ECLAC in the last century, both institutions have not dealt with space matters. Moreover, caution should be taken if LASA is expected to be established under the aegis or sponsorship of a supranational intergovernmental entity, such as the OAS or CELAC. Although in principle the support for the creation of LASA by one of these entities would be a good sign, a political or ideological confrontation between some or all its member states within the framework of this entity may endanger the well-functioning of LASA. Many experiences of failed regional integration mechanisms have existed in Latin America in the last decades,[227] and it would not be convenient that LASA be

[225] Agencia Espacial Mexicana, "Avanza mecanismo regional para constituir la Agencia Latinoamericana y Caribeña del Espacio", 16 November 2020, www.gob.mx/aem/articulos/avanza-mecanismo-regional-para-constituir-la-agencia-latinoamericana-y-caribena-del-espacio-257272?idiom=es.

[226] "Brazil steps out from CELAC, because of its failure "to protect democracy"", *MercoPress*, 17 January 2020, https://en.mercopress.com/2020/01/17/brazil-steps-out-from-celac-because-of-its-failure-to-protect-democracy.

[227] Pablo Garcés gives some examples in this regard. He also considers that Latin American integration is not only an attempt to solve a problem, as a policy usually seeks to be, but it is itself a problem, in: Garcés Velástegui Pablo, "Latin America at a Crossroads: A Cultural Theory to Address the Wicked Problem of Regional Integration with Clumsy Solutions", *Revista de Relaciones Internacionales, Estrategia y Seguridad*, Vol. 14(2), July–December 2019, pp. 33–57.

dependent on a political or institutional forum without officially belonging to it (as a subsidiary body or an inter-American specialized organisation, for example).[228]

All things considered, CELAC and RELACA-Espacio are likely the current suitable regional options to initiate the debates on LASA due to their leading efforts to carry out regional space projects and their growing influence in the region. UNCOPUOS is also a workable option, although this body could be more useful by giving its technical support to creating LASA than by being the ideal forum to discuss the matter, namely because it is not a regional forum. Lastly, an independent forum established with the purpose of discussing and preparing LASA is a further actual option, but its concretisation will depend on political, financial and logistical support of the interested countries. Therefore, the selection of the suitable discussion forum will require political agreements between all interested countries. Even after the selection of the forum, a possible challenge could be the continuity of the political dialogue between all interested countries within that forum.[229]

Even if a proposal for LASA has been backed by several countries and people throughout the region, some additional obstacles may prevent its materialisation, such as the difficulty of obtaining funds to operate the agency and implementing its programmes[230] and the lack of previous Latin American space projects that serve as precedents of effective regional space cooperation initiatives. In this regard, the Costa Rican astronaut Franklin Chang-Díaz, one of LASA's main supporters, considers that before venturing to the establishment of LASA it would be appropriate to invest in regional space programs that will become the building blocks of the future regional space agency.[231] Mexican space lawyer Cynthia Jiménez shares his view by arguing that the discussion on the promotion of space cooperation in Latin America should primarily focus on the definition of a specific Latin American space project rather than on its institutionalization.[232] She highlights that the LASA proposal could be work for

[228] During the negotiations of ESRO in the 1960s, there were several propositions from sponsoring organisations and countries, including the U.S. (through NASA), the Soviet Union, the North Atlantic Treaty Organization (NATO), and the European Communities. All options were discarded because they would be incompatible with the idea of creating a "peaceful and real European character" of the future space organization and because ESRO's founders wanted to avoid political considerations in the operation of ESRO. At the end, the founders accepted the support of the Committee on Space Research (COSPAR). Nevertheless, it was impossible to rule out the political dimension of ESRO due to the different political views and interests of the European countries. Krige and Russo, *A History of the European Space Agency, 1958–1987* (*Vol. 1–ESRO and ELDO, 1958–1973*), pp. 17–23.

[229] Elías Camhaji, "ALCE, el sueño de la conquista latinoamericana del espacio", *El País*, 21 November 2020, https://elpais.com/mexico/2020-11-21/alce-el-sueno-de-la-conquista-latinoamericana-del-espacio.html.

[230] Carlos F. Moreira, "A New Kid on the Block: ALCE—Latin America's Space Agency", Georgetown University Space Initiative, 13 January 2021, www.guspaceinitiative.org/contentmaster/a-new-kid-on-the-block-alce-latin-americas-space-agency.

[231] "Reaping the Benefits of Latin American Space Cooperation, Interview with Astronaut Franklin Chang-Díaz", *21st Century Science & Technology Magazine*, 21 February 2002.

[232] Jiménez proposes the creation of a Latin American EO satellite constellation for water management called "AQUARELSat", in: Jiménez, *Legal and Institutional Aspects of Latin-American Space Cooperation*, p. 33 and Chap. 4.

a short time in the political sphere, but it would not be sustainable on a practical long-term basis.[233] In addition, she points out that there is no consensus about the necessary elements to implement space cooperation in Latin America due to the lack of specific objectives, a regional space project and concrete space applications.[234] Nevertheless, Jiménez adds that once national space capabilities exist in Latin American countries, among other conditions, space cooperation in the continent could be materialized into LASA.[235] In turn, José Franco, doctor in Physics from the University of Wisconsin, considers that the absence of clear scientific guidelines, together with insufficient national budgets dedicated to the space sector and the lack of continuity of regional initiatives, may be important challenges for the establishment of LASA.[236]

A further problem that a LASA proposal may face is the lack of interest by some countries of the region to join this entity, an issue that could reduce the regional impact of LASA in the international sphere and diminish the possibility of undertaking ambitious collective space programmes. Perhaps the most reticent country will be Brazil. For years, Brazil has shown no interest in the creation of a regional space agency in the Americas. José Monserrat, advisor to the Brazilian Space Agency (AEB), has stated that a regional space agency would imply a lot of bureaucracy, produce few results, and would harm the pocket of Brazilians due to the needs required by such a big country, which would finish up by pay all the bill. According to him, the cons of the proposal are more than the pros.[237] Moreover, if LASA is established within CELAC's framework (the ALCE initiative surged from this forum) it would be difficult to convince Brazil to join ALCE due to its refusal to participate in CELAC's activities.[238] However, Conrado Varotto, former director of the National Commission of Space Activities of Argentina (CONAE), considers that sooner or later Brazil will join LASA because there will be projects that one country could not face alone.[239] Other countries that may not be willing to join LASA are Central American countries—except, perhaps, from El Salvador, which has already signed the ALCE Declaration—and Dominican Republic because these countries have their own initiative to create a space agency in this subregion. In this regard, these countries, most of which have incipient space capacities, may not be prepared to joint two regional initiatives at the same time. A similar situation may happen with Peru, which is a member of APSCO. It could be hard for this country to fulfil its obligations under the framework of two regional space organisations, especially if they have

---

233 Ibid., p. 66.

234 Ibid., p. 33.

235 Ibid., p. 179.

236 Camhaji, "ALCE, el sueño de la conquista latinoamericana del espacio", *El País*, 2020.

237 Júlio Ottoboni, "AEB recua e extingue criação da Agência Espacial Latino Americana", 21 May 2015, www.defesanet.com.br/space/noticia/19200/AEB-recua-e-extingue-criacao-da-Agencia-Espacial-Latino-Americana/.

238 Bnamericas, "How politics will likely ground LatAm space agency proposal", 14 October 2020, www.bnamericas.com/en/analysis/how-politics-will-likely-ground-latam-space-agency-proposal.

239 Varotto: "A fines del año que viene deberíamos tener un lanzador satelital", TSS, Universidad Nacional de San Martín, 12 October 2017, www.unsam.edu.ar/tss/varotto-a-fines-del-ano-que-viene-deberiamos-tener-un-lanzador-satelital/.

similar goals. Other countries, such as Chile, Colombia and Ecuador, may need some time to develop governmental—civilian—space capacities before joining LASA. The advantage of these countries is that non-governmental entities (Colombian and Ecuadorian Space Agencies) and the military sector (Chilean and Colombian Air Forces) already contribute to the development of their respective national space sectors.[240] Finally, if LASA is intended to be a specialized space organization, for example, to develop an EO satellite programme, it should be considered that several Latin American countries have adopted agreements in this field with international partners and that they may deem it inconvenient to spend more resources on related space programmes.[241] In this sense, the interests of all Latin American countries must be listened to so as to design the best possible space agency for the region. Furthermore, Latin American countries should not discard the possibility of receiving technical and human support from other countries, institutions or organisations to prepare LASA. UNOOSA and Latin American organisations, networks and entities could contribute valuable insights.[242]

---

[240] Froehlich/Amante Soria et al., *Space Supporting Latin America: Latin America's Emerging Space Middle Powers*, Springer (2020).

[241] For instance, in 2018 Brazil, Chile and Colombia signed cooperation arrangements with the European Commission. Under these arrangements, the three Latin American countries will gain access to the wide range of applications of the Copernicus EO programme and data provided by the European Sentinel satellites using connections between data centres in exchange for access to in-situ data from the regional observatory networks of the three Latin American countries, including geophysical and meteorological networks. Moreover, Copernicus will also gain full, free and open access to Brazilian EO satellite data, see: UN-SPIDER, "European Commission signs Earth observation cooperation arrangements with Colombia, Chile and Brazil", 13 March 2018, https://un-spider.org/news-and-events/news/european-commission-signs-earth-observation-cooperation-arrangements-colombia.

[242] The support by some countries and organisations in founding LASA will not be simple. Some of them may not be currently willing or capable to contribute to this project. In 1987, a member of the U.S. Department of State, referring to a report about the creation of a regional space agency in the Americas, among other issues, declared the following: "First, existing and foreseeable budgetary constraints render impossible the achievement of all that we would like to do assist our Latin American neighbours in fully exploiting advanced science and technology. In particular, we determined that the innovative and highly appealing notion of an inter-American space agency to stimulate advanced science and technology capabilities and applications and to respond to deep aspirations in Latin America was premature. Such an agency would inevitably require commitments of resources in this country as well as in Latin America that are not now available. Moreover, the uneven distribution of advanced science and technology capabilities in the region could create internal stresses within such an organization which neither we nor our Latin American colleagues wish to see developed.", *Hearing before the Subcommittee on International Scientific Cooperation of the Committee on Science, Space, and Technology of the U.S. House of Representatives*, One Hundredth Congress, First Session, July 30 1987, U.S.-Latin American Cooperation in Science and Technology, Washington, 1988, p. 4. Although more than 30 years have passed since the U.S. considered its support to create a regional space agency in the Americas, this country could currently maintain a similar position on the matter. In Europe, there are not yet institutional statements concerning European support in the creation of LASA. On 14 December 2020, during an informal EU27—Latin American and Caribbean Ministerial Meeting, the EU just declared that "Ministers welcomed the recent creation of the Latin American and Caribbean Space Agency (ALCE)", see: "EU 27—Latin America and Caribbean Informal Ministerial Meeting (14 Dec. 20)", Joint

## 3.5 Conclusion

Setting-up a space agency in Latin America requires a set of conditions that the countries of the region must meet before or during the formal negotiations of this entity. It is appropriate that these countries have a look at other regional space agencies to understand how they function and to consider which of their features may be replicated in Latin America. In addition, Latin American countries must determine the number and level of development of other preliminary conditions to create LASA. These conditions may include the establishment of a regional space database, the foundation of national space agencies in all Latin American countries, the adoption of a regional space policy and strategy, as well as the elaboration of a Latin American space program.

Apart from these conditions, the Latin American countries must decide on the appropriate forum to discuss, study and prepare the creation of LASA. The choice of potential forum, including a forum not analysed in this work, will require a strong political commitment from the interested countries. It is important to note that the fact that a particular forum or body does not currently deal on space issues should not necessarily constitute an impediment to discussing a LASA proposal. In this case, Latin American countries could give the appropriate authority the competence to deal with these issues. In any case, it would be convenient that the chosen forum, be it regional or international, general or specialized, institutional or non-institutional, is supported by specialized fora, organizations, institutions and experts dealing with space matters and Latin American integration and cooperation mechanisms. The participation of academic and industrial sectors, as well as user-communities could also be considered to this end.

Lastly, Latin American countries will likely confront a set of important obstacles—political, economic, technical—to establishing LASA. There is not an ideal formula to go to on this project, but countries should be creative and politically willing to establish an integrated, efficient, permanent and successful space agency so that all Latin American countries can be proud.

Once the necessary conditions to establish LASA are met and the regional obstacles and political disagreements have been overcome, Latin American countries could start the preparation of the LASA Convention.

---

Communiqué: France Diplomacy, www.diplomatie.gouv.fr/en/country-files/americas/news/article/joint-communique-eu27-latin-america-and-caribbean-informal-ministerial-meeting. Meanwhile, it is possible that APSCO (and indirectly China) may not strongly support the creation of LASA due to the fact that this organisation wishes to extend its membership to further Latin American countries. More LASA members of the Pacific coast of the Americas could mean fewer APSCO members of the same region. Finally, it is doubtful that Russia will support a LASA project like ALCE because this country is currently supporting the creation of the AECA in Central America and Dominican Republic, a region with which Russia has established significant ties in the space field in recent years, see: "PARLACEN inaugura programa de Educación Espacial Rusia, Centroamérica y el Caribe", *El Caribe*, 17 March 2021, www.elcaribe.com.do/destacado/parlacen-inaugura-programa-de-educacion-espacial-rusia-centroamerica-y-el-caribe/; see also the related publication posted on 16 March 2021 in the PARLACEN Facebook's official page, www.facebook.com/parlacen.

# Chapter 4
# The Convention of the Latin American Space Agency

*When you must fight the most is when you are closest to the goal.*
Rodolfo Neri Vela, Mexican Astronaut.

**Abstract** Creating a Latin American Space Agency requires the fulfilment of several conditions, one of which is the constituent instrument that will formally establish this entity. How this instrument will be prepared, and what will be its legal status and content, will be decided by the interested Latin American countries. Nevertheless, these countries may learn from the experiences of other regions of the world in establishing regional space agencies. This chapter aims at providing some ideas that could be helpful for Latin America to prepare the convention of its regional space agency. The chapter is divided into two main sections. The first section deals with the preparatory work for the adoption of the Convention of a Latin American Space Agency, while the second section examines the potential content or provisions that this instrument may include by considering the structure and features of some regional models.

## 4.1 Introduction

As seen in Chap. 3, the establishment of a Latin American Space Agency (LASA) requires several conditions to be met, whose number and degree of fulfilment will be defined by the interested states. Moreover, it is up to these states to decide on the appropriate forum, institutional or non-institutional, to discuss the creation of LASA and assess the possibility of using a model of a regional space agency. Once these conditions are met, the next natural step is the definition of the preparatory work and the content of LASA's constituent instrument (LASA Convention),[1] including

[1] This study uses the word "Convention" as a wide concept that comprises different options of constituent instruments.

 
A. Froehlich and D. A. Amante Soria, *A Regional Space Agency for Latin America*, Studies in Space Policy 32, https://doi.org/10.1007/978-3-030-79434-7_4

LASA's legal status. However, proceeding to this stage is not uncontroversial because the definition of these elements may be consciously or unconsciously influenced by the forum in which the subject is discussed or within which the regional space agency is expected to operate. In other words, if Latin American countries wish to create an entity like the European Space Agency (ESA) or the Asia–Pacific Space Cooperation Organisation (APSCO), they should adopt an international legal instrument, likely through a non-institutional forum. Conversely, if they prefer to establish LASA as a subsidiary body of an inter-governmental organisation like the African Space Agency (AfSA)—an organ of the African Union (AU)—or the European Global Navigation Satellite System Agency (GSA)—an Agency of the European Union (EU),[2] the LASA Convention would probably be a resolution adopted by an organ of this organisation.

A more difficult task, however, would be the preparation of the LASA Convention to be like the AfSA Statute by a non-institutional forum, or the elaboration of the LASA Convention like the ESA Convention by an institutional forum. In such cases, Latin American countries could struggle to replicate the constituent instruments due to the fact that the conditions are not similar as they were for those models. To avoid this problem, Latin American countries, wishing to use an archetype of regional space agency, should prepare the LASA Convention like the constituent instrument of that agency and give it an analogous content, but bearing always in mind the different regional contexts. Of course, this situation would not exist if Latin America just used some features of one or more models of constituent instruments of regional space cooperation mechanisms that are not strictly related to the conditions or circumstances in which these instruments have been adopted. Even though the definition of the preparatory work and content of the LASA Convention falls to the interested states, it is possible to identify certain procedures and contents that may facilitate the preparation and adoption of this instrument.

## 4.2 The Preparatory Work

Once Latin American countries agree to go ahead with a LASA proposal in a particular forum, they must determine the preparatory work of the LASA Convention among the available options offered by that forum. If Latin American countries submit a LASA proposal within the OAS framework, there are a few possibilities to prepare the respective constituent instrument. The OAS has several organs that can formulate studies on the creation of this instrument, such as the Inter-American Juridical Committee (CJI), the General Secretariat and the Permanent Council.[3]

[2] The AfSA was created by a resolution of the AU Assembly in 2018, and the GSA was established by the Regulation (EU) No 912/2010 adopted by the European Parliament and the EU Council in 2010, see: Chapter 3 (3.1).

[3] See: Chapter 3 (3.3.1.1).

Moreover, in 1999 the OAS Assembly approved a resolution[4] containing "Recommended guidelines for preparing and adopting Inter-American Legal Instruments", which provides recommendations on preparing different types of inter-American legal instruments in a flexible manner and where a procedure has not already been expressly provided for or the states have not agreed on the corresponding procedure for a specific case. This procedure consists of the following phases: proposal, preliminary study, preparatory works and initial drafts, and final draft.

- *Proposal*: in this phase every OAS member state, at any time within the appropriate forum, has the authority to propose any topic for consideration as the subject matter for an inter-American legal instrument.[5] If the proposal is accepted by the corresponding forum, a preliminary study will be requested.
- *Preliminary study*: in this phase, the General Secretariat will prepare a preliminary study within a reasonable time,[6] and may request the advice of other organs, agencies, and entities as appropriate. When the preliminary study has been initiated, the General Secretariat shall notify the Permanent Council, and when the study has been completed, it shall forward it to the forum that requested it. If the forum concludes that it is advisable to prepare an inter-American legal instrument, the matter will be submitted to the Permanent Council for consideration. If this organ gives its approval, it will specify the procedure for preparing the instrument.
- *Preparatory work and initial drafts*: at this stage, OAS member states are notified of the preparatory process and the opportunity for consultations. They may also complete questionnaires, present views and provide written comments on the drafts. In addition, the Secretariat for Legal Affairs of the General Secretariat will provide advisory services and legal support and transmit information to the states throughout the entire preparatory process and negotiating phase of the inter-American legal instrument. All member states shall be timely notified on the meetings and developments concerning the preparation of the legal instrument. Then, the Permanent Council will instruct a working group of that organ to carry out the preparatory work[7] and draw up the initial drafts. This working group may establish standards, guidelines, and objectives to govern the preparation of the draft, and entrust the drawing up of the initial draft to the CJI, the proposing organ, or to any other suitable body. Moreover, prior to negotiations and adoption

[4] *Procedures for Preparing and Adopting Inter-American Legal Instruments within the Organization of American States*, OAS Assembly, AG/RES. 1634 (XXIX-O/99), 7 June 1999.

[5] The resolution provides that for the purposes of this instrument, an "inter-American legal instrument" means any treaty, convention, or any other agreement having legal effect adopted by the member states within the framework of the Organization.

[6] This study will contain three elements: specification of existing legal instruments in force on the proposed topic; specification of current projects to prepare international legal instruments on the proposed topic, and a recommendation as to the need for preparing an inter-American legal instrument on the topic. Additionally, the study may include a recommendation on the method to prepare the legal instrument, and a recommendation on the desired type of legal instrument.

[7] The preparatory work may include an analysis of the preliminary study, consideration of comments by member states, and consideration of comments made by the institutions from which they have been requested.

of the final draft, member states shall have the sufficient time to analyse the initial draft.

- *Final draft*: when all versions of the final draft—in all OAS official languages[8]—are ready, they shall be reviewed by a drafting committee before presentation to the member states. The distribution of this draft to the member states shall be made well in advance for its consideration by the Permanent Council, which may determine procedures for possible adoption.

This procedure could be a suitable option for the preparation of the LASA Convention if Latin American countries (and possibly other OAS member states) wish to create LASA as part of the inter-American system and, therefore, be related in some way to the OAS framework (as a subsidiary body or as a specialized organisation, for instance). Nevertheless, this procedure could hardly be followed if LASA is projected as an independent entity (not linked to the inter-American system) and, thus, the LASA Convention would not have the status of an inter-American legal instrument.

Nevertheless, the OAS options and procedures are not the only possible options to elaborate and adopt the LASA Convention. In a non-institutional forum, Latin American countries may create an ad hoc procedure to carry out the preparatory work and adopt the LASA Convention. These countries may even consider the example of the preparatory procedures of the constituent instruments of other regional space cooperation mechanisms. In this regard, the history of the European Space Research Organisation (ESRO), one of the two ESA predecessor organisations,[9] provides a useful example of the preparatory work of the ESRO Convention—the first international legal instrument of a regional space agency in the world.[10] The concept of ESRO came from the idea of an Italian scientist, Edoardo Amaldi, in 1959, who wanted to create

[8] Spanish, English, French and Portuguese.

[9] The second predecessor was the European Organisation for the Development and Construction of Space Vehicle Launchers (ELDO). ESRO and ELDO were established by the ESRO and ELDO Conventions adopted in March and June 1962, respectively, in: ESA, "Key dates 1960–2018", www.esa.int/About_Us/ESA_history/Key_dates_1960-2018 (All websites cited in this chapter were last accessed and verified on 24 March 2021).

[10] The history of the ESRO Convention is relevant because the ESA Convention took most of the content of that instrument. The preparatory works of the APSCO, EUMETSAT and AfSA constituent instruments may also provide interesting insights (for instance, the African Commission called for consultations to elaborate the AfSA Statute, and a drafting group was formed to prepare the APSCO Convention). However, public information on these procedures is not easily available. A valuable testimony of the history of ESA and its predecessors is the well-documented project called "A History of the European Space Agency 1958–1987", which was led by Prof. John Krige and Profs. Arturo Russo and Michelangelo de Maria in the 1990's. The project was published by ESA in April 2020 in two volumes: "Volume I. The story of ESRO and ELDO, 1958–1973" by J. Krige and A. Russo, and "Volume II. The story of ESA, 1973 to 1978" by J. Krige, A. Russo and L. Sebesta, which are available at www.esa.int/esapub/sp/sp1235/sp1235v1web.pdf (Volume I) and www.esa.int/esapub/sp/sp1235/sp1235v2web.pdf (Volume II).

a European organization exclusively for space research, and foresaw that the organization would be ready in four or five years.[11] Amaldi shared his proposal with Pierre Auger, a French scientist who would help Amaldi to promote his idea across Europe. Then, Amaldi's proposal was discussed in informal meetings attended by scientists and science administrators from the European countries that had participated in the formation of the European Organization for Nuclear Research (CERN).[12]

In 1960, governmental representatives of these countries joined the meetings and all together established the European Research Space Group (GEERS),[13] a study group responsible for defining the areas of space cooperation in Europe, drafting an agreement establishing the preparatory commission that would eventually create the ESRO Convention (the commission would be supported financially and administratively by Switzerland, the Organization for European Economic Co-operation (OEEC)[14] and national authorities),[15] and convening a conference of duly authorised representatives to sign the agreement.[16] This conference was held from 28 November to 1 December 1960 in Meyrin, Switzerland, in which delegations of scientists and governmental foreign relations representatives from eleven countries participated. The Meyrin Conference adopted a draft agreement called "Preparatory Commission to Study the Possibilities of European Collaboration in the Field of Space Research", which set up the European Preparatory Commission for Space Research (COPERS).[17] The agreement also established COPERS' bureau (COPERS meetings were held in Paris), a budget for one year and a contributions scale.[18] The initial responsibilities of COPERS were the definition of ESRO's scientific programme, its necessary infrastructure and budget, as well as the preparation of the ESRO Convention for signature by European governments. COPERS' structure consisted of an office—a vice-president, two vice-presidents and the executive secretary—and two working groups: The Interim Scientific and Technical Working Group (STWG),[19] which was in charge of the preparation of the scientific programme, and the Legal,

[11] J. Krige and A. Russo, *A History of the European Space Agency, 1958—1987 (Vol. 1—ESRO and ELDO, 1958—1973)*, European Space Agency (2000), pp. 13–15.

[12] In French, l'Organisation Européenne pour la Recherche Nucléaire (formerly the Conseil Européen pour la Recherche Nucléaire (CERN)).

[13] In French, Groupe d'Études Européen pour la Recherche Spatiale (GEERS).

[14] In 1961, the OEEC became the Organisation for Economic Co-operation and Development (OECD).

[15] Krige, *A History of the European Space Agency, 1958—1987 (Vol. 1)*, p. 27.

[16] Ibid., p. 32.

[17] In French, Commission Préparatoire Européenne de Recherche Spatiale (COPERS). COPERS was officially established on 27 February 1961, ESA, "A digital record of the European space pioneers", www.esa.int/About_Us/ESA_history/A_digital_record_of_the_European_space_pioneers.

[18] Krige, *A History of the European Space Agency, 1958—1987 (Vol. 1)*, p. 36; see also: ESA, "The ESRO Convention and 'just retour'", 14 June 2014, www.esa.int/About_Us/ESA_history/The_ESRO_Convention_and_juste_retour.

[19] In its third meeting, the STWG presented a 77-page document known as the "Blue Book", which covered an outline of ESRO, a scientific programme, its technology centre, its data handling, and ranges and vehicles, in: Krige, *A History of the European Space Agency, 1958—1987 (Vol. 1)*, p. 48.

**Fig. 4.1** COPERS meeting, 1960. *Source* ESA

Administrative and Financial Working Group (LAFWG), which was responsible for drafting the ESRO Convention and estimating ESRO's financial budgets, among other tasks. On 14 and 15 June 1962, COPERS put the draft of the ESRO Convention before an intergovernmental conference in Paris, which was ratified on 20 March 1964 (Fig. 4.1).[20]

A similar procedure that led to the adoption of the ESRO Convention could be established for the LASA Convention. In addition, Latin America could use several OAS recommendations to prepare this legal instrument although LASA would be prepared outside the OAS framework. Thus, a forum other than the OAS could create a group of experts to elaborate the preliminary study of a given LASA proposal. This body could ask for information, advice and suggestions from different national, regional and international entities or persons. Once this body finishes the preliminary study, it would present it to the same forum for revision and approval. Then, the forum would create a preparatory commission to do the preparatory work and elaborate the first draft of the LASA Convention.[21] This preparatory commission

[20] ESA, "The ESRO Convention and 'just retour'", 14 June 2014, www.esa.int/About_Us/ESA_history/The_ESRO_Convention_and_juste_retour.

[21] Different from the OAS framework, in which several organs and bodies participate in the preparatory work of an inter-American legal instrument, it would probably be more efficient and less expensive if only one body created by the appropriate forum is responsible for this work.

could be established by an international agreement[22] which would include its objectives, guidelines, methods, tasks, structure, composition, budget, and calendar.[23] It could also undertake consultations with the interested states and, if by then a Latin American space policy, strategy or programme has been agreed,[24] consider it for the preparation of the LASA draft convention. When the first draft is ready in the agreed languages, the preparatory commission would submit it to the corresponding forum for consideration. Then, the final draft could be approved by the main body or conference of the forum (in a summit of heads of state, for example), which would determine the procedure for the adoption and ratification of the LASA Convention. This procedure, for instance, could be used by the Community of Latin American and Caribbean States (CELAC) to give birth to the proposed Latin American and Caribbean Space Agency (ALCE).[25]

## 4.3 Content of the Convention

To define the content of the LASA Convention, Latin American countries could resort to models of constituent instruments of regional space agencies. There are many examples. However, only the following ones will be examined in this section: the ESA Convention, the APSCO Convention, the AfSA Statute, and the Convention for the establishment of a European Organisation for the Exploitation of Meteorological Satellites (EUMETSAT Convention).[26] This selection follows the models of regional space agencies analysed in Chap. 3, except for the European Global Navigation Satellite System Agency (GSA).[27] Although these instruments have notable differences, they also share many similarities, especially the conventions of the ESA,

---

[22] This agreement does not have to be a treaty or international agreement. It could be a declaratory document or a political resolution.

[23] As in the case of ESRO, it would be useful if the preparatory commission were joined by scientists, science administrators, government representatives and technical experts to have inter-disciplinary contributions.

[24] See: Chapter 3 (3.2.3 and 3.2.4).

[25] In October 2020, Argentina and Mexico adopted the Declaration for the creation of a Latin American and Caribbean cooperation mechanism in the space field commonly known as the Latin American and Caribbean Space Agency—Agencia Latinoamericana y Caribeña del Espacio (ALCE), see: Chapters 2 (2.1.3) and 3 (3.3.2.3).

[26] Convention for the Establishment of a European Space Agency, adopted on 30 May 1975, and entered into force on 30 October 1980 (ESA Convention); Convention for the Asia–Pacific Space Cooperation Organization, Beijing, People's Republic of China, adopted on 28 October 2005 and entered into force on 12 October 2006 (APSCO Convention); Convention for the Establishment of a European Organization for the Exploitation of Meteorological Satellites (EUMETSAT), adopted on 24 May 1983; entered into force on 19 June 1986 (EUMETSAT Convention).

[27] The legal framework of the GSA will not be analysed here. In December 2020, the European Parliament and the EU member states reached a political compromise to approve in second reading a new EU Regulation that will modify the legal framework of the GSA, as well as to establish the European Space Programme for the years 2021–2027. It is expected that the EU Regulation will

EUMETSAT, and APSCO. This is not only because they are international treaties and binding multilateral agreements adopted by state parties that fall under the formalities of the international law of treaties[28]—these instruments are not actually too different from the constitutive instruments of many other international organisations, but also because they took inspiration from one or more legal instruments. For example, the ESA Convention is based on its predecessors, the ESRO and ELDO Conventions, while the EUMETSAT and APSCO Conventions were inspired by the ESA Convention. Concerning the AfSA Statute, although it shares some similarities with the above instruments, its content presents more distinctions than the others due in part to its status as an internal legal instrument of the AU. A further remark is that the regulatory frameworks of most of these regional space agencies go beyond their constituent instruments. They include other regulations or instruments such as protocols, internal rules, and international cooperation agreements. In this regard, certain matters that are regulated in the constituent instruments of some space agencies may be regulated in additional instruments of other space agencies. Nevertheless, this section will be mainly focused on the constitutive instruments of the regional space agencies.

Given these clarifications, a brief analysis of the overall content of these instruments now follows. Independent of their legal status, all the constituent instruments of the regional space agencies are divided in two general sections: a preamble and a substantive section (Table 4.1). The preamble determines the political motivations that have led the interested countries, in their individual capacity or through their representation by the competent authority, to adopt the corresponding instrument. It may also state the way a regional space policy, vision, mission, strategy or programme is expected to be implemented by the regional space agency. In the case of the AfSA Statute, the preamble also summarizes the historical background and legal basis of the adoption of this instrument. The substantive section, which is divided in articles, mainly determines the general regulatory framework of the regional space agency, as well as the rights and obligations of the parties vis-à-vis the constituent instrument and other legal documents. The average number of articles in all constituent instruments is 25, although there are more articles in adjoining documents of some of them, such as the five annexes of the ESA Convention.[29] The four constituent instruments deal with the following matters: establishment of the regional space agency, legal status, purposes and objectives, membership, headquarters and other facilities, organs, financial issues, privileges and immunities, as well as provisions

be approved by the EU Parliament and the EU Council in the course of 2021, European Commission, see: "Commission welcomes the political agreement on the European Space Programme", 16 December 2020, https://ec.europa.eu/commission/presscorner/detail/en/IP_20_2449; see also: Chapter 3 (3.1.5).

[28] Malcolm N. Shaw, *International Law*, Seventh Edition, Cambridge University Press (2014), p. 944.

[29] The five annexes are: Annex I. Privileges and Immunities; Annex II. Financial Provisions; Annex III. Optional Programmes Covered by Article V, 1 b of the Convention; Annex IV. Internationalisation of National Programmes, and Annex V. Industrial Policy. These annexes are an integral part of the ESA Convention.

**Table 4.1** Comparative chart of constitutive instruments of regional space agencies

| Content | ESA Convention | APSCO Convention | AfSA Statute | EUMETSAT Convention |
|---|---|---|---|---|
| Day of opening for signature | 30 May 1975 (ESA functioned de facto from 31 May 1975) | 28 October 2005 | 29 January 2018 | 24 May 1983 (amended by a protocol adopted on 5 June 1991) |
| Date of entry into force | 30 October 1980 | 12 October 2006 | 29 January 2018 | 19 June 1986 (Protocol: 19 November 2000) |
| Content | • 26 articles<br>• Five annexes<br>• Council rules of procedure: ten articles and one annex | 34 articles | 21 articles | 22 articles |
| Preamble | Yes | Yes | Yes | Yes |
| Establishment of the agency | Art. I | Art. I | Art. II | Art. I |
| Legal status | Art. XV | Art. III | Art. III | Art. I |
| Headquarters | Arts. I and XV | Art. I | Art. XVII | Art. I |
| Definitions | | Art. II | Art. I | |
| Membership | Art. I | Art. IX | Art. I | Art. I |
| Purposes or objectives | Art. II | Art. IV | Art. V | Art. II |
| Information and data | Art. III | Arts. VI, XXI and XXII | | Art. VIII |
| Technology safeguards and export control | Art. XI | Art. XXIII | | |
| Intellectual property rights | Art. III | Art. XXII | | |
| Liability | | | | Art. IX |
| Audit | Annex II | | | Art. XII |
| Exchange of persons | Art. IV | Art. XX | | |
| Activities and programmes | • Arts. I and V<br>• Annexes III and IV | Arts. VI–VIII | | Arts. II, III and V |
| Facilities and services | Art. VI | Art. I | | |
| Industrial policy | Art. VII<br>Annex V | Art. V | | |

(continued)

**Table 4.1** (continued)

| Content | ESA Convention | APSCO Convention | AfSA Statute | EUMETSAT Convention |
|---|---|---|---|---|
| Launchers and other space transport systems | Art. VIII | | | |
| Use of facilities, assistance to member states, and supply of products | Art. IX | Art. XXVI | | |
| Organs | • Arts. X–XII<br>• Council Rules of Procedure and Annex | Arts. X–XVII | Arts. VI–XV | Arts. I, IV–VII |
| Financial provisions | • Art. XIII<br>• Annex II | Art. XVIII | Art. XVI | Arts. II, III, X–XII and XVI |
| Cooperation | Art. XIV | Arts. VI and XXIV | Art. V | Art. II |
| Coordination with national space agencies | • Arts. II, V and VII<br>• Annex V | | Art. V | |
| Common positions on multilateral topics | | | Art. V | |
| Privileges and immunities | • Art. XV<br>• Annex I | Art. XXV | Art. XVIII | Art. XIII |
| Amendments | Art. XVI | Art. XXVII | Art. XX | Art. XVIII |
| Disputes | Art. XVII | Art. XIX | | Art. XV |
| Non-fulfilment of obligations | Art. XVIII | Art. XXXII | | Art. XIV |
| Continuity of rights and obligations | Art. XIX | | | |
| Signature and ratification | Art. XX | Art. XXVIII | | Art. XVI |
| Entry into force | Art. XXI | Art. XXIX | Art. XXI | Art. XVII |
| Accession | Art. XXII | Art. XXX | | Art. XVI |
| Notifications | Art. XXIII | Art. XXXI | | Art. XXI |
| Denunciation | Art. XXIV | Art. XXXIII | | Art. XIX |
| Dissolution | Art. XXV | Art. XXXIV | | Art. XX |
| Registration | Art. XXVI | Art. XXXV | | Art. XXII |

(continued)

**Table 4.1** (continued)

| Content | ESA Convention | APSCO Convention | AfSA Statute | EUMETSAT Convention |
|---|---|---|---|---|
| Use of languages | Annex I of the Council Procedure Rules | | Art. XIX | Art. I |

*Note 1* this chart only presents the main topics regulated in each regional model, some of which are distributed in several articles in the different Conventions and may be complemented by additional regulations. For this reason, some articles may not be mentioned in the chart; *Note 2* the ESA Convention uses the Roman numerals while the other instruments use the Arabic ones. For the purposes of this chart all articles are shown in Roman numerals

concerning the amendments and entry into force of the constituent instrument. This means that at least these issues are essential in all constitutive instruments. Thus, in the negotiations of the LASA Convention, Latin American states could consider it necessary to include these matters.

Meanwhile, in most models—practically, the three international conventions—the following issues are also regulated: information and data issues, activities and programmes, cooperation relations, dispute resolution, non-fulfilment of obligations, working languages, as well as provisions concerning the dissolution of the space agency and the adoption of the international legal instrument, including signature, ratification, accession, notification, denunciation, and registration. Because the adoption of international treaties creating inter-governmental entities usually takes a long time and modifying them may be hard if there is insufficient support by the parties, it is understandable why the negotiators of the three international conventions wished to include these elements. In particular, the activities and programmes and the cooperation relations with the state parties and other partners are of vital importance for the good performance of the regional space agencies. In this sense, Latin American countries may consider appropriate to include these matters in the LASA Convention to facilitate the coordination and implementation of its space activities, especially if they decide to give the convention the status of an international treaty. Conversely, if LASA is created as an organ of an international organisation like the AfSA, it would not be necessary to include certain issues in its constitutive instrument, such as the procedural provisions on the adoption of an international treaty, but sooner or later other issues—activities and programmes, and working languages, for example—will probably have to be defined in a further document.[30]

Lastly, the topics regulated by one or two constituent instruments are the following: definitions, coordinated work with national space agencies, regional position in multilateral space issues, technology safeguards and export control, liability, audit, exchange of persons, industrial policy, launchers and other space transport systems, continuity of rights and obligations, as well as use of facilities, assistance to member states and supply of products. The fact that these matters are regulated in few constituent instruments may be for different reasons, such as the level of political

[30] The AfSA Convention has no provisions on the types of programmes and activities of the agency.

engagement achieved in those matters (e.g., the development of launchers in the ESA Convention), their political relevance (e.g., regional positions in multilateral topics in the AfSA Statute), practicality (e.g., the definitions in the case of the APSCO and the AfSA legal instruments), and specificity (e.g., the provisions related to the continuity of the rights and obligations of ESRO and ELDO provided in the ESA Convention). In this regard, Latin American countries may decide on the inclusion of these issues in so far as they are willing to legally comply with them. Furthermore, it is possible that the LASA Convention has some provisions that are not present in the four models of international conventions, such as relations with the inter-American system if the agency is created under the aegis of the OAS.

In sum, Latin American countries must decide on the issues that will be included in the provisions of the LASA Convention, and the issues that could be integrated in other documents, such as annexes, protocols, and internal rules. The matters dealt with in the different models of constituent instruments may be included in the LASA Convention, namely the matters common in all models. Provisions on further subjects may also be included if Latin American countries agree. Likely, there is not an ideal model of constituent instrument that Latin America could strictly replicate for the LASA Convention because all regional instruments have been prepared through diverse negotiation processes, in separate times and by different countries; in other words, every instrument is the result of the political commitment achieved by the countries of the respective region and a reflection of the context in which it was adopted.

Considering the provisions of the different models of constitutive instruments, the following sections will deal with several issues that Latin American countries may include in the LASA Convention.

### *4.3.1 Preamble, Purposes and Objectives*

The preamble of the LASA Convention could express the reasons and motivations of Latin American countries that led them to the adoption of this instrument and the creation of LASA. It might also state the historical background, possible legal basis, and the preparatory work of the Convention. Moreover, this instrument may call for the implementation by LASA of a Latin American Space Policy (LASP), strategy, space programme or regional vision that would be adopted before, during or after the adoption of the Convention (Fig. 4.2).[31]

In the statutory section of the Convention, Latin American countries could determine the purposes and objectives of LASA. Examples of these elements include the wish and necessity to develop the space sector in Latin America; increase regional independence and regional integration; carry out joint programmes and activities in space science, technology and its applications in the benefit of Latin American people; protect and use natural resources of Latin America in an efficient, rational and

[31] See: Chapter 3 (3.2).

**Fig. 4.2** Crew members of the ESAA-01 mission (LATCOSMOS-C), the first Latin American suborbital mission expected to be launched in the coming years. *Source* LATCOSMOS

sustainable way; promote international space cooperation between the countries of the region and with other regional and international partners; develop a regional space industry; foster the construction of space infrastructure and the formation of human resources, as well as contribute to the multilateral efforts in promoting the peaceful uses of outer space, the development of international space law and the sustainability of space activities, among others. Moreover, as in the preamble, this section could provide that LASA shall implement a LASP, a strategy or another Latin American agreement. In case LASA is projected to be a specialized space organization, its purposes and objectives would be defined in its field of competence (for instance, the exploitation of meteorological satellites or remote sensing satellites, research and development of space science and technology, or the exploitation of GNSS). Therefore, there are many possibilities for the purposes and objectives of LASA to be included in its constituent instrument. The ALCE Declaration,[32] for example, advances some possible purposes and objectives of this regional space cooperation mechanism, such as the coordination of activities with the relevant institutions of Latin American and Caribbean countries to address the priorities identified in the space field, and the role of LASA as a catalyst for regional space efforts to support

[32] See: Chapter 2 (2.1.3 and 2.2).

the well-being and prosperity of the region.[33] Meanwhile, the proposal to create the Space Agency for Central America and the Caribbean (AECA) within the framework of the Central American Integral System (SICA)[34] provides that AECA should foster the scientific, political and social development of Central America and Dominican Republic through the space sector, giving special importance to the promotion of space education.[35]

### 4.3.2 Establishment of the Agency, Legal Status, and Privileges and Immunities

For the formalization of LASA, its constituent instrument must have a provision concerning the establishment of this entity and its legal status, including, if applicable, the corresponding legal basis. Some possible provisions are the following:

- If LASA is to be an international organisation with multiple fields of competence, the provision could be similar to the respective provisions of the ESA and APSCO Conventions[36]: "*A Latin American Organisation, called the "Latin American Space Agency", hereinafter referred to as "the Agency" or "LASA", is hereby established*";
- If LASA is to be a specialized space international organisation, it could use a similar provision of the EUMETSAT Convention: "*A Latin American Organization for the Exploitation of Meteorological Satellites, hereinafter referred to as "LAMETSAT", is hereby established*"[37];
- If LASA is to be a specialized organisation (SO) of the inter-American system, the provision could be like those of the constituent instruments of the SOs of this system[38]: "*The Inter-American* (or *Latin America*, if applicable) *Space Agency is a Specialized Organisation of the Organisation of American States, in charge of...* (competence). *As an Inter-American Specialized Organization, the Agency*

[33] ALCE's inauguration ceremony can be watched on Facebook's official page of the Mexican Ministry of Foreign Affairs, 9 October 2020, www.facebook.com/watch/?v=3844787895554615.

[34] Agencia Espacial de Centroamérica y el Caribe (AECA); Sistema Integral Centroamericano (SICA), see: Chapter 2 (2.1.3 and 2.2).

[35] Sistema Económico Latinoamericano y del Caribe, "Centroamérica trabaja para crear su agencia espacial", 28 September 2020, www.sela.org/es/prensa/servicio-informativo/20200928/si/69163/centroamerica.

[36] Article 1 of both Conventions.

[37] LAMETSAT is a suggested acronym for the Latin American Organisation for the Exploitation of Meteorological Satellites. It is likely that the real name and acronym of the Latin American space agency will be written in Spanish because this language is the most widely spoken language in this region.

[38] See: Chapter 3 (3.3.1.1.4).

*shall enjoy the fullest technical autonomy in planning and carrying out its objectives, within the limits established by the Charter of the Organization, the Standards for the implementation and Coordination of the Provisions of the Charter related to Inter-American Specialized Organizations, and the present Statutes* (or *Convention, Constituent Instrument...*)",[39] and
- If LASA is to be constituted as an organ of the OAS, the provision may be as follows: "*The Inter-American Space Agency* (or *Latin American*, if applicable), *hereinafter referred to as "IASA"* (or *LASA*), *is hereby established in accordance with article 53 of the Charter of the Organisation of American States as an organ* (or *agency*) *of this Organisation*".

A further issue that should be included in the LASA Convention is the legal personality of LASA. In international law, the international legal personality is one of the attributes of most international organisations,[40] which means that they are subjects of international law and capable of possessing international rights and duties, and that they have capacity to maintain their rights by bringing international claims.[41] The EUMETSAT Convention, for example, provides that "EUMETSAT shall have legal personality",[42] while the APSCO Convention states that APSCO "shall be a non-profit independent body with full international legal status".[43] Moreover, although it is possible that LASA's legal personality could be inferred by the functions it performs on the international plane, it is advisable that this attribute be expressly stated in the LASA Convention,[44] just as in the constituent instruments of the ESA, APSCO, EUMETSAT and the AfSA. Equally important is that the LASA Convention includes the capacity of LASA to conclude international treaties,[45] sign declarations of acceptance of rights and obligations of international treaties (such as some international agreements relating to activities in outer space) and become a member of international organizations. Within the OAS framework, if LASA is formed as an

[39] This formula is used by articles 1 and 2 of the Statutes of the Inter-American Children's Institute, amended in the framework of the 77th Meeting of the Directing Council, 13 to 15 May 2002, in Washington, D.C., U.S..

[40] James Crawford, *Brownlie's Principles of Public International Law*, Eight Edition, Oxford University Press (2012), pp. 167–168.

[41] ICJ Reports 1949, pp. 174 and 178–179.

[42] EUMETSAT Convention, art. 3.

[43] APSCO Convention, art. 3.

[44] The objective legal personality of international organizations, an attribute that is independent of recognition by performing certain functions on the international plane is widely acknowledged. The criteria for the possession of legal personality by an international organization are generally the following: (1) a permanent association of states, or other organizations, with lawful objects, equipped with organs; (2) distinction, in terms of legal powers and purposes, between the organization and its member states; and (3) the existence of legal powers exercisable on the international plane and not solely within the national systems of one or more states, in: Crawford, *Brownlie's Principles of Public International Law*, p. 169.

[45] Shaw, *International Law*, p. 944.

SO, the legal personality may be established in its constituent instrument.[46] Even if LASA is created as an organ of the OAS or another international organisation, it could still possess legal personality and be regarded as a separate legal person,[47] although its capacities and independence would be restricted compared to those of the respective international organisation.[48] Moreover, as in the case of the AfSA and its statute, LASA's legal personality may be granted in instruments other than a treaty, such as a resolution of a conference of states or through a uniform practice.[49]

Additionally, the LASA Convention should contain provisions on the legal capacity, privileges and immunities of LASA.[50] LASA's legal capacity may include the capacity to contract, acquire and dispose of movable and immovable property and to be party to legal proceedings. LASA's immunity should comprise immunity from jurisdiction and execution, with the possibility of including waivers in particular situations. Privileges and immunities should also be granted to LASA's staff and experts, as well as to representatives of its member states for the effective exercise of their functions and the accomplishment of its purposes.

Complementary provisions on these issues may be determined in the LASA Convention or in attached instruments, such as annexes or protocols.[51] Furthermore, to carry out its functions with independence, LASA should conclude an agreement with the headquarters country, as well as agreements with other states that will host LASA's offices and establishments for the well-functioning of the agency. In the framework of the OAS, if LASA is created as an SO its privileges and immunities and those of its personnel, as well as of the officials of the OAS General Secretariat, shall be determined in a multilateral agreement, without precluding the adoption of bilateral agreements if necessary.[52] If LASA is established as an organ of the OAS, the provisions of the OAS Charter on privileges and immunities shall apply[53] and,

---

[46] For example, the Inter-American Institute for Cooperation on Agriculture (IICA) possesses international legal personality, Convention on the Inter-American Institute for Cooperation on Agriculture, art. 2, 1979, http://repositorio.iica.int/bitstream/handle/11324/2620/BVE17038700e.pdf;jsessionid=97F20F27AF0A47F2517CAA9590E07969?sequence=1.

[47] In the EU, the legal status of the GSA should be such as to enable it to act as a legal person in the discharge of its tasks, see: *Regulation (EU) No 912/2010 of the European Parliament and of the Council*, 22 September 2010, Preamble, para. 7, and art. 1.4 (the GSA "shall have legal personality").

[48] Crawford, *Brownlie's Principles of Public International Law*, pp. 170–171.

[49] Ibid., p. 170.

[50] In the EU, the GSA enjoys in each of the member states the most extensive legal capacity accorded to legal persons under their law. It may, in particular, acquire or dispose of movable and immovable property and be a party to legal proceedings, see: *Regulation (EU) No 912/2010 of the European Parliament and of the Council, 22 September 2010, art. 4.2.*

[51] For example, article XV of the ESA Convention contains a general rule on privileges and immunities, but it is Annex 1 of the same Convention that regulates these issues in detail. In the case of EUMETSAT, there is a *Protocol on the Privileges and Immunities of EUMETSAT* adopted on 1 December 1986 and entered into force on 6 January 1989.

[52] OAS Charter, art. 135.

[53] OAS Charter, art. 133.—"The Organization of American States shall enjoy in the territory of each Member such legal capacity, privileges, and immunities as are necessary for the exercise

if applicable, the Agreement on Privileges and Immunities of the Organization of American States adopted in 1949.[54]

### 4.3.3 Headquarters, Facilities and Services

As happens with other regional space agencies, LASA's headquarters will be defined by the state parties in the LASA Convention or in another instrument. In the ESA and EUMETSAT Conventions, the city of the headquarters of the respective agencies is expressly mentioned, while in the APSCO Convention only the headquarters country is defined. Therefore, Latin American countries may decide to designate or not the location of LASA's headquarters. An advantage in defining only the host country and not the city is that it gives time for this country to prepare the most appropriate location of the agency's headquarters while the ratifications required for the LASA Convention to enter into force are gathered. However, it is possible that the LASA Convention does not specify the location of LASA's headquarters, such as in the AfSA Statute. In that instrument, however, there is a provision stating that the AfSA's headquarters shall be determined by the AU Assembly in accordance with the criteria adopted by the AU in 2005.[55] These criteria, which apply for AU member states hosting or proposing to host AU organs, are the following[56]:

- The host country shall provide, at its expense a secure structure with furnished and equipped office premises for the seat of the organ on the basis of the objective requirements of office space,
- The premises offered by the host country should be such that the organ shall be easily accessible,
- The host country shall meet the requirements of a conducive political atmosphere and adequate logistical facilities,
- There should be appropriate and efficient modern infrastructure especially telecommunication facilities to enable the office to function efficiently,

of its functions and the accomplishment of its purposes"; art. 134.—"The representatives of the Member States on the organs of the Organization, the personnel of their delegations, as well as the Secretary General and the Assistant Secretary General shall enjoy the privileges and immunities corresponding to their positions and necessary for the independent performance of their duties.".

[54] *Agreement on Privileges and Immunities of the Organization of American States (C-13)*, adopted in Washington, D.C., U.S., on 15 May 1949, and entered into force on 4 June 1951. Only the following countries have ratified or acceded to this Agreement: Bolivia, Brazil, Chile, Colombia, Costa Rica, Cuba, Ecuador, Haiti, Honduras, Nicaragua, Paraguay, Peru and Uruguay, see: OAS, Department of International Law, "Multilateral Treaties", www.oas.org/dil/treaties_C-13_Agreement_on_Privileges_and_Immunities_of_the_Organization_of_American_States_sign.htm.

[55] AfSA Statute, art. 17.

[56] *Criteria for Hosting the AU Organs*, adopted by the 7th Ordinary Session of the Executive Council and endorsed by the 5th Ordinary Session of the Assembly held in Sirte, Libya, on 1–2 and 4–5 July 2005, respectively, African Union, Doc. EX.CL/195 (VLL) Rev. 1, Annex III.

- There shall be available housing, hotel accommodation and health infrastructure to meet the functional needs of the organ,
- Without prejudice to these criteria, nothing in these criteria shall be taken to preclude a member state from offering more facilities. In this regard, a member state offering to host an organ of the Union (AU) is encouraged to provide, at its expense, where the Head of the Organ is required to be resident at the seat, an appropriate furnished and equipped official residence.

Apart from these criteria, further conditions must be stated, including the ratification of international treaties on privileges and immunities by the potential host states,[57] the setting up of an independent team to make a fact-finding mission to the member state or states offering to host organs of the AU to inspect the proposed site and submit the corresponding report, as well as the elaboration of a model Headquarters Agreement by the AU Commission.[58] Accordingly, in February 2019 the AU Assembly adopted a resolution choosing Egypt as the AfSA's headquarters country.[59]

Taking the African example, Latin American countries could consider the inclusion of similar criteria in the LASA Convention to decide the location of LASA's headquarters. Even though the headquarters location is defined in this Convention, the AU criteria may still be used to choose the location of other LASA's facilities.

Concerning LASA's facilities and services, the LASA Convention may contain provisions on the formation and use of these establishments in the headquarters country—that would be complemented by the headquarters agreement—or in other member states—to be detailed in bilateral agreements.[60] There could also be provisions on the necessity to establish and operate facilities for the execution of LASA's programmes, and to use or manage national facilities for the execution of these programmes by, or in cooperation with, national institutions of LASA member states. Moreover, to avoid the creation of new establishments for the regional space agency and save significant costs, the LASA Convention may include a provision concerning the use, as far as possible, by LASA and its member states of their existing facilities and available services as a first priority, and to rationalise them. In this regard, LASA

[57] The international treaties are the *General Convention on Privileges and Immunities of the Organisation of Africa Unity* (OAU), the *Vienna Convention on Diplomatic Relations* of 1961, and the *Vienna Convention on Consular Relations* of 1963.

[58] Additionally, the document provides a detailed procedure to examine the fulfilment of these criteria and determine the host country by the AU Assembly.

[59] Assembly/AU/Dec.748(XXXII) on the *Decision on the High-Level Panel's Report for Assessing Candidate Countries to Host the African Space Agency*, Doc. EX.CL/1118(XXXIV), 32nd Ordinary Session of the Assembly, 10–11 February 2019, Addis Ababa, Ethiopia, available at: https://au.int/sites/default/files/decisions/36461-assembly_au_dec_713_-_748_xxxii_e.pdf.

[60] Article 1 of the APSCO Convention has two provisions in this regard: the first provision states that APSCO may establish branch offices and relevant facilities within the territory of the host state (People's Republic of China) in consultation with the government of this state, while the second provision provides that APSCO may establish branch offices and relevant facilities within the territory of any other member state in consultation with the other member states. These provisions are an example of China's dominance over the rest of APSCO member states because there is no need to consult the latter to set up facilities and branch offices within the territory of China.

**Fig. 4.3** Alcântara Launch Center, Brazil. *Source* Defensa.com

member states shall not set up new facilities or services without having first examined the possibility of using the existing means.[61] A further provision may be the possibility for any member state to use LASA's facilities for its own programmes, provided that the cost is covered by the member state and that this use does not compromise the use of the facilities by LASA for its own programmes and activities (Fig. 4.3).[62]

Therefore, Latin American countries must decide on the necessary provisions concerning LASA's facilities, including the location of its headquarters. Although the LASA Convention excludes details in this regard, it is important, if Latin American countries wish to grant LASA an international character and allow the development of the space sector in all its member states, that these states include a provision in the convention on the desirability or necessity to distribute LASA's facilities among its members, perhaps through the inclusion of the principle of geographical distribution of facilities.

[61] These provisions are regulated by article VI of the ESA Convention.

[62] See: articles IX and 26 of the ESA and APSCO Conventions, respectively.

### *4.3.4 Membership*

The LASA Convention will define who can become party to this instrument and, therefore, a member of LASA. The issue of LASA's membership is relevant because the definition of who may become members of this agency may influence or determine certain characteristics of LASA itself, such as the location of LASA's facilities, the distribution of LASA's financial contributions and industrial contracts, and the use of certain languages. The LASA Convention may provide the terms and conditions of LASA's membership or determine that an organ of LASA shall decide on the accession of new members.[63] Ideally, the use of "Latin American" in the name of the space agency would imply that all Latin American states may become members of LASA.[64] However, the negotiators of the constituent instrument may decide that other states or entities can also be members of LASA or have a special status, such as associate members or observers. Examples of this possibility are found in the different proposals for the establishment of a space agency in the Americas.[65] In this regard, while some proposals refer only to Latin American countries, others include the Caribbean countries.[66] This is the case of the ALCE proposal, which is currently under development.

Within the OAS framework, due to the fact that the OAS is a Pan-American organisation, it is likely that LASA's membership will be open to all OAS member states, including Canada, the U.S., and the Caribbean countries. Indeed, it would be possible that the space agency's name would include "Inter-American" instead of "Latin American". In any case, if LASA is created as a subsidiary body of the OAS, there could be a provision in its constituent instrument stating that all OAS member states shall[67] or can[68] be members of LASA. There is also the possibility that LASA may not have "members" as such and, therefore, there would not be a membership provision in its constituent instrument. This situation may arise if LASA interacts

---

[63] According to Article I of the ESA Convention, the members of ESA shall be the states which are parties to this Convention in accordance with articles XX and XXII. Article XX provides that the ESA Convention shall be open until 31 December 1975 for signature by the states which are members of the European Space Conference, while Article XXII establishes that after the entry into force of this Convention, any state may accede thereto following a decision of the Council taken by a unanimous vote of all member states.

[64] For instance, the APSCO Convention provides that APSCO is open to all members of the UN in the Asia–Pacific region (the APSCO Convention was opened for signature until 31 July 2006), and that any of these states may accede to the convention with the unanimous approval of the APSCO Council, Arts. 9.1 and 30.1, respectively.

[65] See: Chapter 2 (2.1).

[66] There are also proposals of subregional space agencies, such as the creation of a South American Space Agency (SASA) and the Space Agency for Central American and the Caribbean (AECA), see: Chapter 2 (2.1).

[67] Article 1 of the AfSA Statute (Definitions) provides that "member states" means member states of the AU.

[68] Article 4 of the *Reform of the Statute of the Inter-American Telecommunication Commission* (CITEL) determines that all member states of the OAS and other American states that are not members of the OAS can be members of CITEL.

**Fig. 4.4** Tolhuin station for satellite monitoring, Argentina. *Source* Télam

with the OAS member states like other subsidiary bodies of this organisation.[69] Furthermore, if LASA is created as an SO of the OAS, the terms and conditions of membership shall be determined in the respective constituent instrument (Fig. 4.4).[70]

Thus, the conditions to become a member of LASA may include at least belonging to a specific region (Latin America, Latin American and the Caribbean, or the Americas) and the conclusion of the membership procedure established in the LASA Convention or another instrument. Further conditions could comprise, for example, being a member state of the UN or a member of the forum in which the LASA Convention has been prepared or negotiated (OAS, CELAC, the United Nations Committee on the Peaceful Uses of Outer Space (UNCOPUOS), the United Nations Economic Commission for Latin America and the Caribbean (ECLAC), etc.),[71] and

[69] In the EU, there is no membership provision in the GSA's constituent instrument, see: Chapter 3 (3.1.5).

[70] For example, Article 7 of the Statutes of the Inter-American Children's Institute (IIN) provides that the OAS member states are members of the IIN, and Article 5 of the Convention of the Inter-American Institute for Cooperation on Agriculture (IICA) provides that the IICA member states shall be the member states of the OAS or of the Inter-American Institute of Agricultural Sciences (IICA's predecessor) that have ratified the IICA Convention, and other American states whose admission has been accepted by the affirmative vote of two thirds of the member states on the Inter-American Board of Agriculture, and which accede to the IICA Convention. Conversely, the Statute of the Inter-American Commission of Women (CIM) does not have a membership provision. Instead, Article 2 provides that "the mission of the CIM (…) is to support the member states of the Organisation (the "member states") in their efforts…", and Article 5 provides that the CIM "shall be composed of one Principal Delegate from each member state, accredited by the government thereof…", see: *Statute of the Inter-American Commission of Women*, available at www.oas.org/en/cim/docs/CIMStatute-2016-EN.pdf.

[71] In Noichim's proposal of a space agency within the Association of Southeast Asian Nations (ASEAN), membership would be open to all states located in the South-East Asian region which

the completion of a set of stages in a gradual procedure such as applies to be an ESA member state. Currently, to become a full member state of the ESA, the interested candidate state must complete five stages: (1) the adoption of a framework cooperation agreement with the ESA, (2) the joint adoption of a European Cooperation State Agreement (ECS Agreement), (3) the definition of a Plan for European Cooperation State (PECS),[72] (4) the conclusion with the ESA of an Associate Membership Agreement,[73] and (5) the conclusion with the ESA of a Full Member Accession Agreement (Table 4.2). This long procedure, that may last from 13 to 18 years, responds to the necessity to stimulate relations with interested European countries, expanding the overall European scientific and industrial base, and enrich the ESA as a research and development (R&D) organisation.[74] Moreover, the procedure aims at preparing the candidate states to join the ESA, to integrate their national space industries in the space supply chain, and to achieve a satisfactory geographical return.[75]

In sum, the membership procedure adopted by the ESA in the last two decades has facilitated newcomers to integrate with the regional space agency and participate in its activities and programmes, as well as to improve their national space industries. In Latin America, the negotiators of the LASA Convention will assess the possibility to establish a similar procedure for LASA's candidate member states.[76] This would allow small countries of the region to develop their space sectors and participate in a more active way in LASA's activities and programmes, in particular in the basic and mandatory activities. However, a membership procedure like that of the ESA would make sense if one of LASA's purposes is the development and implementation of an industrial policy. Moreover, the assessment of integrating ESA's membership procedure must bear in mind the differences between the European and Latin American contexts. In this regard, it should be considered that the ESA took more than 25 years to adopt its current membership procedure. By then, the agency had already developed a strong industrial policy and many European member states possessed competitive space industries. In Latin America, LASA would be the first regional institutional space cooperation mechanism, and just a few countries of the hemisphere have developed a national space industry.[77] Thus, adopting a lengthy and strict membership procedure to join LASA may be counterproductive and could discourage some states, namely the smaller ones, to participate in the regional space

are also members of ASEAN, in: Chukeat Noichim, *The Asean Space Organisation, Legal Aspects and Feasibility*, Leiden (2008), p. 146.

[72] Bulgaria, Cyprus, Lithuania and Slovakia are currently in this stage, see: ESA, "PECS, General Overview", www.esa.int/About_Us/Plan_for_European_Cooperating_States/General_overview.

[73] Slovenia and Latvia are currently in this stage, Ibid.

[74] ESA, "Members States and Cooperating States", www.esa.int/About_Us/Corporate_news/Member_States_Cooperating_States.

[75] Ibid.

[76] The current ESA membership procedure is not specified in the ESA Convention. However, Article XIV of this instrument provides the legal basis of the different types of cooperation between ESA and non-member states and other partners.

[77] See: Annette Froehlich/Diego Alonso Amante Soria et al., *Space Supporting Latin America: Latin America's Emerging Space Middle Powers*, Springer (2020).

**Table 4.2** ESA's membership procedure

| Stage | Cooperation instrument | Duration | Characteristics |
|---|---|---|---|
| 1 | Cooperation agreement (or framework agreement) | Indefinite | Provides a common basis and the appropriate operational arrangements for efficient and mutually beneficial cooperation with regard to space activities for peaceful purposes, on a no-exchange-of-funds basis |
| 2 | European cooperating state (ECS)—agreement | One year | The ECS Agreement defines the legal basis for developing the specific plan for the ECS (PECS Charter) which must be in place and signed within the next twelve months. It also allows a country to participate in ESA procurements and activities. To be a candidate for an ECS Agreement, a country must be European and already have signed a Cooperation Agreement with ESA |
| 3 | Plan for ECS (PECS Charter) | Five years, renewable for a similar period | The function of PECS is to pave the way forward for the ECS towards ESA. It aims at bridging the gap between newcomers and full member states. Working on a basis of guaranteed return of contributions, participants gain technical knowledge and support, stimulus for industrial activities and familiarity with ESA standards and procedures. For ESA, PECS allows it to harness national technical expertise for its space projects and the opportunity to extend its harmonisation of space R&D further across Europe, coordinating activities to minimise duplication of effort and boost overall return on investment. The five years spent under the PECS Charter enables a country to increase its knowledge of ESA and develop its space industry, thus improving its chances of winning contracts in the future. There is a PECS Committee which monitors and controls the execution of the Plan, in coordination with ESA |

(continued)

**Table 4.2** (continued)

| Stage | Cooperation instrument | Duration | Characteristics |
|---|---|---|---|
| 4 | Associate membership agreement | Variable (currently seven years) | At the end of the five-year period of the PECS, the progress of the country's industry is assessed, and a decision is made by ESA and the respective country on becoming an associate member. This category implies that a non-member state may contribute at least to the studies of future projects under Article V, 1 *a* (i) of the ESA Convention (basic activities). The detailed arrangements for each associated membership are defined by the ESA Council by a two-thirds majority of all member states. Delegates and advisers of the associate member are entitled to attend meetings of the ESA Council and its subordinate bodies, and to vote on questions relating to the activities and programmes in which the state participates in its capacity of "Participating State" in the case of optional programmes. Dedicated access to agency facilities and services will be provided to the associate member national space projects |

(continued)

**Table 4.2** (continued)

| Stage | Cooperation instrument | Duration | Characteristics |
|---|---|---|---|
| 5 | Full member accession agreement | Indefinite | In this stage, the associate member acquires the status of a full ESA member state after the adoption of an accession agreement in accordance with article XXII of the ESA Convention |

*Source* ESA/*Note*: the procedure of the different stages may vary depending on the specific agreements between ESA and the interested state effort. Therefore, Latin American countries should consider whether the criteria and conditions to become a member of LASA should be determined in its constituent instrument.

Meanwhile, the LASA Convention may have provisions on the rights and obligations of its member states, such as their right to vote in the decisions of their organs and the necessary privileges and immunities of its representatives, and the obligations to participate in certain activities and programmes and contribute to the common costs of the agency.

Finally, the LASA Convention may allow additional categories of membership, such as associate members[78] and observers.[79] The terms, conditions and rights of these categories may be determined in additional instruments to the Convention.

### *4.3.5 Organs*

To fulfil the purposes and objectives of LASA, its constituent instrument will determine the necessary main organs of the space agency. It is possible that these organs be at least two, such as in the case of the ESA, APSCO and EUMETSAT, which are a decision-maker and legislative body, and an executive organ. In the case of the AfSA, the space agency comprises two additional organs: a secretariat and an advisory committee.[80]

#### 4.3.5.1 The Decision-Maker and Legislative Organ

In the four models mentioned above, the supreme organ, policy-making and legislative body is the Council. However, in the case of the AfSA, due to its status as an organ of the AU, the African Space Council (AfSA Council) reports to the AU

---

[78] For example, Article 9 of the APSCO Convention determines that membership is divided into three categories: member states, associated member states and observers. The first category is open to all UN member states in the Asia–Pacific region. They have full voting rights, shall be entitled to participate in APSCO cooperation programs and activities, and shall make financial contributions to the organization. The second category is open for any UN member state outside the Asia–Pacific region. APSCO's Council grants the associated member status by consensus. Finally, observer status is open to any UN member state or any international organization involved in space activities. APSCO's Council unanimously grants this status. Both associated members and observers cannot vote in APSCO's Council meetings.

[79] For instance, Canada, the U.S. and the Caribbean countries may become associate members of LASA because these countries are part of the Americas. Extracontinental countries, international organizations or even overseas territories of European countries in the Americas—such as French Guiana—could be LASA observers.

[80] Article 6 of the AfSA Statute provides that the Secretariat is an organ of the AfSA. However, there are no specific provisions in the Statute containing information about this organ, except from the provisions about the "staff" that shall support the Director General of the agency. It is likely that this staff be part of the Secretariat of the AfSA.

Assembly through the Heads of State and Government on Education, Science and Technology.[81] In Latin America, the supreme body, decision maker and legislative body of LASA could be the "LASA Council", although another entity could have the final word if LASA is created as a subsidiary body of an international organisation (the OAS General Assembly, for example). It is up to the negotiators of the LASA Convention to decide on the composition, structure, voting rights, functions and responsibilities of the Council.

Concerning its composition, the LASA Council may be composed similar to the APSCO Council, which is made up of ministers or ministerial representatives of national space agencies,[82] or take different forms, such as the ESA Council, which gathers at delegate level (composed of national delegates) and ministerial level (composed of national ministers competent for space), and functions as a forum of inter-governmental cooperation.[83] If LASA is established as a specialized space international organisation such as EUMETSAT, the composition of its Council may be similar to the EUMETSAT Council, which is made up of no more than two representatives of each member state, one of whom is a delegate of the country's National Meteorological Service.[84] Being an organ of the OAS, LASA may have a Council like the AfSA Council,[85] which is composed of 26 high level experts with high moral character elected by the AU Assembly.[86]

Concerning its structure, the LASA Council may elect a chairman and one or more vice-chairmen for two years with one possible re-election (as in the four models), and it could be assisted by a bureau. About the voting rights, each member state could have a vote in the Council, although a member state may not vote on matters exclusively concerning a programme in which it does not participate.[87] There could also be a provision stating that all Council's decisions shall be taken, if possible, by consensus.[88]

---

[81] AfSA Statute, art. 10.3.

[82] APSCO Convention, art. 11.2.

[83] *The European Space Agency as mechanism and actor of international cooperation*, ESA Legal Services Department, March 2014, prepared for the 53rd session of the UNCOPUOS Legal Subcommittee, Doc. A/AC.105/C.2/2014/CRP.28, 28 March 2014, p. 5; ESA Convention, Arts. 11.1 and 11.2.

[84] EUMETSAT Convention, art. 4.1.

[85] AfSA Statute, art. 6.

[86] Ten elected persons from the member states, two per each of the five African regions (Central Africa, Eastern Africa, Northern Africa, Southern Africa, and Western Africa), four representatives of the AU Commission, and two representatives of the Bureau of the Chairperson (Director General of Communications and the Legal Counsel of the AU), see: AfSA Statute, art. 6; in Latin America, the geographic regions could be North America (Mexico) and the Caribbean, Central America, and South America.

[87] For example, see: ESA Convention, art. XII.6 a). This Convention also determines the motives for which a member state can lose its right to vote in the activities and programmes of the agency (art. XII.6 b)). The AfSA Statute provides that the members of the Council have voting rights, except from the representatives of the Commission (art. 8).

[88] For example, see: APSCO Convention, art. 14.

Finally, the responsibilities of the LASA Council may be similar to those of the four models: approve and oversee the activities and programs of the agency, adopt work plans, budgets and financial arrangements, issue policies, regulations and recommendations, decide on the admission on new members and the deprival of membership, approve cooperation agreements, and create subsidiary bodies. Furthermore, it could be up to the Council to elaborate its own rules of procedure.[89]

#### 4.3.5.2 The Executive Organ

In the four types of regional space agencies, the executive organ is the authority responsible for implementing the activities and programmes adopted by the Council. This organ is headed by a chief executive officer, who is also the legal representative of the agency. In the ESA, EUMETSAT and AfSA, the chief executive officer and legal representative is the Director General (DG), while in APSCO the head of the executive organ—the Secretariat—is the Secretary General (SG). These officers are supported by a secretariat, a staff, and other bodies, which usually represent most of the agencies' administrative structures (Table 4.3). In the ESA, the DG is supported by ten Directors, each of whom is responsible for one of ESA's programmes or for administering part of the agency.[90] The DG is also assisted by scientific, technical, administrative or clerical staff, which is recruited on the basis of their qualifications and takes into account an adequate distribution of posts among nationals of the member states.[91] In APSCO, the Secretariat is supported by a staff and is structured in five departments,[92] while in EUMETSAT the Secretariat comprises four departments and the Management Board, which is composed of the DG and the Directors of these departments.[93] In the AfSA, the DG, who also serves as Secretary of the AfSA Council, is assisted by the necessary staff for the running of the agency.[94] The term of the different executive officers varies depending on the respective agency.

The responsibilities of the executive organs include drawing up reports, working plans and financial budgets; submitting proposals on programs, activities and measures to the Council; recruiting staff and appointing experts that are not regular staff members; negotiating and signing international cooperation agreements, and being the legal representative of the agency.[95] Furthermore, the ESA

---

[89] For example, see: *ESA Council Rules of Procedure*, approved by the Council at its 7th Session (10–11 May 1976) and amended at its 29th Session (27–28 February 1979).

[90] ESA, "ESA top management", www.esa.int/About_Us/Corporate_news/ESA_top_management.

[91] ESA Convention, art. 12.4.

[92] APSCO, "APSCO Structure", www.apsco.int/html/comp1/content/APSCOStructure/2019-02-28/68-258-1.shtml.

[93] EUMETSAT, "About EUMETSAT, Management", www.eumetsat.int/who-we-are/management.

[94] AfSA Statute, art. 15.2.

[95] Article 15.4 of the AfSA Statute determines that the Rules of Procedures shall define the powers and duties of the Director General, while Article 7.1 of the EUMETSAT Convention provides that specific provisions concerning the staff are established in the Staff Rules adopted by the Council. This article also states that when the Rules of Procedure are not applicable to the conditions of

**Table 4.3** Executive organ's structure of regional space agencies.

| ESA's director general | EUMETSAT's director general | APSCO's secretary general |
|---|---|---|
| Director of Technology, Engineering and Quality, and Head of ESTEC | Department of Programme Preparation and Development | Department of Administration and Finance |
| Director of Human and Robotic Exploration | Department of Operations and Services to Users | Department of Education and Training |
| Director of Industry, Procurement and Legal Services, and Head of ESA Headquarters | Department of Administration | Department of External Relations and Legal Affairs |
| Director of Space Transportation | Department of Technical and Scientific Support | Department of Program Operation and Data Service |
| Director of Earth Observation, and Head of ESRIN | | Department of Strategic Planning and Program Management |
| Director of Navigation | | |
| Director of Science, and Head of ESAC | | |
| Director of Telecommunications and Integrated Applications, and Head of ECSAT | | |
| Director of Internal Services | | |
| Director of Operations, and Head of ESOC | | |

*Source* ESA, EUMETSAT, APSCO

and EUMETSAT Conventions provide that the responsibilities of the DG and the staff are exclusively international in character. This means that they shall not seek or receive instructions from any government or authority external to the agency when discharging their duties, and the respective member states must respect those responsibilities (Fig. 4.5).[96]

In this regard, the LASA Convention could create an executive organ for the implementation of the activities and programmes of LASA. This organ may comprise a chief executive officer—LASA's legal representative—and a secretariat, as well as the necessary departments and staff. Mariano Imbert, for example, proposes an

employment of a staff member, they are governed by the law applicable in the country where the person concerned is carrying out his duties.

[96] ESA Convention, art. XII.4, and EUMETSAT Convention, art. 6.5.

**Fig. 4.5** Large millimetre telescope Alfonso Serrano, Mexico. *Source* INAOE

organization structure of a potential Latin American and Caribbean Space Agency made up of seven Directorates[97]:

- Space Programme Planning and Development
- Space Education
- Space Research and Applications
- Space Infrastructure
- Latin American and Caribbean Space Access
- Administration and Finances
- Legal and Foreign Affairs.

[97] Mariano Imbert, *A Latin American and Caribbean Space Organization to be Delivered in the Space 2030 Agenda*, IAC-20-E3.1, 71st International Astronautical Congress—The CyberSpace Edition, 12–14 October 2020, p. 7.

Therefore, Latin American countries must define the structure of the executive organ of LASA. It is possible that the LASA Convention may only have a provision concerning the possibility of the executive organ being supported by the necessary staff and having the power to create supporting bodies for the fulfilment of its tasks. Thus, the detailed provisions on the executive organ and the responsibilities of its staff and supporting bodies could be established in further LASA documents.

#### 4.3.5.3 The Advisory Committee

Apart from the decision-maker/legislative and executive organs, LASA could have additional main organs to achieve the purposes and objectives of the space agency. An example is an advisory committee that supports the work of the Council and the executive organ. In this sense, Latin American countries may take the model of the Advisory Committee of the AfSA.[98] This body aims to provide necessary advice to the AfSA Council. Specifically, it reviews and recommends strategic plans, annual work plans, budgets, external audit reports, policies, regulations and guidelines to the Council.[99] It is composed of five Director Generals of the National Space Agencies of member states, one from each of the five geographic regions of the AU based on the principle of rotation and geographic representation; one representative of the eight Regional Economic Commissions (RECs) recognized by the AU; two experts from academia admitted through the African Academy of Sciences and whose membership shall be drawn from the five regions of the AU, based on the principle of rotation and geographic representation; and four Chief Executive Officers of four African private sector entities, each representing one of the four space sectors: EO, satellite communication, navigation, and space and Astronomy.[100] Except for representatives of the RECs, who are rotated every two years, the term of office of the members of the Advisory Committee is three years renewable once.[101]

Therefore, it might be useful that LASA has a space advisory committee as in Africa. This body could be made up of representatives of the different subregions of Latin America, and representatives of the national space agencies (governmental and non-governmental) of LASA's member states, academia (universities and research centres) and industry (focused on space related sectors) of Latin America to give advice to the LASA Council and other appropriate organs. Moreover, members of Latin American space associations, organisations and networks, such as the Regional Centre for Space Science and Technology Education for Latin America and the Caribbean (CRECTEALC), the Latin-American Society in Remote Sensing and Spatial Information Systems (SELPER), and RELACA-Espacio, could participate in this body.[102] Within the OAS framework, the advisory committee of LASA could

[98] AfSA Statute, art. 12.

[99] Ibid., art. 13.

[100] Ibid., art. 12.

[101] Ibid.

[102] See: Chapter 1 (1.2.3).

**Fig. 4.6** First Paraguayan (Guaranisat-1, left) and Guatemalan (Quetzal-1, centre) satellites, and third Chilean satellite (Fasat-Charlie, right). *Source* ABC, UVG and UACh, respectively

be composed of representatives of some organs of the OAS, such as CITEL and the CJI.

## *4.3.6 Activities and Programmes*

During the negotiations for the LASA Convention, Latin American countries must discuss the different types of space activities and programmes of LASA. There is a great array of activities that LASA could carry out, from space education and space science research to the development of space technology and its applications, including the collection and dissemination of satellite data, and the construction of launchers and space transportation systems.[103] In sum, LASA activities and programmes should fulfil the purpose and objectives of the space agency. A Latin American space programme, as well as a regional space policy or strategy could facilitate the determination of the activities and programmes of LASA, and some ideas may be obtained from the different instruments issued by the regional fora dedicated to space matters, such as the declarations and plans of action of the Space Conferences of the Americas (SCAs) and the proposals on the establishment of a regional space agency in the Americas.[104] For instance, the ALCE Declaration states that ALCE will promote cooperation in the development of space sciences (Fig. 4.6).[105]

---

[103] Article 6 of the APSCO Convention establishes that APSCO shall carry out activities in the following fields of cooperation: space technology and programs of its applications; EO, disaster management, environmental protection, satellite communications and satellite navigation and positioning; space science research; education, training and exchange of scientists/technologists. The article also includes the establishment of a central data bank for development of programs of APSCO and dissemination of technical and other information relating to the programs and activities of the organisation. Further cooperative programs may also be carried out by APSCO member states.

[104] See: Chapter 2 (2.1.2).

[105] EUMETSAT Convention, art. 2.

As in previous sections, the models of constituent instruments of regional space agencies may provide guidance on the possible activities and programmes of LASA and the procedures to adopt them.[106] The ESA, APSCO and EUMETSAT Conventions define two main kinds of activities: mandatory and optional activities.[107] In mandatory activities, which usually cover the basic activities and the management and maintenance of the establishments of the space agency, all member states are obligate to participate. Conversely, in the optional activities some or all member states decide to participate in a voluntary basis. In the case of the ESA, for example, the legal difference between both activities is that mandatory activities are decided and carried out by ESA, while optional activities are decided by some of all ESA member states on an inter-governmental basis at any moment through international agreements called "Programme Declarations" and are carried out by ESA.[108]

The mandatory and optional activities and programmes of these organisations correspond to the purposes and objectives established in their respective constituent instruments,[109] so they differ between each other, namely between the general space international organisations (ESA and APSCO) and the specialized space international organizations (EUMETSAT). For example, the mandatory activities of ESA include education, documentation, studies of future projects and technological research work; the scientific programme, including satellites and other space systems; the collection and dissemination of data; the provision of advice and assistance for the harmonisation of international and national programmes; and the maintenance of contact with technology users.[110] APSCO's mandatory activities comprise setting up plans for space activities and development; research on space science, technology and its applications, space education and training; and management and maintaining of APSCO

---

[106] The APSCO and EUMETSAT Conventions took some inspiration on this matter from the ESA Convention, especially as regards the different kinds of activities that the regional space agencies may carry out. Conversely, the AfSA Statute does not contain specific provisions on the programmes and activities of the AfSA. Article 5 just provides that the agency shall "promote and coordinate the implementation of programmes and activities approved by the African Space Council".

[107] The APSCO Convention uses the term "basic" instead of "mandatory", while the EUMETSAT Convention uses the term "programmes". EUMETSAT "activities" are those activities not linked to a specific programme, including the basic technical and administrative infrastructure of the organisation, EUMETSAT Convention, art. 2.5.

[108] See: *The European Space Agency as mechanism and actor of international cooperation*, ESA Legal Services Department, p. 7. In EUMETSAT, the mandatory programmes are established through the adoption of a Programme Resolution by the Council, while the optional programmes are adopted through a Programme Declaration by the interested member states according to the objectives of EUMETSAT and approved by the Council in an Enabling Resolution (EUMETSAT Convention, art. 3). In APSCO, Article 8 of the Convention provides that in addition to its basic activities, the organisation shall recommend and organize suitable space science, technology and their applications programs for joint implementation by its member states, which choose to participate in such programs. Furthermore, there is a provision (art. 12 e) stating that one of the responsibilities of APSCO's Council is the adoption and approval of cooperative programs and their financial budgets.

[109] Noichim, *The Asean Space Organisation, Legal Aspects and Feasibility*, Leiden (2008), pp. 136–140.

[110] ESA Convention, art. V.1 a).

branch offices, facilities and network system.[111] In turn, EUMETSAT's mandatory programmes include the Meteosat Operational Programme, as well as the basic programmes required to continue the provision of observations from geostationary and polar orbits.[112]

Concerning the optional activities, ESA's activities include the design, development, construction, launching, placing in orbit, and control of satellites and other space systems, as well as the design, development, construction, and operation of launch facilities and space transport systems;[113] and in APSCO, the optional activities may comprise programmes on space science, technology and their applications.[114]

Apart from the mandatory and optional activities, ESA and APSCO may undertake additional activities. For instance, ESA may undertake operational activities on space applications for other agencies. In this case, the Council, by a majority of all member states, defines the conditions for undertaking these activities. ESA can place its own facilities at the disposal of the operating agencies; ensure the launching, placing in orbit and control of operational application satellites, and carry out other activities required by the users and approved by the Council.[115] Furthermore, ESA can place its facilities at the disposal of any member state to carry out its own programmes.[116] Operational activities are carried out at the cost of the concerned state and in so far as the activities do not jeopardise ESA's activities.[117] In the same vein, EUMETSAT may carry out activities requested by third parties, which shall be approved by the Council and must not be in conflict with the objectives of EUMETSAT.[118]

After this analysis, it is possible that LASA has activities and programmes similar to those of the other regional space agencies, perhaps not in the same cooperation fields or level of development—this will depend on the political agreement achieved by Latin American countries after considering the financial and technical capacities of the region—but at least in terms of the procedure to implement those activities and programmes. In this regard, the LASA Convention could provide for the implementation of mandatory or basic activities and optional activities. To maintain LASA, it should be appropriate that the mandatory activities cover at least the management and maintenance of the establishments of the agency, including the payment of contracts for services and the hiring of staff. Moreover, it could be suitable that LASA has a mandatory programme (scientific, for example) in which all member states participate. This would not only prevent that all the budget of LASA goes to the payment

[111] APSCO Convention, art. 7.

[112] EUMETSAT Convention, art. 2.7.

[113] ESA Convention, art. V.1 b).

[114] APSCO Convention, art. 8. The EUMETSAT Convention does not give examples of optional programmes.

[115] ESA Convention, art. V.2.

[116] *The European Space Agency as mechanism and actor of international cooperation*, ESA Legal Services Department, p. 7.

[117] Ibid.

[118] The cost of these activities shall be covered by the third party concerned, EUMETSAT Convention, art. 2.9.

of administrative costs, but to give LASA a real international character, increase the place of Latin America in the international space arena, and contribute to the development of national space capacities in all member states. As in the regional models, LASA's mandatory or basic activities might include space education and training, as well as space science research. Further mandatory activities may comprise the development of space technology and its applications, and the collection of satellite data and its dissemination in the region. These activities would enable Latin America to achieve technological independence. As to the optional activities, the LASA Convention could provide that the agency can implement programmes on space science, technology and its applications, including the construction of satellites and a regional launcher (perhaps in the long-term). Optional activities would be suitable for those Latin American countries that wish to go further in their space cooperation relations by taking advantage of LASA's capacities. Finally, LASA could implement space programmes of the member states provided they do not interfere with LASA's activities and programmes, and the costs are covered by the interested states.

### *4.3.7 Financial Provisions*

For the operation and management of LASA and the implementation of its activities and programmes, Latin American countries must decide on the necessary financial provisions. In the regional models, the financial provisions are mostly detailed in instruments additional to the constituent instruments, namely financial regulations and arrangements adopted by the councils. Conversely, the constituent instruments mainly define issues related to the financial contributions of member states to the common costs of the agency and its activities and programmes, the agency's budget, as well as internal and external auditing.

In the ESA, EUMETSAT and APSCO, all member states are obliged to contribute to the common costs of the agency in accordance with a scale adopted or reviewed by the Council every three years. For instance, in EUMETSAT the annual contributions of member states to the general budget (and mandatory programmes) comprises the programmatic frame for all EUMETSAT core and prospective activities. Core activities are those activities not linked to a specific programme and represent the basic technical and administrative infrastructure of EUMETSAT including core staff, buildings and equipment. Prospective activities mean preliminary activities authorised by Council in preparation for future programmes that are not yet approved.[119] Meanwhile, in the case of the AfSA, the budget of the agency is borne by the AU within the budget of this organization.[120]

[119] EUMETSAT Convention, art. 2.5; see also: EUMETSAT Programmes, chapter on General Budget, in: *EUMETSAT Basic Documents*, created by EUMETSAT on 9 May 2020.

[120] AfSA Statute, art. 16.1.

To calculate the scale of contributions, different economic magnitudes are used in the three international inter-governmental space agencies: the average national income in ESA for the three latest years for which statistics are available,[121] the Gross National Income (GNI) according to statistics issued by the statistical office of the EU (EUROSTAT) in the case of EUMETSAT,[122] and the level of national economic development and the average Gross Domestic Product (GDP) per capita in APSCO.[123] However, the contributions of each member state shall not be required to exceed a specific percentage of the total amount of contributions assessed by the Council (25% in the case of ESA and 18% in APSCO).[124] Moreover, in the case of APSCO, each member state is required to make a minimum financial contribution decided by the Council.[125] The regional space agencies may also accept voluntary contributions, donations, gifts and legacies provided that they are compatible with the objectives, activities and principles of the agency[126] or are not inconsistent with its purposes.[127] For example, the APSCO Convention provides that the funds of the organization shall be provided through contributions of the member states, voluntary grants from the host government (China) and other member states, donations/subsidies received from other organizations, and services provided to others.[128]

Apart from the contributions to the common costs of the agency, member states shall contribute to the mandatory activities and programmes and, if applicable, to the optional ones. In ESA, each member state shall contribute to the costs of the mandatory activities in the same terms as for the common costs. For the optional activities, the participating states[129] contribute to their costs on the basis on the average national income for the three latest years for which statistics are available, and the specific interest to invest in such programmes, unless all participant states decide otherwise.[130] In both cases, no member state shall be required to pay contributions in excess of 25% of the total amount of contributions to the programme

[121] ESA Convention, art. XIII.1.

[122] Article 10.2 of the EUMETSAT Convention provides that for the calculations of the scale of contributions the average Gross National Product (GNP) for the three latest years for which statistics are available shall be used. Current EUMETSAT financial documents refer to the GNI instead of the GNP, *Scale of Contributions for Mandatory Programmes and General Budget*, Applicable from 1 January 2018 until today, see: Doc. *EUMETSAT Programmes*, last amended on 30 June 2020, EUMETSAT, www-cdn.eumetsat.int/files/2020-07/pdf_leg_programmes.pdf.

[123] APSCO Convention, art. 7.4.

[124] ESA Convention, art. XIII.1 a), and APSCO Convention, 18.6.

[125] APSCO Convention, art. 18.5.

[126] EUMETSAT Convention, art. 10.9.

[127] ESA Convention, art. XIII.6, and APSCO Convention, art. 18.7.

[128] APSCO Convention, art. 18.1.

[129] Article XIII.2 of the ESA Convention provides that each member state shall contribute to the costs of each optional programme covered by Article V, 1 b), unless it has formally declared itself not interested in participating therein and is therefore not a participant.

[130] *The European Space Agency as mechanism and actor of international cooperation*, ESA Legal Services Department, p. 10.

concerned.[131] According to the EUMETSAT Convention, member states are bound to pay their contributions to mandatory programmes under the same terms of the general budget and up to maximum of 110% according to the corresponding decision of the Council,[132] while for optional programmes the general rule is that each participating member state shall pay an annual contribution on the basis of the scale agreed for the programme.[133] Finally, the only provision in the APSCO Convention on the contributions to its activities determines that optional activities are carried out through the principle of return of investment, which means that the return on an optional activity shall be obtained in proportion to the investments by the participant member states.[134] Finally, the ESA and EUMETSAT Conventions provide that the payments of all contributions of the member states shall be made in a specific currency (Euros).[135]

Concerning budgetary issues, only the ESA (Annex II) and EUMETSAT Conventions have some provisions in this regard. Both instruments establish rules on the financial year of the agencies, and the procedure to adopt the general budget and budgets for mandatory and optional programmes.[136] In addition, both Conventions have provisions governing the financial control of the agency. The ESA Convention (Annex II) has several provisions on the internal and external (independent audit) controls, as well as provisions on accounting principles, while the EUMETSAT Convention has a few provisions concerning the annual audit of the organisation.[137]

Given the above, Latin American countries might consider the possibility of adopting in the LASA Convention financial provisions similar to the regional models. Even if it is decided that most of the financial provisions shall be defined in secondary instruments, it would be convenient if the LASA Convention at least had provisions on

---

[131] ESA Convention, art. XIII.

[132] EUMETSAT Convention, Arts. 10.2 and 10.4.

[133] EUMETSAT Convention, art. 10.5. Article 10.6 of this Convention provides that "in the case of an optional programme is not fully subscribed within one year after the date at which it has taken effect in accordance with Article 3.2 the existing participants are bound to accept a new scale of contributions whereby the deficit is distributed pro rata, unless they agree unanimously on a different solution".

[134] APSCO Convention, art. 8.7.

[135] ESA Convention, Annex, II, art. I, and EUMETSAT Convention, art. 10.6. Actually, the EUMETSAT Convention provides that all contributions shall be made by European Currency Units (ECU) as defined by the European Communities. However, the *EUMETSAT Financial Rules* changed the application from ECUs to Euros (from 19 November 2000). Article 2 of this instrument defines that "the budgets and all other financial documents circulated by EUMETSAT shall be established in Euro". The ECU was the former currency unit of the European Communities that was used from 13 March 1979 to 1 January 1999; this currency was only an electronic unit of account without any official coins or notes that could be used for cash transactions, see: Eurostat Statistics Explained, "Glossary: European currency unit (ECU)", https://ec.europa.eu/eurostat/statistics-explained/index.php/Glossary:European_currency_unit_%28ECU%29.

[136] EUMETSAT Convention, art. 11.

[137] Ibid., art. 12.

the contributions of the member states to the general budget of LASA,[138] including the scale of contributions and the formula for its calculation. For instance, in his proposal for a Latin American and Caribbean Space Agency, Imbert proposes the use of the GDP of the member states for the contributions to the budget of the main space programmes of the agency.[139] Equally important is the consideration of rules governing the contributions to the activities and programmes of LASA, whether they are mandatory or optional. Furthermore, LASA's budgetary rules and financial controls, including the currency of payments should also be considered in the Convention or in complementary financial rules.

Finally, within the OAS framework, if LASA is created as an organ of this organization, its budget could be covered by the OAS budget. Further financial provisions may be determined according to OAS practices and procedures.

### *4.3.8 Industrial Policy*

Latin American countries could decide that one of LASA's main functions shall be the elaboration and application of an industrial policy.[140] In ESA and APSCO,[141] the industrial policy aims at fostering the competitiveness of the industries of the member states in a cost-efficient manner, promoting and developing their industrial and technological capacities, and ensuring their participation in an equitable manner in implementing the agency's activities and programmes and in the associated development of space technology.[142] Moreover, the agencies, for the execution of their

[138] Efraín Guadarrama, a representative of the Mexican Ministry of Foreign Affairs, has stated that ALCE will start operations with the budget that have been already assigned by the different Latin American countries to their space programmes, in: Elías Camhaji, "ALCE, el sueño de la conquista latinoamericana del espacio", *El País*, 21 November 2020, https://elpais.com/mexico/2020-11-21/alce-el-sueno-de-la-conquista-latinoamericana-del-espacio.html. An alternative could be the creation of a mixed fund made up of governmental, institutional and private funds to finance LASA, in: Laura Fernández Zapata and Silvia Romero Aguilera, *Derecho y Política Espacial Latinoamericana. Una Vía a la Integración*, Santiago, Chile, 2015, p. 151.

[139] Imbert, "A Latin American and Caribbean Space Organization to be Delivered in the Space 2030 Agenda", p. 10.

[140] ESA Convention, art. II d), and APSCO Convention, art. 5.

[141] In ESA, the industrial policy is designed to meet the requirements of the European and the coordinated national space programmes in a cost-effective manner; improve the world-wide competitiveness of European industry; ensure that all member states participate in an equitable manner in implementing the European space programme and in the associated development of space technology, and exploit the advantages of free competitive bidding in all cases, except where there is incompatibility with other objectives of industrial policy, ESA Convention, art. VII.1; in APSCO, the industrial policy has two main goals: the industrial policy has two main goals: the development of competitive Asia–Pacific industry through free competitive bidding, and the distribution of relevant technologies among the member states to foster capacity-building in the benefit of APSCO's programmes and activities, APSCO Convention, art. 5.5.

[142] In ESA, the industrial policy is vital in the procurements of ESA to develop capacity in the industry of its member states to meet market demands in the most efficient and economical

programmes, grant preference to the fullest extent possible to industry in all member states, which shall be given the maximum opportunity to participate in the work of technological interest undertaken for the agencies.[143]

The industrial policy is based on the geographical distribution of contracts, which is governed, among other special rules, by the fair geographical return (or principle of "fair return" or "juste retour principle"). This principle implies that there shall be an equitable distribution between the total value of all contracts awarded among all member states and their total percentage contributions.[144]

In Latin America, the LASA Convention could provide that one of main LASA's functions shall be the elaboration and application of a Latin American industrial policy. This policy would generate a competitive Latin American space industry and contribute to the development of space technology in all member states. Furthermore, the implementation of the principle of geographical distribution would allow all member states to benefit from the implementation of LASA's activities and programmes, whether mandatory or optional. However, Latin American countries should be aware of the technical challenges concerning the implementation of an industrial policy. In this sense, they should consider the necessity of adopting technical instruments related to LASA's procurements and creating subsidiary organs aimed at ensuring fair procurement procedures and the correct application of the return principle in the distribution of LASA's contracts.[145]

---

way, ESA, "Industrial policy and geographical distribution", www.esa.int/About_Us/Business_with_ESA/How_to_do/Industrial_policy_and_geographical_distribution.

[143] ESA, "ESA, an intergovernmental customer", www.esa.int/About_Us/Business_with_ESA/Business_Opportunities/ESA_an_intergovernmental_customer. More specifically, in the placing of ESA's contracts, ESA shall give preference to industry and organisations of the member states, and in case of optional programs, preference shall be given to industry and organisations of participating states. ESA's contracts are awarded directly by the Director General, but in some specific cases the Council decides on the matter. Specific provisions on ESA's industrial policy are provided in Annex V of the ESA Convention. In the case of APSCO, the agency shall give preference/opportunity to the maximum possible extent to the industry of all member states to participate in the tasks related to the implementation of those programmes and activities. APSCO shall aim at strengthening competitiveness of the industries of its member states by making use of the existing industrial potential of these countries, developing and maintaining space technology and the products thereof, and encouraging the development of industrial structure according to market demands, APSCO Convention, art. 5.

[144] In ESA, the geographical distribution of all the agency's contracts is governed by the following general rules: a member state's overall return coefficient is the ratio between its percentage share of the total value of all contracts awarded among all member states and its total percentage contributions; for the purpose of calculating return coefficients, weighting factors are applied to the value of contracts on the basis of their technological interest, and ideally the distribution of contracts placed by the agency should result in all countries having an overall return coefficient of 1, see: ESA Convention, Annex V, art. IV (1–3).

[145] In ESA, there are several instruments containing technical provisions on ESA procurements and ESA's industrial policy: ESA Procurement Regulations and related Implementing Instructions, general clauses and conditions for ESA contracts, and Industrial Policy Committee Terms of reference. Furthermore, ESA has created an Industrial Ombudsman responsible to guarantee

### 4.3.9 Cooperation

To achieve its purposes, LASA could be empowered by the LASA Convention to carry out cooperation relations with multiple partners, from international organisations and institutions to governments, institutions and organisations of non-member states.[146] This cooperation, for instance, may include participation in LASA's activities and programmes. Should LASA be granted with treaty-making power, an aspect of international legal personality,[147] it could adopt different legal cooperation instruments, including cooperation agreements, implementing arrangements,[148] memoranda of understanding (MoU) as far as they contain legal obligations, exchanges of letters as far as they contain legal obligations, and other international agreements. Moreover, LASA could grant associate membership and observer status to non-member states and international organizations to foster international cooperation. Conversely, LASA may be a member, observer or participant in international organizations or institutions, such as UNCOPUOS and its two Subcommittees, the Group on Earth Observations (GEO), the International Committee on GNSS (ICG), and the International Telecommunication Union (ITU). LASA could also participate in international initiatives and collaborate with international and regional partners to foster common goals, including UNCOPUOS and its secretariat UNOOSA, CRECTEALC, SELPER, RELACA-Espacio, CITEL,[149] the Space Frequency Coordination Group (SFCG),[150] ESA, APSCO, AfSA, the International Astronautical Federation (IAF),

---

that ESA procurements are carried out within the principles of transparency, impartiality and non-discrimination, ESA, "Ensuring fairness competition in ESA procurements", www.esa.int/About_Us/Business_with_ESA/How_to_do/Ensuring_fairness_of_competition_in_ESA_Procurements.

146 ESA may cooperate and conclude agreements with international organisations and institutions, as well as with governments, organisations and institutions of non-member states, ESA Convention, art. XIV.

147 See: Chapter 4 (4.2.2).

148 In ESA, cooperation agreements establish the legal framework and outline the principle of cooperation with a certain partner (purpose, areas of cooperation, modalities of implementation, liabilities, settlement of disputes), while implementing arrangements particularise a concrete project-based cooperation to be undertaken under the general framework. Cooperation agreements require unanimity at Council level to ensure that the cooperation is based on a solid political mandate from all ESA member states, while implementing arrangements are approved by two-thirds majority of participating states to give ESA a rapid reaction to carry out cooperation with its partners with whom cooperation in principle is already established and formalised, *The European Space Agency as mechanism and actor of international cooperation*, ESA Legal Services Department, pp. 12–14.

149 Should LASA develop and operate space missions, it must coordinate with CITEL (OAS) to have an efficient use of the radio spectrum in Latin America and other states of the Americas, as well as to prepare regional positions before the World Radiocommunication Conferences (WRC), see: Chapter 1 (1.2.3.5).

150 The SFCG is a radio-frequencies collegiate of space agencies and related national and international organizations through which global space systems spectrum resources are judiciously managed for the benefit of humanity. The SFCG adopts resolutions and recommendations with express technical and administrative agreements to make best use of allocated bands and to avoid interference. LASA could participate in SFCG meetings and follow its recommendations for the best

**Fig. 4.7** Signature of the Outer Space Treaty, 1967. *Source* UN

and the Space Generation Advisory Council (SGAC). Furthermore, it could be appropriate that LASA adopts some guidelines to conduct its cooperation relations with international partners and harmonise cooperation activities with its member states. Equally important should be the consideration of creating a subsidiary body within LASA's framework to support LASA's international cooperation, such as the International Relations Committee (IRC) of ESA. In this regard, the IRC has the following functions[151]:

- To assist the ESA Council in concerting member states' space policies with the aim of arriving at common positions in international bodies,
- To prepare the Council decisions relating to ESA's international relations,
- To provide the Council with opinions regarding international relations, and
- To submit views and recommendations to other delegate bodies of ESA or the Director General.

Meanwhile, LASA could contribute to the codification, progressive development and implementation of international space law. In this regard, LASA could decide on the acceptance of rights and obligations of the following international space treaties:

use of the assigned allocated bands of LASA member states while coordinating with the missions of other space agencies, SFCG's website: www.sfcgonline.org/About/default.aspx#Mission.

[151] The IRC meets three or four times during a calendar year and receives reports and information to accomplish its duties on space activities of non-member states and international organisations or notes on questions of international law and space law, *The European Space Agency as mechanism and actor of international cooperation*, ESA Legal Services Department, p. 13.

- The 1968 Agreement on the Rescue of Astronauts, the Return of Astronauts and the Return of Objects Launched into Outer Space (ARRA)[152];
- The 1972 Convention on International Liability for Damage Caused by Space Objects (REG)[153];
- The 1975 Convention on Registration of Objects Launched into Outer Space (LIAB), and
- The 1979 Agreement Governing the Activities of States on the Moon and Other Celestial Bodies (MOON).

As happens in ESA,[154] the related decisions could be taken in the form of Council "Declarations" unanimously approved by LASA member states, provided that the majority of the member states are parties to these international treaties and to the 1967 Treaty on Principles Governing the Activities of States in the Exploration and Use of Outer Space, including the Moon and Other Celestial Bodies (OST),[155] and acknowledge that the establishment of rules and procedures for outer space activities would contribute to the strengthening of international cooperation (Table 4.4).[156]

In addition to the UN outer space treaties, LASA might commit to respecting or implementing non-legally binding international instruments on outer space, including:

- International instruments on space debris mitigation, such as the UNCOPUOS Space Debris Mitigation Guidelines, the Inter-Agency Space Debris Coordination Committee (IADC) Space Debris Mitigation Guidelines, and the International Organization for Standardization (ISO): Standards and technical reports,[157]
- UNCOPUOS Recommendations on enhancing the practice of states and international intergovernmental organizations in registering space objects[158];

---

[152] All international space treaties and other related documents can be consulted at: *International Space Law: United Nations Instruments*, UNOOSA, United Nations, May 2017, www.unoosa.org/res/oosadoc/data/documents/2017/stspace/stspace61rev_2_0_html/V1605998-ENGLISH.pdf.

[153] In conformity with articles II and IV of the REG, LASA could establish an internal procedure for internal and external registration of LASA space objects like ESA's procedure, Ibid., p. 18.

[154] Ibid., p. 13.

[155] Although international organisations cannot be party to the OST, the majority of the member states of an international organization wishing to accept the rights and obligations contained in any of the other space treaties shall be contracting parties to that treaty and the OST, see: articles VI (ARRA), XXII (LIAB), VII (REG) and XVI (MOON).

[156] *The European Space Agency as mechanism and actor of international cooperation*, ESA Legal Services Department, p. 13.

[157] *Compendium, Space Debris Mitigation Standards adopted by States and International Organizations*, UNOOSA, 19 January 2021, www.unoosa.org/documents/pdf/spacelaw/sd/Space_Debris_Compendium_COPUOS_19_jan_2021.pdf. LASA could also adopt its own policy and guidelines on space debris mitigation.

[158] *Recommendations on enhancing the practice of States and international intergovernmental organizations in registering space objects*, UNGA Resolution 62/101 of 17 December 2007.

**Table 4.4** Latin American countries signatures and ratifications and international organisations declarations of UN outer space treaties

| Country/Organization | 1967 OST | 1968 ARRA | 1972 LIAB | 1975 REG | 1979 MOON |
|---|---|---|---|---|---|
| Argentina | R | R | R | R | |
| Bolivia | S | S | | | |
| Brazil | R | R | R | R | |
| Chile | R | R | R | R | R |
| Colombia | R | S | R | R | |
| Costa Rica | | S | S | R | |
| Cuba | R | R | R | R | |
| Dominican Republic | R | S | R | | |
| Ecuador | R | R | R | | |
| El Salvador | R | R | R | | |
| Guatemala | | | S | | S |
| Haiti | S | S | S | | |
| Honduras | S | | S | | |
| Mexico | R | R | R | R | R |
| Nicaragua | R | R | R | R | |
| Panama | S | | R | | |
| Paraguay | R | | | | |
| Peru | R | R | R | R | R |
| Uruguay | R | R | R | R | R |
| Venezuela | R | S | R | R | R |
| EUMETSAT | | D | D | D | |
| ESA | | D | D | D | |
| EUTELSAT (IGO) | | | D | D | |
| INTERSPUTNIK | | D | D | D | |

*R* ratification, acceptance, approval, accession or succession; *S* Signature only; *D* Declaration of acceptance of rights and obligations
*Source* UNOOSA, Sciences Ministry of Colombia

- UNCOPUOS Safety Framework for Nuclear Power Source Applications in Outer Space,[159] and
- UNCOPUOS Guidelines for the Long-term Sustainability of Outer Space Activities (Fig. 4.7).[160]

---

[159] *Safety Framework for Nuclear Power Source Applications in Outer Space*, Endorsed by UNCOPUOS at its fifty-second session (2009) and contained in A/AC.105/934.

[160] *Guidelines for the Long-term Sustainability of Outer Space Activities*, Endorsed by UNCOPUOS at its sixty-second session (2019) and contained in A/74/20.

### 4.3.10 Settlement of Disputes

The negotiators of the LASA Convention should also consider the establishment of a method of settlement of disputes between LASA member states or between LASA and one or more of its member states concerning the interpretation or application of the LASA Convention. The method could be similar to the methods of the existing regional models. In ESA, EUMETSAT and APSCO, disputes shall first be settled by or through the Council.[161] If the dispute is not settled through this means, it may be submitted to arbitration at the request of any party to the dispute. Instead of arbitration, the EUMETSAT Convention provides that the parties may agree on another mode of settling the dispute.[162] The ESA and EUMETSAT Conventions provide details on the arbitration procedure, which consists in the establishment of an arbitration tribunal made up of three members, two of which shall be nominated by the parties to the dispute—one for each party, while the third member shall be nominated by the two first arbitrators. The arbitration tribunal will determine its seat and establish its own rules of procedure. The award, which shall be made by a majority of its members, shall be final and binding on all parties to the dispute.

A method for dispute settlement in international agreements between LASA and its international partners could be arbitration, although other methods may be implemented.[163]

### 4.3.11 Exchange of Persons, Data Provisions and Transfer of Technology

The LASA Convention might have provisions on the facilitation by member states of the exchange of persons whose activities are related to the competence of LASA. The exchange of persons shall be consistent with the laws and regulations of member states relating to entry into, stay in, or departure from their territories.[164]

The Convention might also govern the exchange of data or information.[165] This means that LASA and its member states should facilitate the exchange of scientific and technical information on space research and technology and their applications. However, a member state should not be required to communicate information

---

[161] ESA Convention, art. XVII, EUMETSAT Convention, art. 15, and APSCO Convention, art. 19. The APSCO Convention provides that the dispute shall be resolved through "cordial consultations in the Council".

[162] EUMETSAT Convention, art. 15.

[163] Arbitration is the common method for dispute settlement between ESA and its international partners, *The European Space Agency as mechanism and actor of international cooperation*, ESA Legal Services Department, p. 16.

[164] See: Articles IV and 20 of the ESA and APSCO Conventions, respectively.

[165] See: Articles III, 21 and 8 of the ESA, APSCO and EUMETSAT Conventions, respectively.

obtained from outside LASA if its inconsistent with its own security or its agreements with third parties. Furthermore, a provision concerning the publication of the scientific results of LASA experiments after their use by the corresponding scientists should be considered. This data could be considered property of LASA. If LASA is created as a specialized space agency like EUMETSAT, apart from granting LASA exclusive ownership of all data generated by its satellites or instruments, it could make available certain data agreed to the National Meteorological Services of third states.[166]

Meanwhile, the LASA Convention could regulate that LASA, when placing contracts or entering into agreements, shall secure the rights of access, disclosure, use and other appropriate rights of its member states and the persons under their jurisdictions concerning the resulting inventions and technical data of the programmes in which they participate. These inventions and technical data would be the property of LASA and communicated and disclosed to its member states, which may use it free of charge.[167] In addition, the LASA Convention may determine that LASA shall abide by international conventions concerning the protection of intellectual property.[168]

Lastly, the LASA Convention could have provisions on the transfer of technology and products. For example, the Council may adopt rules under which authorisation will be given for the transfer outside the territories of its member states of technology and products developed under the activities of LASA or with its help.[169] In addition, the Convention might include technology safeguards to prevent unauthorized access to protected information, items and technologies related to the activities of the agency. To this end, LASA could elaborate and implement technology security plans, and its member states could conclude agreements on technology safeguard measures with competent organizations. A further provision could state that LASA member states shall act in accordance with their respective national regulations and export control legislation concerning the goods and services included in the corresponding export control lists.[170]

### *4.3.12 Miscellaneous Provisions*

Apart from the above provisions, the LASA Convention could have additional rules concerning topics or issues that are not determined in any of the regional models. Furthermore, the LASA constituent instrument might deal with certain issues that are

---

[166] Article 8 of the EUMESTAT Convention provides that EUMETSAT shall make available sets of data agreed by the Council to the National Meteorological Services of member states of the World Meteorological Organization.

[167] See: Articles III.3 and III.4 of the ESA Convention.

[168] See: Article 22.3 of the APSCO Convention.

[169] See: Article XI.5 j) of the ESA Convention.

[170] See: Article 23 of the APSCO Convention. Due to the fact that Peru is a full member of APSCO, these provisions must be strictly respected by this country if it wants to become a member of LASA.

included or regulated in just one or two regional models, such as the provision of definitions (AfSA Statute and APSCO Convention), launchers and space transportation systems (ESA Convention) or liability of member states (EUMETSAT Convention). Meanwhile, there are further provisions that the LASA Convention would probably have if LASA were created as an international inter-governmental organisation such as ESA, APSCO and EUMETSAT,[171] which are explained in the following sections.

#### 4.3.12.1 Use of Languages

The LASA Convention might define the working languages of LASA. Because LASA is envisaged as covering the Latin American region, the languages of the agency would probably be at least Spanish, Portuguese and French. If LASA membership were extended to other countries of the Americas, such as the Caribbean countries, English and Dutch might also be working languages (Fig. 4.8). In addition, Latin American countries could consider the inclusion of one or more indigenous languages as LASA's working languages, especially those languages largely spoken in the continent, such as Quechua, Aymara, Guarani and Nahuatl.[172] Even if none of these languages are predominant languages in the countries where they are spoken, their inclusion in LASA's daily work could be applauded by the international community and allow indigenous people to become interested in space issues and contribute to the activities of the agency. Nevertheless, it is more likely that the definition of LASA's languages will be influenced by the signatories to the LASA Convention, although other criteria could also be considered, such as the facilitation of presentation of member state's views in LASA's main bodies or the economical use of funds.[173] In this case, for example, the English language could be LASA's working language due to its worldwide and practical use,[174] even though no English speaker country may become a member state. Conversely, if Brazil or Haiti do not participate in the negotiation or signature procedures of the LASA Convention, Portuguese and French could be omitted as LASA's working languages. Lastly, if LASA is settled

---

[171] Even though LASA is established as an internal organ of an international organization like the OAS, its constituent instrument may also provide related provisions.

[172] There are hundreds of languages spoken in Latin America and the Caribbean, including 560 indigenous languages, some of which are spoken by millions of people in different countries of the region, such as Quechua (9 million speakers in Bolivia, Ecuador and Peru), Aymara (2.2 million speakers in Bolivia and Peru), Guarani (5 million speakers in Paraguay) and Nahuatl (1.5 million speakers in Mexico), see: One World Nations Online, "Official and Spoken Languages of the Countries of the Americas and the Caribbean", www.nationsonline.org/oneworld/american_languages.htm; The World Bank, "Languages at risk in Latin America and the Caribbean", 22 February 2019, www.worldbank.org/en/news/infographic/2019/02/22/lenguas-indigenas-legado-en-extincion.

[173] See: final provisions of the ESA Convention, and article VI and Annex I (Resolution No 8: Use of Languages) of the ESA Council Rules of Procedure.

[174] The ALCE Declaration was adopted in three languages: Spanish, English and French.

**Fig. 4.8** Predominantly spoken languages in Latin American and Caribbean countries. *Source* Nations Online

as an organ of the OAS, its official languages would probably be OAS' official languages: Spanish, English, French and Portuguese.[175]

### 4.3.12.2 Signature, Ratification and Accession

The LASA Convention must have essential provisions concerning the legal procedures to become a party to it. In the regional models, these procedures are signature, ratification and accession.[176] Signature of the LASA Convention could be open until a specific date for the states participating in the signature official ceremony[177] (for instance, a conference of plenipotentiaries), in the forum in which the instrument has been negotiated and adopted (for example, in CELAC or in the Space Conference of the Americas (SCA))[178] or by the states defined in its Convention (e.g., all countries of Latin America).[179] These states could become parties to the LASA Convention either by signature not subject to ratification, acceptance or approval, or by the deposit of one of these instruments with the depositary if the Convention was signed subject to ratification, acceptance or approval.[180] Then, the corresponding instruments are to be deposited with the depositary.[181]

Once the LASA Convention enters into force, or after the expiration of the signing period, any state may accede to it with the unanimous decision of the Council. The procedure to accede to the Convention may start with a notification to the head of the executive organ, followed by the notification of this person to the member states of that request at least three months (usual interval in the regional models) before it is submitted to the Council for decision. In addition, the Council may determine

[175] The OAS Charter makes no reference to the use of official languages; these references are found in Article 51 of the *Rules of Procedure of the General Assembly* adopted in 1970, www.oas.org/xxxiiga/english/docs_en/genasam_rules.htm. According to Article 19 of the AfSA Statute, AfSA's working languages shall be those of the AU.

[176] ESA Convention, arts. XX and XXII, EUMETSAT Convention, art. 16, and APSCO Convention, Arts. 28 and 30. A further mode could be similar to that of the AfSA Statute (art. 1), in which all member states of the AU are automatically parties to that instrument.

[177] The EUMETSAT Convention is open for signature by the states that took part in the Conference of Plenipotentiaries on the setting-up of a European Organisation for the Exploitation of Meteorological Satellites.

[178] The ESA Convention was opened for signature by the states that were members of the European Space Conference (ESC). The ESC was a forum created in 1972 to formalise the amalgamation of ESRO and ELDO and give birth to ESA. It was the third ESC held on 15 April 1975 at Brussels—the first and the second ones were held in December 1972 and July 1973, respectively—that approved the terms of the final draft of the ESA Convention, which was signed at the Conference of Plenipotentiaries, in Paris, on 30 May 1975, see: ESA, "European Space Conference, 1975", www.esa.int/About_Us/ESA_history/European_Space_Conference_1975.

[179] The APSCO Convention establishes that the Convention shall be subject to the ratification or acceptance by members of the UN in the Asia–Pacific region (art. 28).

[180] The two options are available in EUMETSAT, while only the first option is available in ESA and APSCO.

[181] The depositary shall be determined in the LASA Convention, which could be the headquarters state.

the terms and conditions[182] for the accession of the state in question.[183] Finally, the instrument of accession shall be deposited with the depositary.

#### 4.3.12.3 Entry into Force

The LASA Convention must determine how it will enter into force. To this end, it could replicate a mode established in one of the regional models. The ESA Convention conditions its entry into force when ten defined European states—which were members of ESRO and ELDO—have signed it and have deposited with the depositary their instruments of ratification or acceptance.[184] The APSCO Convention provides that it shall enter into force when at least five states in the Asia–Pacific region, which are members of the UN, have signed it and have deposited with the host government their instruments of ratification or acceptance.[185] Finally, the EUMETSAT Convention determines several technical provisions in this regard. One provision states that the Convention shall enter into force when the aggregate contributions of the member states that have become parties to the Convention not by accession amount to at least 85% of the total amount of the contributions according to a scale defined in the Annex II of the Convention.[186] A second provision refers to the situation where the requirements of the first provision have not been met two years after the date on which the Convention was opened for signature. In this case, the depositary shall, at the earliest time possible, convene the governments of the states that have been parties to the Convention not by accession. These governments may then decide that notwithstanding the requirements of the first provision the Convention shall enter into force among them on a date agreed by them.[187] Furthermore, the three models include a provision stating that the Convention shall take effect for the states that have ratified or accessed to it after its entry into force on the date of the deposit by such state of its instrument of ratification, acceptance or accession.

---

[182] See: Chapter 4 (4.2.4).

[183] Article 16 paras. 5 and 6 of the EUMETSAT Convention have two additional provisions on this issue, respectively: "accession to the EUMETSAT Convention means as a minimum participation in the general budget and in all the mandatory programmes. Participation in optional programmes is subject to a decision of the participating states in accordance with Article 5.3 (c). Any state that becomes a party to the Convention shall make a special payment towards the investments already made taking into account the mandatory and optional programmes in which the state will participate. The amount of payment shall be determined in conformity with Article 5.2 (a) i. as regards mandatory programmes and in conformity with article 5.3 (c) as regards the optional programmes", "If a state accedes to the Convention, the scale of contributions for the general budget and for the mandatory programmes shall be adjusted by the Council. The participating states shall decide about any adjustment of scales of contributions following the accession to any optional programme".

[184] These states are Belgium, Denmark, France, Germany (Federal Republic), Italy, The Netherlands, Spain, Sweden, Switzerland, and the United Kingdom, ESA Convention, art. XXI.

[185] APSCO Convention, art. 28.

[186] EUMETSAT Convention, art. 27.1.

[187] EUMETSAT Convention, art. 27.2.

The three models also regulate that after the entry into force of the Convention and pending the deposit of its instrument of ratification, acceptance or approval, a signatory state may take part in the meetings of the organisation, without the right to vote. Therefore, similar provisions could be included in the LASA Convention. The provisions of the APSCO Convention in this matter seem to be more suitable if LASA is created as an international organisation. Conversely, the provisions of the EUMETSAT Convention may be more appropriate if LASA is established as an international specialized organization. Finally, if LASA is established as a subsidiary body of the OAS, the provision of its entry into force may be similar to the provision of the entry into force of the AfSA Statute, which indicates that the instrument shall enter into force upon its adoption by the Assembly (Fig. 4.9).[188]

**Fig. 4.9** Launch of Bolivia's telecommunications satellite TKSAT-1 from Xichang, China, 2013. *Source* Éxito Noticias

[188] AfSA Statute, art. 21.

#### 4.3.12.4 Amendments

A provision to amend the LASA Convention and its potential annexes could be similar to the respective provisions of the regional models. The amendments procedure includes recommendation by the Council or proposal of an amendment by a member state; the notification of the amendment to the executive organ and all member states; discussion of the amendment and its recommendation by the Council; unanimous acceptance of the amendment by all member states, as well as the notification of entry into force of the amendment. If LASA is created as a subsidiary body of the OAS, amendments to its constituent instrument could be made, for instance, by the General Assembly, which shall come into effect on the date decided by this organ.[189]

#### 4.3.12.5 Non-fulfilment of Obligations and Denunciation

These provisions would deal with two different situations in which a LASA member state ceases to be a member of the agency. The first situation—non-fulfilment of obligations or deprivation of membership—would occur when a member state fails to fulfil its obligations under the LASA Convention, while the second situation—denunciation or withdrawal—would be concretised when a member state voluntarily decides to leave LASA by renouncing its constituent instrument. The ESA, APSCO and EUMETSAT Conventions establish the procedures, conditions and legal consequences of each situation, some of which could be replicated in the LASA Convention.

In general, in the deprivation situation, it is the Council that decides on the matter by a two-thirds majority of all member states.[190] Further conditions are provided in the ESA and EUMETSAT Conventions. Concerning the ESA Convention, the provisions on the denunciation procedure shall apply in such a case (see below), while in the EUMETSAT Convention there is a provision stating that if a member state is excluded from the Convention, the scales of contributions for the general budget and for the mandatory programmes shall be adjusted. Additionally, the participating states shall, in accordance with the rules laid down in the programme declaration, decide on any adjustment of scales of contributions following the exclusion from optional programmes.

As to withdrawal, this can occur once the Convention has been in force for a certain number of years—five years in APSCO and six years in ESA and EUMETSAT. Fulfilling this condition, any member state may denounce the Convention through a notification to the depositary of the Convention (ESA and EUMETSAT) or the

[189] Article 20 of the AfSA Statute provides that the Statute may be amended by the Assembly (of the AU) upon recommendation of the Specialized Technical Committee of the AU.

[190] ESA Convention, art. XXVIII, EUMETSAT Convention, art. 14, and APSCO Convention, art. 32. In the case of EUMETSAT, the Council shall take the decision by a two-thirds majority vote of the member states present and voting representing also at least two-thirds of the total amount of GNP contributions. Moreover, the state concerned shall not take part in the vote on this issue, and the decision shall take effect at a date decided by the Council.

Secretary-General (APSCO).[191] The notification in APSCO shall be made at least one year in advance. Then, the depositary or Secretary-General shall notify the other member states (ESA and APSCO) and the Director General (ESA) or chief of the Council (APSCO). In APSCO, the Council shall call a meeting of the Council within 90 days to consider whether or not to approve the application.

In ESA, the denunciation takes effect at the end of the financial year following that during which it was notified to the depositary, while in the case of EUMETSAT it takes effect for the general budget at the end of the five year period for which the financial ceiling was decided, and for the mandatory or optional programmes at the time of the expiration of the programmes.[192] In addition, the withdrawal is accompanied by a set of conditions and rights for the ex-member state, such as being bound to honour certain financial obligations (ESA and APSCO), indemnifying the agency for any loss of property on its territory, unless special agreements has been adopted in this regard (ESA), and retaining the rights it has acquired up to the date on which the denunciation takes effect (ESA, EUMETSAT and APSCO).[193]

Therefore, the LASA Convention could have provisions on the non-fulfilment of obligations of a member state and the denunciation of the Convention, which would imply the loss of its membership in LASA. It is up to Latin American states to decide on the formalities and conditions on these issues. However, in the case of denunciation, these states should consider that the denunciation of the LASA Convention should only be possible after LASA has become fully operational for several years (not less than five years, for example). This provision comes from the ESRO Convention, whose negotiators were convinced that it was necessary that ESRO member states were committed for some years to participate financially in the first programmes of the agency without compromising the overall joint effort due to early withdrawals to the Convention. Because Latin America has fought hard to reach its regional integration, a provision on this matter would be convenient for a more solid and long-lasting regional space agency.

#### 4.3.12.6 Dissolution

As in most conventions creating international organizations, including the regional convention models, the LASA Convention should have provisions for the dissolution of LASA.[194] In this regard, LASA could be dissolved in three ways. One way is by

[191] The notification to APSCO shall be done at least one calendar year in advance.

[192] The APSCO Convention does not contain a provision on the moment in which the member state loses its membership nor a provision concerning the conditions or reasons for approval or refusal of the withdrawal by the Council.

[193] The EUMETSAT Convention also provides that if a member state ceases to be a party to the Convention, the scale of contributions for the general budget shall be adjusted in accordance with Article 10.2 for the five-year period following the period in which the state concerned denounced the Convention.

[194] ESA Convention, art. XX, EUMETSAT Convention, art. 20, and APSCO Convention, art. 34.

agreement between its member states at any time.[195] A second option is when LASA member states become less than a precise number (for example, less than five).[196] This provision would prevent that a few member states bear high financial burdens to maintain the effectiveness of the activities and programmes of the agency. A third option could be similar to a provision of the EUMETSAT Convention, according to which the agency shall be dissolved if, as a result of the decrease of its member states by withdrawal or denunciation, the contribution rate of each other member state to the general budget and to the mandatory programmes is increased by more than one fifth.[197]

Further provisions on the dissolution of LASA might deal with the appointment of the Council of a liquidation authority—leaving the legal personality of LASA for this purpose—and the distribution among the member states of the potential surplus assets and deficits of LASA.

#### 4.3.12.7 Notifications

The LASA Convention may also have provisions on the notifications that the depositary shall make to all signatory and acceding states, which may include[198]:

- All signatures of the Convention,
- The date of deposit of each instrument of ratification, acceptance or accession,
- The date of entry into force of the LASA Convention and of amendments to this Convention,
- The date of denunciation from the Convention by a member state, or any loss of membership status in LASA,
- The dissolution of LASA.

#### 4.3.12.8 Registration

A further provision that the LASA Convention could have is that of the registration of the Convention with the Secretariat of the UN according to article 102 of the UN Charter,[199] which could be drafted as follows: "*Upon the entry into force of this*

---

[195] See: ESA Convention, art. XXV, and APSCO Convention, art. 24. The dissolution of APSCO shall be done by a consensus agreement among all its member states.

[196] In ESA, this number is less than five, while in APSCO is less than four members.

[197] EUMETSAT Convention, art. 20.2.

[198] See: ESA Convention, art. XXIII, EUMETSAT Convention, art. 21, and APSCO Convention, art. 31.

[199] Article 102 of the UN Charter: "(1) Every treaty and every international agreement entered into by any member of the United Nations after the present Charter comes into force shall as soon as possible be registered with the Secretariat and published by it. (2) No party to any such treaty or international agreement which has not been registered in accordance with the provisions of paragraph 1 of this article may invoke that treaty or agreement before any organ of the United Nations.".

*Convention, and of any amendments to it, the depositary shall register them with the Secretary General of the United Nations in accordance with Article 102 of the Charter of the United Nations*".

## 4.4 Conclusion

Creating a space agency for Latin America implies political compromises between the states of the region concerning the objectives, structure and activities of this entity. The adoption of a regional space policy and strategy could help to concretize the space agency and formulate its objectives in the short, medium and long terms. A regional space programme could also facilitate this task. Nevertheless, it is LASA's constituent instrument or convention where Latin American states will formally define the status and features of the space agency and transform their political intentions into legal obligations. The procedure to adopt the LASA Convention will be decided by the interested states, who could consider the creation of a preparatory commission for the draft convention, and receive the support of different stakeholders, including academics, industry, civil society, as well as governmental and non-governmental international partners. Similarly, the content of the LASA Convention is to be defined by Latin American states through negotiations on the topics that they consider necessary to put into the instrument. To this end, the experiences of other regional space agencies and the provisions of their constituent instruments may be useful for Latin American states in setting-up their own space agency.

However, there needs to be awareness of the multiple contextual differences between Latin America and other regions of the world, including the space capacities, the social and economic circumstances, and the political situation of the region. In this regard, it may be prudent for a multidisciplinary group made up of scientists, science administrators, engineers, lawyers, economists, politicians, and diplomats to prepare the LASA Convention. In the same vein, it could be useful to know the opinions of user communities of space assets in Latin America. In any case, the preparation and adoption of the LASA Convention are only two of the several steps to materialize the regional space agency. The subsequent adoption of this instrument by the highest possible number of countries may require further political agreements at the national and regional levels. This process, like in the regional models, might take several years, but it is important that the interests of all states are considered. Moreover, the most fervent Latin American supporters of the LASA project shall have in mind that the current global pandemic and economic crises could prevent other countries of the region joining the project in the short term, so that the discussions on LASA may need some time to be settled on.

Once the LASA Convention enters into force and the space agency starts its operations and activities, additional efforts must be taken by all member states. As difficult as these tasks may be, Latin American countries must evaluate their position in the international space arena and the current conjunctural regional situation in which two proposals on the establishment of a regional space agency in the Americas (ALCE and

AECA) are in development. In this regard, the potential members of each proposal would not be the same because of their different geographical approaches (the first proposal includes all Latin American and Caribbean countries, while the second proposal only comprises the Central American states and Dominican Republic). Therefore, a possible solution, and probably an urgent one, is that all countries of Latin America, and even of the Caribbean, join together to establish a unique space agency for the overall region. There might be no other chance to do it.

FSC
www.fsc.org
MIX
Papier aus verantwortungsvollen Quellen
Paper from responsible sources
FSC® C105338

If you have any concerns about our products,
you can contact us on
**ProductSafety@springernature.com**

In case Publisher is established outside the EU,
the EU authorized representative is:
**Springer Nature Customer Service Center GmbH**
**Europaplatz 3, 69115 Heidelberg, Germany**

Printed by Libri Plureos GmbH
in Hamburg, Germany